The Neuroscier
the Developing

The Neuroscience of the Developing Child informs Early Years (EY) students, practitioners and parents about the fundamental importance of self-regulation (SR) as a critical skill for young children to develop if they are to go on to lead happy and fulfilled lives. Packed with accessible information concerning the neuroscience of early brain development alongside real-life case studies, this book clearly demonstrates how to put SR theory into action across educational and home settings.

Dr Conkbayir draws upon a wide range of resources to show readers how they can nurture SR through their daily interactions with children and the environment and experiences they offer them. Comprehensive and engaging chapters cover topics such as:

- Examining what exactly SR is (and what it is not)

- Co-regulation's critical role in enabling SR to occur

- Exploring the developing brain

- The importance of sensory integration as part of SR

- Using relational approaches to nurture behaviour in the classroom and at home

- The wider global role of SR in creating a sustainable future.

With real-life case studies and reflective questions in every chapter, this book is essential reading for students and practitioners within the EY sector, as well as anyone beyond the sector wanting to develop their understanding of SR and how to apply it for themselves and others.

Dr Mine Conkbayir is an award-winning author, trainer and researcher passionate about bridging the knowledge gap between neuroscience and the EY sector. A key contributor to the Birth to Five Matters non-statutory guidance for the Early Years Foundation Stage and designer of the first-ever neuroscience-informed qualifications for the EY sector, her latest award-winning book, *Early Childhood and Neuroscience: Theory, Research and Implications for Practice*, is now in its second edition.

The Neuroscience of the Developing Child

Self-Regulation for Wellbeing and a Sustainable Future

Dr Mine Conkbayir

Routledge
Taylor & Francis Group

LONDON AND NEW YORK

Cover image: © Getty Images

First edition published 2023
by Routledge
4 Park Square, Milton Park, Abingdon, Oxon, OX14 4RN

and by Routledge
605 Third Avenue, New York, NY 10158

Routledge is an imprint of the Taylor & Francis Group, an informa business

British Library Cataloguing-in-Publication Data
A catalogue record for this book is available from the British Library

ISBN: 978-1-032-35577-1 (hbk)
ISBN: 978-1-032-35576-4 (pbk)
ISBN: 978-1-003-32747-9 (ebk)

DOI: 10.4324/9781003327479

Typeset in Bembo
by Apex CoVantage, LLC

Printed in Great Britain by Bell and Bain Ltd, Glasgow

Contents

Figures

Tables

Abbreviations

ACEs	adverse childhood experiences
ADHD	attention deficit hyperactivity disorder
CR	co-regulation
EC	Emotion Coaching
ECEs	early childhood educators
ELGs	Early Learning Goals
EY	Early Years
EYFS	Early Years Foundation Stage
PNS	parasympathetic nervous system
SEND	special educational needs or disabilities
SI	sensory integration
SIPT	Sensory Integration and Praxis Test
SNS	sympathetic nervous system
SPD	sensory processing disorder
SR	self-regulation

Acknowledgements

Bu kitabı, mükemmel kızım Delilah'a adıyorum.
Kucak dolusu sevgilerle,

Annen.

Introduction

What to Expect

The premise of this book is simple. It is intended to inform Early Years (EY) practitioners and parents alike about the fundamental importance of self-regulation (SR). At its simplest, SR refers to our ability to manage our thoughts, feelings and behaviour in ways that are healthy and growth promoting. Without SR, our mental health and holistic wellbeing become significantly compromised, along with our relationships and ability to function optimally.

You can therefore expect accessible information concerning the neuroscience of early brain development, combined with abundant real-life case studies, to help place the theoretical knowledge in meaningful, practical contexts – both professionally and personally.

Structure of the Book

This book is designed to be "dipped into" according to your specific area of interest or need. You will notice that Chapters 1 and 2 are particularly comprehensive. This is because these respectively examine SR and co-regulation (CR) in great detail, with plenty of real-life case studies to inform and inspire your current practice. The six chapters are packed with practically useful information, with reflective questions to help consolidate and build knowledge, while encouraging you to think critically. Each chapter ends with a Further Reading list, should you wish to develop your line of inquiry concerning some of the key issues.

The tone of this book is unparalleled and set from the start by an interview with founder of the MEHRIT Centre, Dr Stuart Shanker – the leading light in SR around the world. The Foreword is provided by the executive director of Dr Shanker's MEHRIT Centre and chief executive officer of Self-Reg Global, Dr Susan Hopkins. Their principles and insights shine through in their contributions to this book.

Topics covered include an examination of what SR is – and what it is not. The critical role of co-regulation (CR) in enabling SR to occur is discussed, followed by an accessible and engaging whistle-stop tour of the developing brain. Sensory integration as part of SR is considered, alongside a compelling argument against the use of behaviour management in settings and homes. The book concludes with a forward-looking chapter concerning the underpinning role of SR in the wider global context of building a sustainable future and what action is needed now to achieve this.

The term "disorder" is avoided in this book, with "condition" used in its place, as far as possible. This is in recognition of the fact "disorder" has negative connotations – as if there is something wrong with a person who has a neurodevelopmental or mental health condition. If we are to each help create a truly inclusive and understanding society, we need to eschew such negative and unhelpful labels, as they can have disastrous effects on self-image while doing nothing to progress thinking about neurodevelopmental and mental health conditions.

Where it *is* included in direct citations, it remains, along with widely recognized abbreviations such ADHD (attention deficit hyperactivity disorder).

The terms "parents," "primary carers" and "caregivers" are used interchangeably throughout the book to indicate the main carers of the child.

Why This Book, and Why Now?

This book has implications for us all – both on a personal and professional level. Parents, primary caregivers, EY practitioners, teachers, school leaders, counsellors, social workers and police officers would all benefit from the information. Understanding the fundamental importance of individual SR and the impact this ultimately has on a wider societal level is something we would all benefit from reflecting – and acting on.

Further reasons for the necessity of this book *now* are outlined in the following section and explored in greater detail throughout the book.

Children and their families worldwide have survived the ongoing pervasive impact of the coronavirus pandemic and the consequent repeated lockdowns as part of extensive public health measures in an attempt to thwart the virus. These, combined, have caused long-term disruption and uncertainty in all aspects of society, with millions exposed to situations linked to poor mental health outcomes, such as isolation, job loss and consequent financial difficulties. Such factors have amplified existing difficulties and tensions within families, as well as creating additional challenges – each of which take precious time away from parents connecting with their children. Aligned to this, parents have struggled with their own mental health and their children's, which is exacerbated when parents find it difficult to be emotionally available to co-regulate their children's thoughts, feelings and behaviour. Almost all (98%) survey respondents in a study by the First 1001 Days Movement (Reed and Parish, 2021) said babies their organization works with had been impacted by parental anxiety, stress or depression, which was negatively affecting bonding and responsive care.

Moreover, the government's unhelpful deficit perspective of children in the aftermath of the pandemic has resulted in the prioritization of children "catching-up" academically, resulting in the possibility of longer school days and shorter summer holidays. Children have survived a pandemic – some were already struggling with their mental health and some would have been traumatized, developing poor mental health as a result of the pandemic. It stands to reason that parents and professionals alike must put mental health first – the rest *will* follow.

Inextricably linked to the pandemic is the sharp increase of poor mental health among children and young adults. A recent NHS report (Lifestyles Team, NHS Digital, 2020) into child and adolescent mental health, which captures such experiences of children as young as five, found that the number of mental health conditions has increased since 2017, with one in six (16%) children aged five to 16 years identified as having a mental health condition in 2020. Children as young as eight are reported to be self-harming, due to the cascading effects of the pandemic. The same survey reports a 27% rise in hospital admissions for self-harm by children aged three to nine in England – with admissions jumping 13% among this age group between 2016 and 2017. Poor SR plays a key role – which returns us to parental mental health – where parents are struggling with their own mental health, they are not able to co-regulate their children's emotional responses and behaviour and so the detrimental spiral continues.

Alarmingly, the cascading effects of the pandemic have also resulted in an exponential rise in the abuse of children from birth to two-years-old. Sidpra et al. (2021) reported that in just one month, the number of new cases of head trauma rose by 1493% compared with the same period in the previous three years, pointing to a "silent pandemic" in 2020. The outgoing children's commissioner, Anne Longfield (The Centre for Social Justice, 2021), stated during the launch of the Early Years Healthy Development Review (25th March 2021) that there were approximately 100,000 infants from birth to one-year-old living in families where domestic abuse, severe mental health conditions and addiction were prevalent among parents. Where there is such turbulence and chaos in children's lives during these most influential, formative years, the course of early brain development and behaviour will be adversely affected. These are the infants who are consequently erroneously labelled as "challenging" or "difficult to settle," which can further impede or rupture the bond between them and their parents – ultimately inhibiting the process of CR and SR from taking place.

Furthermore, September 2020 saw the introduction of the SR Early Learning Goals (ELGs) in the Early Years Foundation Stage (EYFS). Reflecting on their meaning and interpretation in their current form (2021: 11), they are immersed in the language of compliance, which is *not* what SR is about. This book will therefore be a particularly useful and necessary resource for the EY workforce to help redress the balance, with extensive knowledge that is more robust, reliable and helpful to both EY practitioners and children.

Key Take-Aways From This Book

Individuals will likely find different aspects of the book pertinent, depending on their life experiences, needs at the time of reading and level of understanding of the neuroscience of early brain development and SR. That said, it is hoped that as a result of reading this book, the reader builds on their knowledge of the precarious process of early brain development and the critical role of the adult in influencing this. The insights and practical strategies provided will help to develop SR and CR skills in a variety of contexts for both children and adults alike, while increasing self-awareness around personal triggers and current coping mechanisms. Ultimately, it is hoped that more relational approaches to understanding and supporting behaviour are adopted and that behaviour management – be this as a parent or practitioner – is eschewed. This means putting an end to controlling behaviour through commonly adopted tactics such as rewards and punishments that are used across schools and in the home. (More on this in Chapter 5.)

So prepare to engage with this book, make notes if it helps – and enjoy this journey of SR.

Foreword

Early childhood educators (ECEs) are difference makers. If you are an ECE reading this book by Dr Mine Conkbayir, you know this is how she sees each and every one of you. It was an honour to write the Foreword for Mine's book, for many reasons, but most of all because I see her as a difference maker. My hope is that some of you who will read this book and engage in more learning with Mine will feel validated in your expertise, honoured for your contributions to the lives of so many children and families over the years and empowered to bring the science and the research into your relationships with children and your practice as an ECE.

As I first got to know Mine several years ago, I was struck by three things. The first is that Mine knows her stuff: she knows the early years, she knows children and what they need to thrive and she know her neuroscience. A long-time ECE and advocate for the wellbeing and rights of children, she grew weary of the expert model of bringing the brain–body science to her field. This isn't to say that she didn't value the research, science and expertise of others — one look at the references that back up this book makes it clear that she embraces all that she can learn from everywhere she can learn it. She recognized that being a neuroscientist, neurobiologist, psychologist or XYZ did not line up with an equally important area of expertise for the mental health, wellbeing and learning of young children — that of an early childhood educator. So she filled that gap with a PhD in neuroscience for the purpose of bringing the science to the field in ways that honoured and aligned with the work of ECEs.

The second thing that struck me about Mine is that she will always boldly stand up for what she believes in. She'll advocate for the voices of ECEs at the decision-making tables. She'll advocate for the rights of every single child every single time. She'll contribute to work that she cares deeply about, and not only when it is an easy thing to do. She'll honour the progress, the successes, the stories of hope. And then she'll get right back to work moving the mountains to bring change into the lives and lived experiences of children in the early years. An example of this integrity-driven mountain moving focus is connected to the origins of this book. Mine was at the advisory table for the new UK EYFS Early Learning Goals (ELG). She celebrated its release as a step in the right direction. And then she set to work writing this book to fill a gap that would be a difference maker for ECEs and the children and families they serve. The problem was this: while the new ELG included "self-regulation," the definition of the term – there are at least 447 definitions out there (Burman et al., 2015) – focused on self-control and the children's need to manage themselves, their attention, their impulses, their emotions, their learning. Mine well knew that this age-old self-control mindset put the onus on children and that the science of brain-body self-regulation, grounded in the original definition of the term, opened the door for a new paradigm for supporting children, parents and ourselves. And she set about getting the brain-body science, the co-regulation practices and quality early years pedagogies that support children's development of growth-promoting modes of self-regulation in motion.

The third thing about Mine that became very apparent, very quickly, was that she was deeply committed to a holistic understanding of being. How can we consider early literacy or early numeracy without considering all the intersecting areas that contribute to a child's learning, behaviour and wellbeing? Mine's view aligns with the science, the experience of ECEs and many diverse cultures and ways of knowing. We are honoured that she found the five-domains framework and the Self-Reg work of Dr Stuart Shanker and our teams at The MEHRIT Centre and Self-Reg Global to be a foundation for her book and the focus of the first chapter. A self-control mindset leaves us seeking behaviour management strategies to "get" a child to be able to "wait for what they want and control their immediate impulses when appropriate." This sounds good as a goal on paper, but what do we do when everything we try doesn't work? Do we look at the child as misbehaving and making poor choices? Through a self-control lens, we would. A Self-Reg (Shanker, 2020; Shanker and Hopkins, 2019; Shanker and Barker, 2018a, 2018b) lens seeks to understand and (1) reframe the behaviour; (2) recognize the stressors that contribute to the child's brain-body state; (3) reduce the stressors in each of the five domains when a child's stress "backpack" is too heavy; (4) enhance brain-body stress state awareness; and (5) restore energy, relationships, attention and hope.

This book makes a terrific contribution to the sector and beyond. All ECEs – and parents – would benefit from reading it.

Susan Hopkins, EdD
ED of The MEHRIT Centre
CEO Self-Reg Global
Co-Author (with Stuart Shanker): *Self-Reg Schools
Handbook for Educators* (Pearson, 2019)

Interview With Dr Stuart Shanker, Founder and Visionary of the MEHRIT Centre and Self-Reg Global

The purpose of this book is to familiarize readers with or, for many, consolidate and extend their knowledge concerning self-regulation and its fundamental role in enabling an individual to fully embrace life. Writing a book on SR, however, cannot be undertaken without giving due regard and respect to the invaluable work of Dr Stuart Shanker and the MEHRIT Centre. In collaboration with Dr Susan Hopkins, their work continues to lead the way in challenging and changing how we see, interpret and respond to the behaviour of infants, children and young adults globally.

I am honoured to have this opportunity to ask Dr Shanker a few questions concerning the increasingly prevalent but often misunderstood concept of SR.

1 **What do you feel is a good workable definition of self-regulation and its key elements?**

Self-regulation, in its original, psychophysiological sense, refers to how we manage stress. We can do so in a manner that is maladaptive – meaning, it reduces stress in the moment but creates even more stress down the road – or in a manner that restores energy and reduces tension.

2 **Why do you feel it is so important?**

Children and teens today are displaying classic signs of being overstressed: e.g. heightened anxiety and impulsivity, poor concentration, social and emotional problems. It is very hard to say whether this is happening because they are dealing with higher levels of stress or because they are more drawn to maladaptive modes of self-regulation. But in either case, they need to practice Self-Reg: the five-step method we have developed to recognize when they are becoming over-stressed, and why, learn how to reduce their stress-load and discover growth-promoting modes of self-regulation that are suited to their individual needs and lifestyle.

3 **What are the key factors or experiences for children in supporting the development of self-regulation?**

We are seeing a generation with diminished awareness: both of what is going inside them and around them. In place of learning what it feels like to be calm, and how to achieve this state, they are seeking to avoid or blunt their awareness. Unfortunately, they are surrounded by activities and products that have been designed with precisely this purpose in mind.

4 **What currently prevents self-regulation developing in young children?**

I would like to reframe this question – per what I said above – to: What is impairing growth-promoting self-regulation in young children? This ability is only developed through the Interbrain: that is, it is only by being regulated by a caregiver or educator that a young child learns mindful ways of self-regulating. Far too often, caregivers or educators resort to devices or behaviours to keep the child quiet, which is not only fundamentally different from but actually opposed to helping them learn what calmness feels like and how to be in such a state.

5 **What would enhance self-regulation in young children?**

Young children have a remarkable capacity to learn when they are becoming overstressed, and the reasons why. But only if their caregiver or educator understands the difference between *misbehaviour* and *stress-behaviour*: recognizes the signs of when a child is *becoming* overstressed and remains calm herself in order to "lend her calm to the child."

6 **What most concerns you about the current education system and why?**

Two things. First, we have not thought seriously enough about the needs and demands on educators. And second, we jump far too quickly to the belief that a child is not "working hard enough" when the truth is the exact opposite: i.e. the child is "working far too hard." What we have seen in the work we have done with schools across the country is that children learn best when they – and their educators – feel emotionally as well as physically safe and the stresses they are exposed to are positive and enriching. In other words, we have to develop a better understanding of stress across five domains: physical, emotion, cognitive, social and prosocial. Only then can we start to manage stress-loads in a manner that allows learning to flourish.

7 **While many do appreciate the importance of self-regulation in achieving and maintaining wellbeing, there remains resistance to meaningfully embedding this in policies and practice. Why do you think this might be the case?**

To be honest, we are not seeing all that much resistance these days. This might have been the case a short while back, when the distinction between *self-regulation* and *self-control* was not fully understood. But everywhere we go now, we are seeing educators and administrators who not only recognize the importance of this distinction for student wellbeing and academic achievement but understand its importance for their own wellbeing as well.

8 **There is some debate concerning whether cognitive self-regulation is more significant than emotional self-regulation. My understanding (or position) is that if the brain is in a state of anxiety or hyper-/hypo-arousal, it cannot access those higher regions required for executive functioning. What are your thoughts?**

This is a great question, although once again I would want to reframe it a little. Self-regulation simply refers to managing stress. But the point that your question is making is that there are the different domains of stress that I mentioned above. In this case, you are asking whether it is more important to regulate cognitive than emotional stress. To stick with your example, we do know that heightened anxiety has a huge impact on a student's capacity to learn. Not only is working memory compromised, but the very speed at which new information can be absorbed is significantly reduced. My own view is that this is not an Either/Or situation, but an And/And. That is, when we work on Self-Reg, we always address all five stress-domains: even – or perhaps especially – in those cases where one domain in particular stands out.

9 **What is your vision for early childhood programmes and education, and how might this be achieved?**

This is the easiest of all your questions to answer. The ECE has one of the most important roles of any educator in helping young children learn how to manage their stress in a manner that establishes a healthy trajectory. We now have a mountain of science to turn this theory into practice. And what we have seen, over and over, is that when ECEs master this material, it is not just their students, but they themselves who flourish.

10 **You have said that the MEHRIT Centre is "laying the foundation for a paradigm-revolution built around the science of self-regulation" – can you outline three key ways individuals and organizations could play their part in realizing this paradigm revolution?**

  1   Individuals and organizations need to sign up for the TMC Foundations Course, "Self-Reg & Early Childhood Development Certificate Program" (https://self-reg.ca/learn/online-courses-with-dr-shanker/early-childhood-development/)

2   They need to encourage parents to sign up for TMC's "Self-Reg Parenting Course" (https://self-reg.ca/learn/self-reg-parenting-course/)

3   They need to help everyone in our society understand that: "There is no such thing as a bad kid, a lazy kid, or a stupid kid."

Dr Stuart Shanker, thank you so much for taking the time to respond to these questions and setting the tone for this book.

Self-Regulation – What It Is and What It's Not

Self-regulation. Where to begin with this fundamentally important set of skills which are critical to life itself? Bronson's (2000: 1) comprehensive explanation starts us on the right path:

> Self-regulation begins with life itself. The capacity for conscious and voluntary self-regulation is central to our understanding of what it is to be human. It underlies our assumptions about choice, decision making and planning. Our conceptions of freedom and responsibility depend on it.

What to Expect in This Chapter

This chapter presents diverse definitions of SR, along with an examination of the five domains of SR and the stressors in each of these five domains, as proposed by Dr Stuart Shanker (Shanker and Hopkins, 2019). The domains and their stressors will be revisited across the six chapters, in line with the issues examined. The fundamental, life-long importance of SR will be explored alongside discussion of how this should begin through CR from birth (or even in utero). Readers will also learn about the inextricable link between SR and how this influences executive functioning. The introduction of SR as part of the revised EYFS ELGs will also be explored, with close attention paid to their unsuitability and the reasons for this. Questions are included to help consolidate the reader's understanding and to help the reader to challenge particular arguments that are put forward. A Further Reading list concludes the chapter.

By the End of This Chapter, You Will Be Able to:

■ Define and describe SR

■ Identify and explain the five domains of SR

DOI: 10.4324/9781003327479-1

■ Identify the stressors in each of the five domains

■ Understand how dysregulation disrupts emotional wellbeing

■ Understand and discuss the interconnectedness of the emotional and cognitive domains of SR

■ Understand and discuss Bruce Perry's neurosequential model of brain development (2006)

■ Explain when SR develops

■ Explain how SR develops

■ Describe the impact of maternal stress on the foetus

■ Understand the concept of dysregulation and how it affects children

■ Compare and critique the role of SR in the EYFS.

What Is Self-Regulation?

At its simplest, SR is our ability to regulate (or manage) our thoughts, feelings and behaviour. Being able to self-regulate helps us to remain calm and attentive and helps us to respond, rather than react, in the face of our many strong emotions and responses to stressors in life. When a child can self-regulate, they are able to think before they act, self-calm or re-organize when they are met with overwhelming or stressful input.

This might look like a child choosing to walk away from an argument, instead of staying in it and fighting back. It might be a child not giving up while working on a task, even if they are finding it difficult. It also includes a child being able to calm themselves down by taking slow deep breaths instead of "flipping their lid" (which is explored in Chapter 3). Without SR, children struggle to develop meaningful relationships, communicate reciprocally, succeed at school or thrive personally. This is why *SR is not self-control. SR is what makes self-control happen.* This makes sense when we reflect on SR in the context of its 10 attributes, listed here:

■ Managing own feelings and behaviours

■ Self-soothing/bouncing back from upset

■ Being able to curb impulsive behaviours

■ Being able to concentrate on a task

■ Being able to ignore distractions

■ Behaving in ways that are prosocial (like getting along and empathizing with others)

- Planning

- Thinking before acting

- Delaying gratification

- Persisting in the face of difficulty.

The key to living a fulfilling and successful life is one's ability to manage one's own thoughts, emotional responses and consequent behaviour; to know how to control those big, overwhelming feelings such as anger or fear in order to get on with the serious business of play, learning and building and maintaining relationships. In short, being able to self-regulate means taking responsibility for our thoughts and behaviours and being able to choose how we respond to the stressors in our lives. When we reflect on this, we must also bear in mind that the capacity to self-regulate varies greatly from one child (or adult) to the next and is dependent on a range of factors that interact with each other, including:

- Genetics

- The presence of any special educational needs or disabilities (SEND)

- Parenting styles

- Caregiver support

- Environmental context

- Age of the child.

SR is an important predictor of mental health and wellbeing (Compas et al., 2017). Yet definitions of SR remain difficult to agree upon (Early Years Coalition, 2021; Conkbayir, 2021; Bronson, 2000; Schunk and Zimmerman, 1994), with continued lack of integration among definitions (McClelland et al., 2013), resulting in some division concerning its meaning and purpose. Some definitions focus on the cognitive aspects of SR, like metacognition and motivation (Pino-Pasternak et al., 2014), while others emphasize its emotional characteristics, such as resilience and the capacity to recover from dealing with stressors – both internal and external to the individual (Porges, 2021; Shanker, 2020; Hughes and Baylin, 2012). Despite there being over 447 definitions of the term (Burman et al., 2015), cognitive interpretations of SR continue to be advocated over other domains of SR, arguably to the detriment of, for example, the emotional capacities that are necessary in ensuring self-regulatory abilities. The complexity underpinning the interplay between the emotional and cognitive domains of SR will be examined further on in this chapter.

Definitions also depend upon which school of thought one most identifies with, be it psychodynamic theories (Freud, 1989; White, 1963; Erikson, 1959), behaviourist theories (Skinner, 1976; Thorndike, 1932; Pavlov, 1897), social learning theories (Dweck, 2017; Bandura, 1977; Dollard and Miller, 1950), the Vygotskian perspective (1978) or the Piagetian perspective (Piaget and Inhelder, 1972). Of course, such theories and perspectives are ever-evolving, being revised in light of current research, its methodologies and conclusions. As you reflect on the definitions presented in this section, you may find echoes of each of the theoretical perspectives outlined previously, while instinctively veering towards some more than others.

Some of the definitions of SR included in this section demonstrate the emphasis on its different attributes. The regarded definition by Schunk and Zimmerman (1994: 309) explains SR as being:

> The process whereby students activate and sustain cognitions, behaviours and . . . affects, which are systematically oriented toward attainment of their goals.

Their choice of the word "student" is noteworthy, as it lends itself to a more cognitive, academic perspective of SR, whereas affect is cited last. Similarly, some psychologists suggest that emotion regulation may be understood as a form of self-regulated, goal-directed behaviour (Erber and Erber, 2000; Larsen, 2000; Tice and Bratslavsky, 2000), whereas the non-statutory guidance for the EYFS – Birth to Five Matters (Early Years Coalition, 2021: 20) emphasizes the role of attuned relationships in the development of SR, as opposed to cognitive capacities being uppermost:

> Self-regulation, like many elements of development and learning, is not something children do by themselves. It is a process that grows out of attuned relationships where the caregiver and baby or child are closely attentive to each other and engage in sensitive, responsive exchanges.

Given the complex nature of SR, this document also goes on to highlight the inextricable link between the emotional and cognitive domains of SR, which is sometimes a source of contention:

> It can be most helpful to focus on the interlinked aspects of emotional self-regulation and cognitive self-regulation, and how these work together to enable children to manage thoughts, feelings and behaviour.
>
> Early Years Coalition (2021: 20)

Here, the child's agency in regulating their own emotions and behaviour is acknowledged – as opposed to these being controlled externally, by the adult. This brings us to the well-regarded definition of SR by Hughes and Baylin (2012: 50), who are unequivocal about what SR is – and what it is not:

> What is self-regulation? We'll begin with what it's not: it is not suppression. Rather, it is the resilient capacity to "feel" and "deal," to experience a full range of affect and to modulate all kinds of feelings effectively enough to trust oneself to be able to cope well with the full range of human experience and to be an emotionally trustworthy partner and parent.

Again, their definition puts the responsibility on the individual in interpreting a situation (or their emotional response to a situation) and being *able* to *choose* how to respond and behave in ways that are not self-limiting but instead helpful to themselves and those around them. With this in mind, my personal favourite definition of SR is one offered by Shanker and Barker (2018b: 23). This is because their comprehensive definition of SR captures the complex feat of a child trying to regulate their energy states, emotions and behaviour while explaining what this might look like when a child finds it difficult to self-regulate. They explain SR as:

> The ability to manage stress and the neural processes that control the energy expended to deal with a stressor and then recover. When an individual's stress levels are too high, various systems for thinking and metabolic recovery are compromised. The signs of dysregulation show up in the behaviour, or mood, or attention and physical wellbeing.

The last three sentences of that quote are particularly important for you to reflect on as parents or EY practitioners: that signs of dysregulation show up in behaviour, mood, attention or physical wellbeing. Think about all the times you may have reprimanded a child for misbehaving. Did you pause to consider that they might be feeling unheard, tired, hungry, thirsty, unwell, anxious, experiencing difficulty concentrating or feeling overwhelmed?

With this more holistic perspective of SR, we seek to understand the stressors that cause behaviours which are often misunderstood and labelled as "naughty," "challenging" or "defiant" – instead of trying to simply stop the behaviour. When we reflect on how much children have to contend with in their lives, we are able to understand how easy it is to become dysregulated (frustrated or angry, for example) and how easy it is for us to misinterpret the signs and wind up dysregulated ourselves. At school, children have the daunting task of managing all the transitions that occur as part of the daily routine; making and maintaining friendships; organizing themselves and meeting work deadlines; ignoring distractions while focusing on multi-step instructions from their teacher; managing their biological needs such as being hungry or thirsty, articulating when they are unwell; when they need to use the bathroom and when they need time away from the hustle and bustle to feel calm.

If we were to look at a brain scan of a child who has not yet managed to self-regulate in a certain situation, we would see that their limbic system – commonly referred to as the "downstairs brain" (Siegel and Bryson, 2012) has become activated and therefore lit red, with reduced activation in their prefrontal cortex (PFC). This is discussed in Chapter 3. This is activated and therefore lit red, with reduced activation in their prefrontal cortex (PFC). On the other hand, a child who can self-regulate will have minimal activation in the limbic system, but a PFC (a key part of the "upstairs brain," also discussed in Chapter 3) that is highly activated and lit red. This indicates that the PFC is "in charge" – instead of the limbic system (which is always first to be activated if someone is or perceives themselves to be in danger).

Studies (McClelland et al., 2013; McClelland and Wanless, 2012) demonstrate that children's self-regulatory abilities at four-years-old were a significantly stronger predictor of academic achievement and emotional wellbeing at age 25 than a range of other developing abilities, including early numeracy and literacy accomplishments. This important finding highlights the importance of SR as an all-encompassing set of skills which actually provides the foundation from which all other skills and abilities can unfold. Academic or professional success as an adult means little if an individual cannot regulate their own thoughts, emotions and behaviour in ways that are socially acceptable and ever-evolving, as opposed to ways that are self-limiting or harmful to others. When we are able to self-regulate, we are better able to support babies and children to develop this set of essential life skills.

Self-regulation is the greatest gift we can give to children.

Hopefully, you have added to your understanding of SR and some of its diverse definitions. Clearly, it is not the role of this book to include all existing definitions. It is up to you to continue reading widely around the subject to compare and critique definitions and reach your own conclusions.

The Five Domains of Self-Regulation

In order to develop a robust understanding of SR, it is important to understand that it is not a one-dimensional skill that resides in just one part of the body or brain region. According to Shanker (2020), there are five domains of SR – each affecting the other and each with its unique stressors. These domains are vital to hold in mind when trying to figure out the root cause of children's (and young adults') emotional responses and consequent behaviours – as opposed to only reacting to the surface behaviours we see – which is sadly what all too often happens. Take a look at Table 1.1 and reflect on the triggers. Some may bring to mind triggers in your provision that you previously did not think posed a problem. Note that the list is not exhaustive but serves as a catalyst for further thinking and research.

Table 1.1 The Five Domains of SR

Domain	*Stressors*
Biological domain 	This domain focuses on physical health and wellbeing. Stressors include insufficient sleep, poor diet, physical abuse, having to be sat still for extended periods, lack of exercise, lack of fresh air, energy levels, illness, pain, sensitivity to certain fabrics (clothing), excessive visual stimulation (brightly coloured wall displays and hanging displays), bright lighting and feeling too hot or cold.
Emotional domain 	This includes a child's ability to monitor, consider and (as a result) change their behaviour. Stressors affecting this domain include abuse, trauma, bullying, bereavement, transitions, changes in routine, as well as feeling embarrassed, unwelcome, anxious, depressed or scared. It also includes difficulty in coping with strong emotions (such as excitement and anger).
Cognitive domain 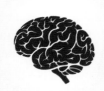	This domain involves the mental processes involved in building knowledge, such as paying attention, perception, memory and problem-solving. Difficulties in the other domains will impact a child's ability to pay attention, which often gets them in trouble at school. Stressors include abuse, lack of intellectual stimulation, confusion, difficulty concentrating and prioritizing tasks, poor memory and low frustration tolerance.
Social domain 	This includes verbal and non-verbal communication, empathy, active listening, managing friendships and overcoming conflict. Stressors include abuse, a lack of friends, being isolated or bullied at school, not having anyone to play with during break times, difficulty in understanding social norms and understanding the impact of own behaviour on others, feeling awkward in social situations, large groups, disagreements and feeling defensive.
Prosocial domain 	This includes the capacity to care about others' feelings and to help them manage their feelings – to co-regulate them during emotionally charged times. Stressors include abuse, difficulty reading others' cues and coping with other people's stress, sharing, telling the truth and knowing right from wrong. It also includes injustice, unfairness, expectations of others, being late and being exploited by others.

When we reflect on these five domains with regard to children (or, indeed, teenagers and adults), it is easy to understand how each domain is mutually dependent on and inextricably linked to the other, with each being of equal importance. Consider a child who attends a hectic, cluttered setting and is expected to sit for extended periods without sufficient room and opportunity to move. Add to this an inflexible approach to behaviour and a routine that is focused on academic outcomes over emotional well-being, and you might appreciate the impact across the five domains of SR. Children are likely to be "fidgety" and get easily frustrated; they may find it difficult to concentrate and learn and therefore get into trouble. This can result in low self-esteem and navigating interactions and friendships may prove challenging – all five domains triggered on a daily basis. What makes this all the more concerning is that SR and its five domains are not embedded in teacher training programmes or EY professional development programmes, yet such knowledge could do much to inform EY pedagogy, how EY environments are furnished and resourced and how the daily routine is planned.

We will now take a closer look at each of the domains in turn to help broaden and deepen your understanding of each domain, how they are affected by internal and external factors and what this means for children's holistic wellbeing.

Biological Domain

While factors including nutrition, sleep and general physical health and wellbeing underpin the biological domain of SR, it is also important to understand the fundamental role of the developing brain and the rest of the nervous system as being integral to maintaining homeostasis (balance in the body) by controlling and regulating the other parts of the body. Early brain development occurs at an exceptionally rapid rate from birth to two-years-old, with experiences, relationships and interactions shaping this precarious process for good or bad – and their legacy lasts across the life trajectory. In this early phase of life, infants are at the mercy of their nervous system and need to be regulated by attuned and responsive adults in order to achieve SR. It certainly will not be achieved by "letting babies cry it out" or not picking them up when they need to be held or comforted. We would not turn away a friend or relative who is crying or expressing the need for comfort. So how can we deem this ethical when it comes to our youngest and most vulnerable, whose nervous systems and consequent ability to regulate themselves are still nascent and thus wholly dependent on us for regulation? Where a child is aware of their brain-body responses to stressors in their environment, they are able to self-regulate them in order to reach a state of calm – but this comes at a cost. The more energy an individual expends on trying to recover from overcoming a stressor, the less capacity they have to be emotionally and cognitively present. This may look like difficulty in concentrating, lethargy or being "spaced out." As Shanker et al. (2017: 16) remind us:

> Self-regulation is concerned with the manner in which an individual deals with stress, in all its many forms, and then recovers from the energy expended. An

individual (be they a child, parent or early educator) exposed to too much stress in the early years, may develop a "kindled alarm system," in which even relatively minor stressors can send them into fight-or-flight or freeze.

The four neural mechanisms (or the four Fs) for dealing with stress are also key here. They are:

- Fight (hyper-aroused state)

- Flight (hyper-aroused state)

- Freeze (hypo-aroused state)

- Fawn (hypo-aroused state).

The specific arousal states will determine whether a child needs support to up- or down-regulate their emotional responses. The adult's role is thus vital in:

- Knowing the child's background

- Identifying and minimizing triggers

- Identifying whether they have entered a hyper- or hypo-aroused state

- Using the child's preferred ways to help them reach a regulated state.

Arousal states are further discussed in Chapter 4.

When an individual is unable to regulate their nervous system, they become locked in a constant state of fight or flight, being triggered over what are sometimes seemingly innocuous causes, and as a result, feel constantly stressed. During the fight or flight response, signals from the autonomic nervous system stimulate the adrenal gland to start pumping the hormone adrenaline into the bloodstream in order to deal with the perceived or real threat, with adrenaline affecting the heart, lungs, muscles and blood vessels. Its release into the bloodstream brings about the following physiological changes:

- Increased heart rate and blood flow

- Faster breathing

- Raised blood sugar levels

- Increased strength and physical performance.

This surge of adrenaline in the bloodstream is commonly referred to as an adrenaline rush or the fight or flight response, within which another hormone, noradrenaline, plays a complementary role to adrenaline by promoting vasoconstriction (narrowing of the blood vessels), which increases blood pressure. Like adrenaline, norepinephrine also increases heart rate and blood sugar levels to galvanize the brain and body during the stress response.

Usually, when the threat or stressors have passed, hormones, heart rate and blood pressure return to baseline level and other systems that were supressed during fight or flight can resume as normal. However, when stressors are always present and an individual constantly feels (or is) under attack, the fight or flight reaction stays turned on, with stress hormone levels also remaining high. Over time and with persistent activation of the fight or flight response and the related overexposure to the stress hormone cortisol (and other stress hormones), almost all of the body's processes can become disrupted, with overall health being compromised. It is useful to envisage it as an over-reactive alarm system, with the sympathetic nervous system and hypothalamic-pituitary-adrenal (HPA) axis going into overdrive (discussed further on). This increases inflammation and compromises the immune system. These processes contribute to many diseases such as diabetes, cancer and heart disease. Anxiety, depression, digestive problems, weight gain, memory and concentration impairment, headaches and sleep problems are also commonly reported. New evidence suggests that these responses occur in response to perceived social isolation as well as to a physical threat of harm (Shanker, 2020; Siegel and Bryson, 2018; Perry, 2014). Finding healthy ways to identify and manage our personal triggers will not only enable SR to occur but will enable us to more effectively co-regulate children's emotional dysregulation.

Emotional Domain

Babies are wholly dependent on their caregivers to help regulate their nervous system, physiological states and emotional responses. Very young children, who are very emotionally labile, need the support of an attuned adult to guide them through the sometimes frightening and overwhelming world of emotions, to identify where they are coming from, what they are called and how to manage them. The more dysregulated a young child is, the less able they are to reflect on and modify their emotional responses in the future; therefore, *connecting* with the child before trying to re-direct their behaviour is what every adult should strive to do. A child's capacity to regulate their emotions affects every aspect of their life, including their relationships with their family and friends, academic performance and long-term mental health and wellbeing (Raver, 2004). The emotional domain of SR is therefore fundamentally important, providing the very foundation of all other skills and holistic wellbeing.

Cognitive Domain

Executive Functioning (Cognitive SR) and School Readiness

The cognitive domain of SR is arguably the most emphasized of all five domains and the most demanded of in our education system, which is no accident, given the continued prioritizing of academic outcomes over children's emotional wellbeing and mental health in education – which is taking place at an increasingly early age.

Children with SEND can find it difficult to exercise cognitive SR. Behaviours such as fidgeting, an inability to sit still or concentrate for extended periods, make learning very challenging and draining for these children, due to the excessive energy and effort they need to expend on "doing what they're told" or sitting still and "behaving themselves" in order to learn while trying hard to curb their need to move, play or be active. Moreover, when a child feels anxious; is in a state of distress; or feels threatened, stressed or humiliated, they are not able to apply those higher-order, executive functioning skills, such as problem-solving, setting goals, self-motivating, paying attention, following instructions, using their working memory and ultimately learning, because their brain's panic button – the amygdala – has been activated, which causes a swift downward spiral in emotional wellbeing and behaviour (this is explored in Chapter 3). As Immordino-Yang and Damasio (2007: 12) highlight:

> Learning, attention, memory, decision-making and social functioning are both profoundly affected by and subsumed within the processes of emotion.

Discussion concerning executive functioning cannot be complete without due attention being paid to the contentious matter of school readiness (I say contentious because, in my opinion, the question needs to be *how child-ready are our schools?* as opposed to forcing children to be ready for school). Being able to regulate thoughts, emotional responses and behaviour are *necessary precursors* to developing executive functioning skills. SR as *the* foundation for learning and any support necessary for the child is recognized by speech and language pathologist McCalla (2020), who explains:

> Emotional regulation (ER) – the ability to maintain a well-regulated emotional state to cope with everyday stress, plays a significant role in all aspects of cognitive-linguistic function and executive functioning. Emotions may hinder or facilitate problem-solving (Gordon and Hibbard, 1992). If, as Luria states, problem-solving is the basis for executive function skills, ER must be a focus of intervention.

Executive Functioning and Its Development

Executive functioning is the management (or regulation) of cognitive processes, including working memory, reasoning, decision-making, task flexibility, problem-solving and the planning and execution of ideas. Metacognition is a core part of these executive functioning skills, which provides the foundation for all learning. Put simply, metacognition means thinking about thinking: children who can use metacognition have an awareness of their thoughts and can recognize their strengths and areas for improvement, identify the errors they make and why, how they could approach the same problem differently and explain the rationale informing the strategies they choose.

Metacognition helps children to understand how they think and learn so that they can transfer or apply this self-awareness in new situations.

The following are just a few metacognitive questions children may ask themselves during their learning. Upon reading, reflect on whether these are familiar to you:

■ What do I need to do first?

■ Who can I ask for help?

■ Can I explain what I learned?

■ What might happen if I?

■ What did I find difficult?

■ What have I learned from this activity?

■ Can I use my skills in a different activity?

■ How can I improve?

SR is also a skill set to filter distractions, control impulses; focus and re-direct attention; hold and manipulate information; prioritize tasks and set, achieve and adapt goals when necessary. Opportunities for abundant free-flow, child-led play where young children can push their own boundaries, develop their reasoning skills, make decisions, release stress and work through difficult emotions and of great importance – exercise control – are integral to the development of SR and executive functioning – not least because children have not yet developed the top-down cognitive capacities to engage those executive functioning skills. This is recognized by Whitebread (2016: 4), who emphasizes the central, leading role of child-led play in the development of SR and executive functioning skills:

> Playful collaborative activities powerfully support young children's abilities to express their ideas, explain their reasoning and talk about their own learning and, in turn, significantly improve their self-regulatory abilities.

Executive functioning skills are critical for being holistically ready for school and succeeding in academic learning, but we need to understand the deep, inextricable link between the brain regions and circuits associated with executive functioning and the extensive interconnections with deeper brain structures that control the developing child's responses to stress (Siegel, 1999). This is discussed in Chapter 3. Cultivating respectful, nurturing provision that is framed by SR and is trauma-informed will permit and enable practitioners to prioritize children's emotional wellbeing and mental health, which in turn will "free up" the brain to function as optimally as possible.

School Readiness – Not So Fast!

School readiness can be characterized by *three interlinked dimensions:* a) *ready children*, b) *ready schools* and c) *ready families* (UNICEF, 2021a: 5). It is not a set of skills that can or should be hot-housed the term before school begins, as is continually mentioned in this chapter. It begins in utero – with SR being its foundation.

So what else does school readiness involve? Broadly speaking, it requires a child to:

- Be prepared to cope emotionally with separation from their parents/carers

- Demonstrate robust social skills with the adults around them and their peers

- Demonstrate some independence in their personal care

- Demonstrate curiosity about the world and their place in it, through observation and exploration

- Listen and have sufficient language to express themselves

- Feel safe, secure, cared for and resilient enough to be able to take risks and find solutions to the challenges they encounter.

As identified in UNESCO's definition and the previous characteristics, school readiness does not start or end with the child and their executive functioning/academic prowess. It is far broader and longer term than this, requiring ongoing participation and genuine partnership by the current setting, prospective school and family to make the transition less daunting and more enjoyable – and, dare I suggest, even exciting. This triangular relationship, which should provide the foundation to enable the child to feel "school ready" (that is, confident, resilient and encouraged to navigate their new world), needs to continue well after the child has made the transition to school to help ensure parents feel valued and included in the transition process. This is all the more important given the high parental anxiety that often surrounds school readiness. Stories about children not being allowed to take a transition object to their new school, nurseries' efforts at liaising with prospective teachers at the school and parents not being kept informed of their child's progress are common. Yet, actively involving the child in their transition can be immensely beneficial in allaying any fears while helping them to express their thoughts about the experience and what they are looking forward to. One study (O'Farrelly et al., 2019) found that school readiness initiatives would be improved by consultation with the child and encouraging the participation of the child, especially regarding the *child's* priorities.

Ongoing research into school readiness (Blair and Raver, 2015; McClelland et al., 2013; Dignath et al., 2008; Whitebread et al., 2007) emphasizes the respective roles of maturation and of family investments such as parents' provision of sensitive, nurturant and language-rich care as key influences on young children's early social-emotional and cognitive skills. Also highlighted is the necessity of supportive interactions with parents, teachers and peers in positively influencing emotional reactivity and regulation, in the control of attention and in higher-order cognitive functions – chiefly those school readiness skills.

So when you reflect on what SR is, just remember, it is *the foundation* for school readiness! I envisage it as SR = SR:

Self-Regulation = School Readiness

School readiness does not only mean the strictly academic concept of readiness characterized by such skills and abilities as being able to count to 20, to know the letters of the alphabet, to know colours and shapes or to be able to hold a pencil "correctly." It includes being physically well nourished and rested; the ability to communicate wants and needs verbally; to be enthusiastic and curious in approaching new activities; to pay attention and follow directions; to regulate thoughts, emotions and behaviour and to be sensitive to other children's feelings. This is acknowledged by Blair and Raver (2015: 17), who underscore the importance of SR in making the educational experience more equitable for all children, particularly those growing up in poverty:

> An approach to the promotion of school readiness by fostering the development of self-regulation offers the potential to remake early education in a way that is effective for all children. It can help to level the playing field and restore equality of opportunity.

The role of the adult and environment in facilitating school readiness must also be carefully considered and flexible to meet the moment-to-moment needs of children. As Shanker (2020: 57) explains:

> The emphasis on self-regulation in school readiness research is heightened by advances in neurobiology and neuroendocrinology indicating that environmental conditions and interpersonal interactions, both positive and negative, are embedded biologically, shaping or canalizing the development of brain and behaviour.

When we reflect on early brain development and the protective factors that ensure its healthy growth, it stands to reason that in the rush to force children to be "school ready," the wellbeing of children across the other domains of SR suffers. Consider the re-introduction of the once-failed Baseline Assessment of four-year-old children in the United Kingdom, phonics tests, times tables tests and weekly spelling and maths tests, with consequent grouping according to ability, from the nursery. The current education system is squeezing out play in favour of a sub-Victorian, formal education starting far too young, to the detriment of children's wellbeing, self-confidence, imagination and creativity.

Social Domain

Humans are born to be social, seeking to be in close physical proximity to their caregiver from birth to ensure health and survival. Feeling regulated in the social domain of SR includes the ability to read social cues – to know what others are feeling, how their behaviour impacts others and how they can modify their behaviour in response to this. Our mirror neurons enable us to match each other's emotions unconsciously and immediately, so we can anticipate and mirror each other's movements when feeling sympathy for another person or when we are in agreement with them. Some children may find it difficult to read (or infer) emotions from facial expressions or even feel threatened by certain gestures, movements or tone of voice and consequently enter fight or flight mode. This makes it all the more important to co-regulate and demonstrate calming techniques that can help the child to cope with and even begin to enjoy such situations. Where an individual struggles to do this, over time, they may experience difficulty in creating and maintaining friendships. Where tolerable, play experiences are generally a fun, non-pressuring way to build children's SR skills (this is discussed further on in the chapter).

Prosocial Domain

As mentioned, we are relational creatures – we were born to connect. When a child lives with chronic and toxic stressors, they may develop anti-social behaviours – behaviours such as shouting, bullying, intentionally disrupting, fighting and hitting others or shouting, which if left unchecked or worse – a child is continually reprimanded without any connection and addressing of root causes – will increase in severity across the life course. This is highlighted by eminent neuroscientists Immordino-Yang and Damasio (2007: 2), who confirm that:

> In pre-schoolers and school-age children, problems in socioemotional development typically manifest themselves as challenging, socially disruptive patterns of behaviour that, without intervention, can evolve into persistent antisocial behaviour, such as physical aggression and bullying and ultimately adolescent delinquency.

Now that you have read about the five domains of SR, it is clear to see just how complex a concept it is and how much is demanded of children just to be physically, emotionally and cognitively present – and how many obstacles they face on a daily basis. Shanker et al. (2015: 19) are unequivocal about the fundamental importance of SR:

> Self-regulation is not, however, just another root: it is the "taproot" that feeds all the smaller, lateral roots. To understand why this is the case, you need only consider how each of the "roots" serves to reduce the stress created by the stimuli impinging on an infant's senses.

Rewind. Reflect. Write!

1a In your own words, describe what self-regulation is.

1b Reflecting on the definitions of self-regulation in this chapter, which one most resonates with you? Discuss.

2 What factors influence a child's ability to self-regulate?

3a Identify and explain the five domains of self-regulation.

3b Identify the stressors in each of the five domains.

3c Note down any further stressors you can think of across the five domains.

4 Discuss the connection between self-regulation and a child's ability to concentrate.

Top Tips for Practice!

■ If SR is yet to be embedded within your provision, in your next team meeting, introduce it and talk about how you currently support children's ability to self-regulate

■ Support your team (and parents) to understand that emotions drive behaviour

■ When you are next at work, take a close look at your setting (indoors and outdoors) and note down all the potential stressors for children

■ With the support of your team (including the leadership team), plan how you will address these stressors

■ Set the tone first thing in the morning – when children see and sense that you are relaxed and truly welcoming, they will feel calm, happy and ready to explore

- Check in with the children – ask them about things that might be bothering them and whether they had any breakfast (for example)
- Build the children's emotional vocabulary – just one effective way to do this is creating a word wall filled with "feelings" words and faces.

Stop Calling It a Tantrum! – The Disrupting Force of Dysregulation

Now that you have an understanding of the stressors that can trigger a child across each of the five domains of SR, it will be worthwhile looking a little deeper at what happens when a child cannot cope with these stressors and loses the ability to regulate their emotional responses to provocative stimuli – that is, when they enter a state of dysregulation. A dysregulated child is too frequently mislabelled as being "challenging" or "naughty" or "pushing an adult's buttons," "attention-seeking" and, perhaps most commonly, as having a "tantrum." Such terms are dismissive of the child's psychological state during moments of dysregulation and serve to emotionally distance the adult from the child, while doing nothing to practically support them to regain equilibrium. Re-thinking the language used in your setting and home can make a positive change to your mindset and behaviour when supporting dysregulated children.

Dysregulation happens to us all at some point in our lives – babies, children, adolescents and adults all struggle to regulate their emotional responses during their lives, but a persistent inability to regulate our emotions and behaviour can lead to a lifetime of difficulties, including problems with interpersonal relationships, trouble with school performance and the inability to function effectively at work. There is no tickbox approach or milestone as to when an individual should stop getting dysregulated. It is a unique phenomenon, with early adversity playing a pivotal role in a child or adult being able to self-regulate (prevent dysregulation from taking hold). A key factor here is parental SR. Where a parent finds it difficult to self-regulate, their child will quite inevitably mirror their behaviours. This not only results from observing and imitating their parents' dysregulated behaviour, but also because they are physiologically affected – entering a state of fight or flight as a result of bearing witness to this. We can all attest to that – when we are physically close to somebody in a state of distress (particularly if they are someone we care about), we too become dysregulated. This might manifest as fear, panic, agitation or anger.

The Interconnectedness of the Emotional and Cognitive Capacities Underlying SR

Now that we have looked at SR and its five domains and triggers, let us turn our attention to a consistent source of contention when it comes to defining SR. I continue to find myself embroiled in debates trying to reach common ground concerning where its primacy resides – it is this issue and the interconnectedness of the emotional and cognitive domains of SR that warrant closer attention.

We each have our own evidence base on which we draw to help us build informed judgement and consolidate our understanding about matters which concern us. For example, these might in part be due to our own experiences that we recognize and identify with in the literature we read. I believe there is a primacy to the emotional aspect of SR – with SR being primarily born out of emotional abilities, as opposed to cognitive abilities. I thus naturally find myself drawn to some theoretical perspectives more than others in building my understanding of SR and its development. This brings to mind LeDoux's perspective on emotions in underlying neural activity (2002: 320). He explains:

> Emotions play a key role in organizing brain activity, with the net result that emotional arousal penetrates the brain widely and perpetuates itself.

This dominance of emotions plays itself out on a daily basis in children and adults alike: the dysregulated child who temporarily loses the ability to "think rationally" and think before she acts or a child who cannot face a test because "their nerves got the better of them." This is due to the automated responses of our primitive, emotionally reactive brain, which tends to be first to react in emotionally charged situations – be they perceived or real. The result of the limbic system taking over is a cascade of chemical reactions that could cause an individual to enter fight or flight. In a predictable environment with caregiving that is consistently loving and supportive, a child will learn how to regulate their emotions so that they are able to choose how they behave or respond to the stressors they encounter in their lives. It takes consistent nurturing of nascent SR abilities for them to be refined by children and adults alike.

It is my contention that emotion regulation *does* provide the foundation from which all other skills can consequently develop. When we understand how the brain develops – that is, back to front and sequentially – or bottom up (Harvard Centre on the Developing Child, 2021), with those primitive regions responsible for emotion regulation, memory-recall and associating memories with feelings residing here – it stands to reason that these primitive, emotional regions cannot be "bypassed." A child needs to feel psychologically safe and regulated before they are able to access their executive functioning skills (the aforementioned cognitive domain of SR). As Perry (2009: 242) states:

> Simply put, the organization of higher parts of the brain depends upon input from the lower parts of the brain.

It is not the other way round. Stressed brains cannot learn (Shanker, 2020; Siegel and Bryson, 2018) – this is due to the pre-cognitive state a child enters when in fight or flight. There is no rationality to a child's behaviour in this state because they are caught in a limbic state of high arousal and need to regain a state of emotional equilibrium before they can engage their higher-order, thinking skills. So while some could argue that to be successfully self-regulated, we need to employ our cognitive skills to help us to deal with feelings – otherwise we are never self-regulated and only relying on CR forever – again, brain development, much like other areas of development, is sequential. We cannot run before we can walk. The emotion centres of the brain develop first – so these need to be engaged first. Brain regions responsible for those higher-order skills develop later. So while the two are indeed inextricably linked, emotion regulation *does* precede higher-order (or executive functioning) skills. This is illustrated in Figure 1.1.

Brain development

The developing brains and nervous systems of children may be affected by severe and persistent fear and anxiety. As a result, they may face a variety of challenges in school and life, including trouble managing their emotions, solving problems, relating well to others and concentrating.

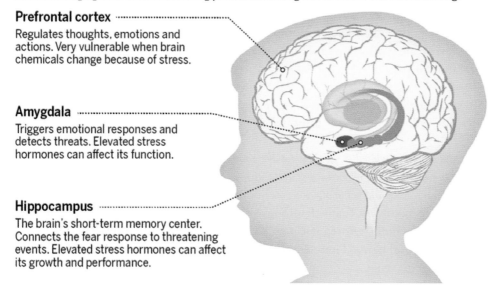

Prefrontal cortex

Regulates thoughts, emotions and actions. Very vulnerable when brain chemicals change because of stress.

Amygdala

Triggers emotional responses and detects threats. Elevated stress hormones can affect its function.

Hippocampus

The brain's short-term memory center. Connects the fear response to threatening events. Elevated stress hormones can affect its growth and performance.

Figure 1.1 Sequential Brain Development

Source: National Scientific Council on the Developing Child (2010). Illustration by Betsy Hayes; adapted with permission from the Centre on the Developing Child.

At the bottom of Figure 1.1 is the brainstem (which develops first and is responsible for our survival, including regulation of heart rate, breathing, sleeping and eating, as well as awareness and consciousness). Developing next, sitting atop the brainstem and buried under the cortex, is the set of primitive brain structures, the limbic system (which is responsible for our behavioural and emotional responses – particularly behaviours we need for survival and fight or flight – and consists of key brain regions like the amygdala and the hippocampus). The frontal lobes, critically the PFC, which regulates our thoughts, emotional responses and behaviour, as well as managing impulse control and focusing our attention, develop last. Shanker et al. (2015: 17) explain:

> The lesson here is parents and early childhood educators alike need to soothe before they try to educate. Identify and reduce whatever stress they can. So, before they try to help the child learn how to monitor, evaluate and modify her emotions, they need to focus on the "three R's" of emotion-regulation: Recognize. Reduce. Restore. Recognize the signs of escalating stress. Reduce the stress. Restore energy. All this sets the foundation from which learning can then take place.

This is all the more important to understand now, with children returning to school, post-pandemic, where many are feeling dysregulated, anxious, stressed and overwhelmed. That is not to say that young children lack all inhibitory control, but there is a neuro-biological sequence to this taking place – and just as with executive functioning skills, emotion regulation skills also require adult support to develop – as does the development of every other skill. SR cannot occur without CR, and this needs to be understood by everyone working with or on behalf of children and young adults. As Bronson (2000: 60) explains:

> Although the child is active in developing her own self-regulatory capacities, she does not and cannot do this in isolation.

Once a child is in a regulated state, they are able to reflect on their behaviour and talk through more helpful coping mechanisms when in a state of distress. They are also able to adopt more prosocial ways of communicating and behaving. Perry's neurosequential model (2006) clearly identifies the bottom-up nature of brain development and the necessity of engaging and regulating the limbic system before expecting a child to access the cognitive capacities of SR. Figure 1.2 is helpful here. (There are many variations of this model available online.)

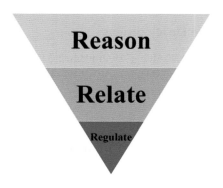

Figure 1.2 Bruce Perry's Three Rs – Reaching the Learning Brain

We must always seek to first soothe and reassure the child in order to calm their fight or flight response. This will depend on the individual child, their triggers and the context. A few in-the-moment strategies include getting down to their level (never leaving them "until they calm down"), speaking in a gentle tone of voice and practicing some deep breathing techniques (further strategies are provided throughout this book). Then, we relate on a deeper level through our attuned relationship and sensitive responses to let the child know that they are seen, heard and understood. By acknowledging their feelings in that moment, even by simply saying "I can see you're upset now and I'm here for you" can go a long way in validating the child's emotions. Once the child feels calmer, we must swiftly seek to understand what happened and talk through alternative ways of behaving which can actually build their SR skills while helping to minimize future instances of dysregulation and dependence on others for CR. Perry (2009: 242) explains the neurosequential model of early brain development, highlighting its hierarchical nature:

> The brain is organized in a hierarchical fashion and organizes itself from the bottom up, from the least (brainstem) to the most complex (limbic, cortical) areas. While significantly interconnected, each of these regions mediates distinct functions, with the lower, structurally simpler areas mediating basic regulatory functions and the highest, most complex structures (cortical) mediating the most complex functions. The cortical areas responsible for abstract cognition have years before they will become fully organized and functional.

So a key issue underlying the need to emphasize emotion regulation largely relates to developmental growth – that CR from caring relationships plays a critical role in supporting a child's development of self-regulatory capabilities. Note, too, that Perry underscores the significance of the cortical brain regions taking years to fully develop (this is examined in Chapter 3). Critically, Perry (2009: 243) goes onto explain the fundamental importance of emotion regulation occurring before more cognitive skills can be accessed by the child. He says:

> In order to most efficiently influence a higher function such as speech and language or socioemotional communication, the lower innervating neural networks must be intact and well regulated. An overanxious, impulsive, dysregulated child will have a difficult time participating in, and benefiting from, services targeting social skills, self-esteem and reading, for example.

As mentioned in the previous paragraph, the need for CR does not suggest a permanent dependency on regulation by others forever – quite the opposite. Where children can depend on being regulated by attuned and responsive others when they need it and through observing and imitating positive role models for SR, they develop their own toolkit of SR skills. Thus, SR is a necessary, ever-evolving process that should occur as needed, across the life course. When we understand that the brain is built bottom up, we cannot expect a baby or young child to access and use their higher-order thinking skills (the cognitive domain of SR) without a solid foundation of emotion regulation. Thus, focusing on the reasoning part of the brain with an expectation of learning will not work so well if a child is dysregulated and/or disconnected from others. In relation to the sequential nature of early brain development, Shanker et al. (2015) pose the question *why self-reg first?* when exploring its relevance to children's wellbeing and ability to learn. They invite us to consider the following explanations:

- Pushing a child to master executive function skills when there are constrictions in his sensory root system can be frustrating for the child (and parents/teachers too!)

- We can't begin to work on these higher stage PFC skills until we understand the child's ability to take in and process different kinds of sensory information.

Note the second point – that providing support to engage the more primitive brain regions responsible for emotions needs to be in place before a child can access the more cognitive capacities of the PFC. When we reflect on how the developing brain is organized and its plasticity – particularly during early childhood – we know that consistent provision of co-regulatory experiences causes changes in the brain's architecture in response to these experiences. With maturation and repetition, these get laid down as neural pathways, ultimately resulting in building a child's capacity for SR.

Both emotional and cognitive abilities are vitally important and need to be understood as fully integrated and inter-related in a completely bi-directional relationship, with one affecting the efficiency of the other. Just as metacognitive abilities support children's developing competence to manage their own social and emotional lives, so are the emotional and social elements of SR essential in supporting the development of children's cognitive regulation, as these enable a healthy relationship with oneself and others across the life course. The conflict here is that while metacognitive abilities do support a child to better manage their emotions and behaviour, these capacities are not sufficiently developed in a baby or young child, so relying on their cognitive abilities is not an option when the regulation of their nervous system is wholly dependent on their primary caregiver co-regulating their biological, physical and emotional states. A crying baby does not have the cognitive capacity to stop themselves from crying in the understanding that they will likely get their needs, for example, for food, milk, comfort or companionship met, nor can they regulate their own temperature. They use the only forms of communicating available to them to get the help they need to return to a state of regulation, as they are not able to do this independently of an adult – this being via their social engagement system (Tronick and Gold, 2020; Porges, 2017). It is through the process of CR that babies and young children gradually develop the skills of SR – the ability to self-soothe in ways that are healthy and conducive to reaching equilibrium (Schaffer, 1996; Sroufe, 1995). As Shanker (2020: 8) says:

Nature's plan was to have a higher order brain regulate a developing organism that is years away from being able to manage this feat on his own. A baby cannot down- or up-regulate herself; it is up to the caregiver to perform this role.

Reflecting on the limbic system – as with the rest of the brain, its experience-dependent nature and dependence on the quality of those initial dyadic interactions cannot be overstated. Responsive interactions and caregiving, with regular opportunities for the child to practice using language and manage their emotions with the support of a sensitive and attuned parent or primary carer thus play a fundamentally important role in the process of SR. Correspondingly, how a child manages their emotions in difficult situations influences pathways created in the brain, which in turn create the "blueprint" for future emotional responses and behaviours (National Scientific Council on the Developing Child, 2011). Neuroimaging studies show that structures including the amygdalae, hypothalamus and PFC are pivotal in producing emotions, memory and the regulation of behaviour and emotions (Trevarthen and Delafield-Butt, 2013; Trevarthen et al., 2006).

The inextricable link between the brain and emotions also becomes clearer – our very being is governed by our emotional states. Emotions are linked with early developing regions of the human nervous system, including structures of the limbic system and the brain stem (Thomson, 2013; Barrett et al., 2007; Bell and Wolfe, 2007).

The ability to make judgements and take risks, respond to frightening situations and learn new skills are all dictated by how secure, confident and happy a child feels. Put simply, emotion regulation is a core component of SR (Murray et al., 2015), and SR is critical for learning, as well as for academic and social success. Shanker (2020: 13) goes on to emphasize the essential role of the attuned adult in nurturing children's emotional development, which provides the foundation for other skills to develop. He explains:

> A limbic-to-limbic connection makes the growth of emotions possible, which then shape a child's communicative, social and cognitive development.

The eminent neurobiologist Dr Daniel Siegel perfectly captures the enduring conflicting perspectives concerning the origins and essence of SR. During one seminar (2020), he quipped:

> There is some controversy regarding emotion being only cortical – which is a very cortical thing to say!

I am in complete agreement with Siegel, as it is my contention that much of the conflicting perspectives do tend to arise from academics who are more in favour of supporting the metacognitive capacities involved in SR.

In conclusion, emotion regulation is indeed a fundamental necessity in early childhood, but as long as CR consistently takes place during this sensitive period of development, it could be argued that instead of emotion regulation being the foundation of everything, the interrelation of emotional and cognitive SR should be emphasized while not removing the roots in early CR and need to support young children's emotion regulation in times of great stress and distress, that is, those moments of dysregulation that are often erroneously and unhelpfully referred to as a "tantrum" or, better, "flipping the lid" (Siegel and Bryson, 2018, 2012). We also need to hold at the forefront of our minds that children who have been exposed to adverse childhood experiences (ACEs) and trauma will predominantly function from their limbic system, which means they will not be so adept at functioning from their more rational "upstairs" brain, which supports the process of SR – a process that is as unique as the individual child.

Rewind. Reflect. Write!

1   In your own words, explain the interconnectedness of the emotional and cognitive capacities underlying SR.

2   In your opinion, is there a primacy to the role of emotion regulation in SR? Explain the reason for your answer, including two references to theory.

3   Do you think there are potential problems in emphasizing the cognitive capacities of SR? Explain the reasons for your answer.

4   Do some online research concerning the emotional and cognitive aspects of SR. Write a paragraph or two about your thoughts on the subject, using your references to support you.

5a Outline Perry's neurosequential model.

5b How far and in which ways do you think it is useful for practitioners and parents to understand?

6   Consider the three Rs in the context of the current education system. Do you think this consistently takes place? Explain your answer.

7a Do you think it is important to move away from terms like "tantrum"? Discuss.

7b Note down some ways to encourage your team and families to consider stopping using this term and replacing it with "dysregulation."

When Does Self-Regulation Develop?

SR is not a set of skills that can be taught via prescriptive tick-box criteria. It is a life-long, ever-fluctuating process that is dependent on influencing factors within and external to each child, beginning in the mutually dependent relationship between mother (or other primary caregiver) and child, from conception (Maltese et al., 2017; Pezzulo and Castelfranchi, 2009; Lockman and Hazen, 1989). In utero, the baby's brain orchestrates every aspect of development – and indeed life itself, regulating cardiac, digestive and temperature control functions. When these functions are in harmony and working optimally, the baby's motor movements and reactions are organized and predictable, in line with their mother's mood, temperament and state of general wellbeing – that is, a state of homeostasis (the body's ability to maintain a stable internal environment despite changes in external conditions). However, where a mother experiences short- or long-term toxic stress, such as domestic abuse, poverty, homelessness, racism or discrimination, or is feeling depressed or anxious, elevated foetal heart rate, increased irritability and susceptibility to certain neurodevelopmental conditions that persist across the life trajectory may result. This is demonstrated by La Marca-Ghaemmaghami et al. (2017: 3), who explain:

> If an expectant mother is strongly stressed over a longer period of time, the risk of the unborn child developing a mental or physical illness later in life, such as attention deficit hyperactivity disorder (ADHD) or cardiovascular disease increases.

This rather shocking statement is sadly far from unique. Studies continue to draw similar conclusions regarding continued maternal stress causing childhood mental health conditions such as anxiety and depression, as well as neurodevelopmental conditions like ADHD and autism (Maté, 2019; MacKinnon et al., 2018; Ruisch et al., 2018; Kingsbury et al., 2016; Walder et al., 2014). Generally, the higher and more persistent the level of stress on the foetus, the more likely the high symptom trajectory for hyperactivity (MacKinnon et al., 2018). Conversely, it is widely understood that some stress is inevitable and necessary to our survival. The hormones released during stress, such as corticotropin-releasing hormone (CRH), actually facilitate childbirth as well as increasing levels of the stress hormone cortisol to prepare us for fight or flight (Porges, 2021; Siegel et al., 2021; La Marca-Ghaemmaghami et al., 2017). This is illustrated in Figure 1.3.

Stress activates the expression of hypothalamic CRH, which stimulates the cascade of events preparing the organism for fight or flight – chiefly the release of cortisol and adrenaline to galvanize the body into action. It is important to note that during pregnancy, the maternal HPA system changes dramatically because the placenta expresses the genes for CRH, with placental CRH (pCRH) markedly increasing during pregnancy, which increases levels to concentrations 1,000 to 10,000 times those found in a non-pregnant individual (Thomson, 2013: 1). As well as persistently raised levels of cortisol during pregnancy adversely affecting long-term physiological and mental health (Lee Oh et al., 2018; Sandman and Glynn, 2009; Felitti et al., 1998), the attachment process may also be adversely impacted: 98% of survey respondents in a study by Reed and Parish (2021) said babies their organization works with had been impacted by parental anxiety, stress or depression which was negatively affecting bonding and responsive care.

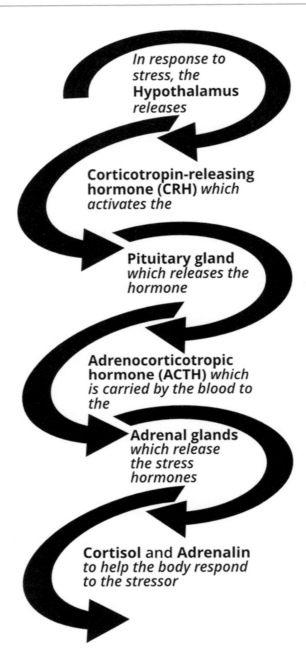

In response to stress, the **Hypothalamus** *releases*

Corticotropin-releasing hormone (CRH) *which activates the*

Pituitary gland *which releases the hormone*

Adrenocorticotropic hormone (ACTH) *which is carried by the blood to the*

Adrenal glands *which release the stress hormones*

Cortisol and **Adrenalin** *to help the body respond to the stressor*

Figure 1.3 The HPA Axis

You may have heard or even made statements such as a baby is "whingey," "upset easily" or "difficult to settle," but when was the last time you paused to attribute any of these behaviours to their prenatal experience? Where an infant has shared the neuro-biological and physiological impact of the toxicity in their mother's life for (approximately) nine months, it will likely affect their internal and external experiences of

the world. This will be all the more amplified if, through their early experiences of being parented, they come to understand that their needs for care, love and companionship will not be met by a loving, responsive parent. They will view the world with anxiety, fear and mistrust, shutting down (or dissociating) to avoid the pain of rejection. This can consequently further derail healthy attachment, through both parent and infant not seeking out one another for companionship, with frequent episodes of dysregulation in the parent and infant resulting. This could ultimately diminish the infant's ability to self-regulate. The need for early emotional connection is emphasized by Trevarthen and Delafield-Butt (2016: 4), who state:

> Simple actions performed in utero and the first gestures in early life, tested in communication with a caring and sensitive caregiver, are brought together, or "chained," to compose habits or projects of action that may reach far into the future.

During infancy, in the mother–infant dyad, the infant begins to learn through interactions with their mother (or primary caregiver) how to self-regulate the experience of intense and potentially overwhelming emotions – both positive and negative. The caregiver's behaviour towards and responses to her baby very quickly begin to shape the baby's ability to self-soothe, with neurological changes in the infant occurring in response to positive interactions with them, such as playing, comforting, holding and communicating, both verbally and non-verbally through smiles, gazing at each other and the caregiver's use of infant-directed speech (IDS) – speech which is characterized by its simpler sentences, slower pace and song-like qualities. Careful attention to the infant's behaviour and responses, in turn, enables the caregiver to understand their infant's desires and intentions and when they may need a break from the interaction and stimuli. This too should be construed as a positive step in their journey to achieving SR, as this indicates that the infant can identify within themselves and express feelings of dysregulation, signalling to their caregiver that they need some "time out." This might, for example, be due to feeling tired or over-stimulated. Where the caregiver is able to notice this and reflects back to the infant that they see they are feeling tired or stressed and gives them the time and space to recalibrate, the infant will eventually develop the confidence and resilience to express their feelings clearly, without fear of reprimand. Perhaps most powerful is the identification by researchers Bush et al. (2017: 4), who explain:

> The foetus' response to stress and the ability to return to baseline may be the earliest sign of a foetus' emerging stress regulation system, which in turn is the foundation of temperament (reactivity and regulation).

How Self-Regulation Develops

SR occurs gradually, over time, through relationships with adults who are responsive, authentic and able to co-regulate the child's thoughts, emotional responses and behaviour – as well as being able to regulate their own thoughts, emotional responses and behaviour. When primary carers have the emotional capacity to meet their infant's early attachment needs, they are positively sculpting their infant's limbic system. This plays a central role in attachment and SR. Infants can build trust and a sense of security and consequently perceive and experience their world with confidence, with every supportive, nurturing and loving interaction helping to build healthy neural pathways in their brains. This is shown in Figure 1.4.

As Figure 1.4 shows, when a baby has a need and their primary carer meets the need in a timely and affectionate way, this helps the baby to trust their primary carer – and so the cycle continues and builds as the baby grows and develops. When a baby's needs are met consistently and affectionately, they too gradually learn how to soothe themselves in ways that are positive and healthy – this is SR. The fundamental importance of this process is highlighted by Dr Allan Schore (2003: 275), who explains:

> The attachment mechanism, the dyadic regulation of emotion, psychobiologically modulates positive states, such as excitement and joy, but also negative states, such as fear and aggression.

Figure 1.4 Infant Attachment Cycle

With this in mind, learning to manage one's emotions occurs over time as a result of complex interactions both within and external to the infant. What is of great importance during this rapid time of growth and change is how the infant's varied (and often intense) emotional states are recognized and nurtured by significant adults. These responses help to create the neurobiological foundations for emotional development and how the infant learns to manage their own emotions. Furthermore, each infant's neurobiological markers are unique, based on their individual experiences and temperament, which also needs to be taken into consideration. This is identified by the National Scientific Council on the Developing Child (2011: 2) which informs us:

> The emotional health of young children is closely tied to the social and emotional characteristics of the environments in which they live.

Conversely, where primary carers do not meet their baby's physiological, intellectual, emotional or social needs, trust cannot be developed by the baby, and they will consequently find it very difficult to be calmed or to calm themselves down. If this misalignment between the baby's needs and their caregiver's persists, over time, this could impair the attachment process while causing the infant to be in a constant state of anxiety. This is illustrated in Figure 1.5.

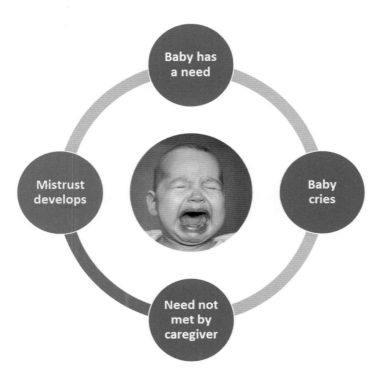

Figure 1.5 Infant Trauma Cycle

The brain is highly receptive to external influences that directly influence its growth and development. When we talk with our babies and children, responding to their babbling or cries, or answering children's questions and giving them the names for everything they feel and see, we are sculpting their brain's architecture – we truly are brain builders! All this rich, respectful and meaningful engagement lays the very foundations on which SR is developed in those early years of life. As Siegel et al. (2021: 39) explain:

> We mammals share attachment, the need for a close relationship between parent and offspring to connect and protect, to soothe and attune. The magic of attachment is that our children internalize our patterns of communication with them, shaping the very structure of their developing brains as they move from the safe haven of our love to set out into the world from the launching pad of home.

It is important to be mindful of the great diversity in children's formative experiences and the quality of attachments in their lives. For example, some children may not have been raised in their biological family's home; some may have been adopted or experienced multiple foster placements – all of which, while signifying the end of the mother–infant attachment process, hopefully will mark the start of new attachments in the child's life. So SR is clearly not an extrinsic set of tick-box skills that we should be forcing children to demonstrate through fear or bribery – which is commonly done across schools through their punishment and reward systems as part of behaviour management policies and procedures (see Chapter 5). Such approaches actually damage mental health (Kohn, 2018; Siegel and Bryson, 2015) while doing nothing to modify the child's behaviour. This is especially important to remember with regard to children who:

■ Have experienced ACEs

■ Have sensory integration difficulties

■ Have SEND.

SR is always determined in the context of an environmental event (Maltese et al., 2017) and is unique to every child, being influenced by the child's temperament, wellbeing at the time, level of support provided (if any) to help the child overcome the stressor and how receptive the child is to the support provided – which is likely to be shaped by the quality of the relationship itself. I use the Building Blocks of SR, as shown in Figure 1.6, to help me remember the key elements involved in nurturing SR.

These building blocks can be an effective way to remember three key components of building SR in a child (or adult). Before trying to re-direct behaviour or model alternatives to the child, you need to be attuned to them. This **attunement** is the first and vital building block in supporting SR. It provides time and space for you to really listen to and engage with the child without judgement or reprimand, to find out what happened, how they are feeling and to help calm them down: just as we would hold a

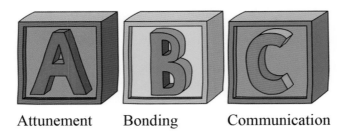

Attunement   Bonding   Communication

Figure I.6 The Building Blocks of SR

baby close to us to help regulate her heart rate and breathing, we do similarly to a child, synchronizing our (limbic, or emotional) brains. Through **bonding** with the child, we can (to some extent) meet unmet emotional needs and build trust, which is especially important where a child has been exposed to ACEs, as they may have few adults they can turn to for consistent care and support. Professor Robert Winston and Chicot (2016: 1) are unequivocal about the fundamental importance of a healthy, secure bond between parent and infant. They tell us:

> Infancy is a crucial time for brain development. It is vital that babies and their parents are supported during this time to promote attachment. Without a good initial bond, children are less likely to grow up to become happy, independent and resilient adults.

Effective communication also needs to be woven throughout all our interactions with children, not only for modelling purposes but to make them feel respected, listened to and safe. Through this reciprocal exchange, children can gradually build trust, which is vital in enabling children to relax and understand what is being said and to encourage them to reach out and express their thoughts and feelings. We all know how difficult it is to pay attention and actively listen to others when we are feeling highly stressed, threatened or anxious.

Developing SR – Child's Play?

Play is also an excellent way to nurture children's SR skills, as it provides a medium without pressure through which they can:

- Test out their skills of cooperating with others
- Not give up when faced with challenges
- Build patience, such as waiting their turn
- Understand the need for rules and follow them

■ Build the confidence to talk to children outside of their friendship group

■ Make and talk through plans with their peers

■ Overcome disagreements in socially acceptable ways

■ Concentrate on the experience

■ Filter out distractions

■ Curb impulses and remain focused on the play.

There are many games that you can play to help develop SR. You can adapt well-known games or make up your own, depending on whether you are supporting babies or children. Babies' SR may be developed through experiences such as singing, gently rocking in your arms, playing with and listening to musical instruments, spending time outside in nature, playing peek-a-boo or providing sensory experiences. Remember that each child will differ in what games they enjoy and what may be beyond their control, depending on their age and stage of understanding and the presence of any SEND (this will be discussed in Chapter 4). Some examples of play experiences that are commonly used to aid the development of SR skills include:

■ Board games

■ Puzzles

■ Drawing/colouring

■ Musical chairs

■ Traffic lights

■ Musical statues

■ Simon/Simone Says

■ Follow my clap

■ Breathing exercises

■ Making and playing with playdough.

Figure 1.7 provides a lovely example of how one setting has built in time for children to take elected "time out" to self-regulate whenever they feel they need to. This simple exercise has proven so effective to soothe children in the moment, that parents are now doing this with their children at home!

The experiences listed above can also be taken outdoors within the daily routine (at home or in the setting), as being outdoors in nature can exert an instantly calming effect on children during times of frustration or anger, relieving feelings of tension, anxiety or stress and generally helping children recalibrate. Juxtaposed against this, however,

Figure 1.7 Two Children Practicing Breathing Exercises at Nursery

is the ever-diminishing importance of play in schools (Gray, 2020a; Bassok et al., 2016), which works against building in time for unfettered, free, child-led play. The drastic reduction of play and the detrimental impact on mental health is drawn to our attention by Gray (2011: 443):

> Over the past half century, in the US and other developed nations, children's free play with other children has declined sharply. Over the same period, anxiety, depression, suicide, feelings of helplessness and narcissism have increased sharply in children, adolescents and young adults. . . . Play functions as the major means by which children: (1) develop intrinsic interests and competencies; (2) learn how to make decisions, solve problems, exert self-control, and follow rules; (3) learn to regulate their emotions; (4) make friends and learn to get along with others as equals; and (5) experience joy. Through all of these effects, play promotes mental health.

Note also Gray's emphasis on the importance of play in supporting children's SR skills. Perhaps now more than ever, with the continued ubiquity and pervasive impact of tech devices in families' lives, alongside parental fears concerning their children's safety and the impact of the COVID-19 pandemic and repeated lockdowns reducing children's interactions with others, it is all the more necessary to re-introduce the fundamental role of play in childhood. Play/playful experiences which draw on children's emergent social and language skills are an excellent way to support young children's abilities to express their thoughts and ideas, explain their thought processes and talk about their own learning and, in turn, significantly improve their self-regulatory abilities, as studies continue to demonstrate (Shanker and Barker, 2018b; Pino-Pasternak et al., 2014).

Rewind. Reflect. Write!

1 When does SR begin?

2 How does SR begin?

3 Discuss how you have used an approach like the ABC of SR to intervene with a child to help regulate them.

4 Where the mother–infant attachment is insecure and a child consequently struggles to demonstrate the ability to "bounce back" from upset, identify three existing strategies you/your team currently use that could be improved, based on your understanding of SR.

5 Identify a baby's emergent SR skills.

6 Discuss two ways you could nurture an eight-month-old baby's emergent SR.

7a Identify three play experiences that help to promote children's SR skills.

7b Explain how each experience promotes these skills.

Top Tips for Practice!

- Try some of the listed games in your setting. It might be at the start of the day, after lunch, before play time or if you see that the children need to be energized or calmed down

- If you don't already, try introducing daily mindfulness for the children in your setting (more on this in Chapter 2)

- Involve primary carers! Share some of these ideas with them to play with their child/ren while taking the time to explain how these help build SR

- Revisit your key person policy – if necessary, revise this in light of your knowledge around the impact of disrupted attachment on early brain development

- Revisit your SEND policy – if necessary, revise this in line with your knowledge of SR.

Caution! – What SR Is Not

Research continually shows that children's ability to self-regulate is a stronger predictor of academic performance than IQ or entry-level maths or reading skills (Robson et al.,

2020; Blair and Raver, 2015; McClelland et al., 2013; McClelland and Wanless, 2012). This is hugely significant and needs to be emphasized as part of SR development in teacher training and EY professional development programmes as standard – and be placed front and centre in EY frameworks for teaching and learning. This last issue is critical and forms this section.

September 2021 saw the introduction of SR as part of the EYFS ELGs. Yet the ELGs are quite some way off the mark, failing to acknowledge the psychological world of children. Associated key issues exist here: given that workforce qualifications do not include any mandatory or consistent embedding of SR, practitioners currently do not have any – or at least not a sufficiently robust – understanding of the concept and its true meaning, nor has the workforce been given any training or resources to understand SR and their role as co-regulators (another key concept that is not mentioned as part of its development). Where practitioners are familiar with SR, this has been achieved through their own interest in the subject and subsequent undertaking of continued professional development (CPD). This is unfair to the workforce and the babies and children entrusted in their care.

The definition of SR and its bullet-pointed descriptors lack accuracy, breadth and depth and coherence, which could consequently exert a detrimental impact on practitioners' facilitation of the ELGs – not least because they fail to encapsulate the psychological foundation of SR. Instead, the SR ELGs (which form part of the personal, social and emotional development [PSED] ELG – not separate and distinct from it) would be recorded as achieved if a child can, for example:

SR ELG:

- Show an understanding of their own feelings and those of others and begin to regulate their behaviour accordingly

- Set and work towards simple goals, being able to wait for what they want and control their immediate impulses when appropriate

- Give focused attention to what the teacher says, responding appropriately even when engaged in activity, and show an ability to follow instructions involving several ideas or actions.

Managing Self ELG:

- Be confident to try new activities and show independence, resilience and perseverance in the face of challenge

- Explain the reasons for rules, know right from wrong and try to behave accordingly

- Manage their own basic hygiene and personal needs, including dressing, going to the toilet and understanding the importance of healthy food choices.

Now that you understand what SR is and how complex and nuanced it is, it is clear to see just how narrow, inaccurate and brief these ELGs are. Those who have written the ELGs have grossly misinterpreted and as a result have misinformed an entire workforce, with children ultimately paying the price, especially those who experience emotional and social sensory integration difficulties and learning disabilities. What we are left with is a vague and inaccurate definition of SR which is disrespectful and dismissive of the child. Take, for example, "regulate their behaviour accordingly" and "manage self" – a young child cannot readily achieve this without CR from an adult. Again, this term does not feature at all by way of explaining how to help children achieve SR. Children's ability to self-regulate is still developing and hence often goes up and down – being able to consistently regulate their own feelings and behaviour is a major task for a young child, and CR is critical to this process, providing them with a healthy "blueprint" of how to respond to triggers – this requires high-quality professional development programmes, as opposed to three vague bullet points with no consistently embedded workforce training.

A child who has become dysregulated needs adult support to help regulate limbic stress-behaviours, as she/he could easily enter fight or flight when ordered to "behave" or to "stop being naughty" or to "say sorry." The concept of SR cannot be confused with expecting a child to eat independently or to resolve conflict without adult support. Practitioners have raised with me the issue of children who have not experienced secure attachments and who consequently lack the ability to self-regulate, as they have not had this modelled to them – what happens to these children under the revised ELGs? Given the deep complexity of SR and the responsibilities of the practitioner in understanding and nurturing it through CR – a wonderful opportunity for the workforce could be lost.

Understanding SR and CR could equip practitioners to be more sensitive and attuned to babies' and young children's emotional states and consequent ability to get on not only at nursery or school but throughout their lives. It would be worthwhile for practitioners to familiarize themselves with the theory and vocabulary, as this can instil confidence when having pedagogical conversations with parents and colleagues – and, most importantly, understanding the theory and language will inform their approach when caring for babies and young children.

> Introducing a weighty concept like SR without aligning this to urgent revision of workforce qualifications, training and CPD to enable staff to know what SR is could prove damaging to children and practitioners alike.

This has implications for practitioners who work with children from birth to three, as they are with these infants from so early on in their lives. If we get it wrong for children during these formative years, we could be setting them up for failure.

Rewind. Reflect. Write!

I   Why do you think that children's ability to self-regulate is a stronger predictor of academic performance than IQ?

2a Given your understanding of SR, what are your thoughts about its inclusion in the EYFS?

2b Discuss the training you have received concerning its inclusion in the EYFS.

2c If you do not already, how do you intend to meaningfully embed SR into your policies and procedures? Take this discussion to your team for planning and implementation.

Concluding Thoughts

The aim of this chapter was to provide you with a deep and broad range of issues related to SR. This was deemed important to do given the persistent paucity of consistent workforce development on the subject. The issues presented should hold you in good stead to reflect on the changes you could make to your provision for children, as well as your interactions with them – be this at home or in the setting. Be brave and bold, and dare to challenge! The books listed in the Further Reading section will also help you on your SR journey.

Further Reading

■ Shanker, S. and Hopkins, S. (2019). *Self-Reg Schools: A Handbook for Educators*. Melbourne: Pearson Education.

This book contains seven chapters and is full of practical tools and strategies which you can use to enhance your setting/classroom so that it embodies the theory of SR for the benefit of all children, their families and staff in your setting.

■ Shanker, S. and Barker, T. (2018). *Help Your Child Deal With Stress – And Thrive: The Transformative Power of Self-Reg*. London: Yellow Kite.

Underpinned by neuroscience, in this excellent, practical book for parents, Dr Stuart Shanker argues that by teaching children the art of SR, it can transform their behaviour and help them to identify, talk about and manage their emotions. This ultimately results in children who feel nurtured and supported.

■ Siegel, D. and Bryson, T. (2018). *The Whole-Brain Child Workbook: Practical Exercises, Worksheets and Activities to Nurture Developing Minds*. Eau Claire, WI: PESI Publishing and Media.

This practical book provides an interactive approach which allows the reader to not only think more deeply about the ideas presented but how these fit their own parenting or teaching approach. Containing lots of clear and practical exercises and activities, this book is useful for parents and educators alike.

2 Co-Regulation – It Takes Two, Baby!

If one could bottle the most effective method to enable SR, it would be a hearty dose of co-regulation.

> The single most important discovery that scientists have made about the early years is that it is by being regulated that a child develops the ability to self-regulate.
>
> (Shanker et al., 2015: 11)

What to Expect in This Chapter

In this chapter, CR will be defined and explored, with the three approaches to CR (Murray et al., 2015) providing the framework to the chapter.

An outline of the different types of CR needed by young children in different phases of early childhood, starting with infancy, will also be presented as part of the discussion, with emphasis throughout the chapter on the importance of the adult's role in facilitating this process. The adult's own ability to self-regulate will be examined as part of the process of CR, with attention paid to the consequences of difficulties in co-regulating children's emotions and behaviour. Case studies and questions are included to help consolidate the reader's understanding and to help the reader to challenge particular arguments that are put forward. A Further Reading list ends the chapter.

By the End of This Chapter, You Will Be Able to:

- Define and describe the process of co-regulation

- Discuss three key theoretical approaches to understanding co-regulation

- Define and discuss young children's co-regulation needs in early childhood

DOI: 10.4324/9781003327479-2

- Outline and critique the three main approaches (Murray et al., 2015) through which co-regulation is achieved

- Use these three main approaches to frame your approach to providing co-regulation in your daily practice

- Use the Stream of Self-Regulation to reflect on your own ability to self-regulate

- Understand and draw on Emotion Coaching to co-regulate emotions and behaviour

- Identify key features of an effective indoor co-regulating environment – and be able to create one in your setting

- Identify key features of an effective outdoor co-regulating environment – and be able to create one in your setting.

What Is Co-Regulation?

CR entered discourses concerning psychology and education in the mid-1990s (Zimmerman and Schunk, 2011), with the concept first being coined by McCaslin and Good (1996). They acknowledged the vital role of SR in learning, specifically in the context of the classroom and the teacher's role in developing characteristics such as personal agency and resilience as part of SR in learning. CR is something that we all do, be this with our children, colleagues or partners, during times of stress, upset or difficulty. It can be described as the supportive process between a caring adult and a child (or other adult) that fosters SR – and it takes place across the lifespan. It includes supportive environments and the strategies demonstrated and used by the co-regulating adult to build an individual's self-regulatory capacity. Many varied definitions of CR exist, some focusing on the adult's role in supporting higher-order thinking skills in an academic context, such as generating ideas, organization, reasoning, planning and creative thinking (Pino-Pasternak et al., 2014; Schunk and Zimmerman, 1994). Other definitions are more holistic, focusing on the need to co-regulate thoughts, emotions and behaviour in order for learning – execution of those higher-order thinking skills – to take place (Perry, 2021; Shanker, 2020). Murray et al. (2015: 14) provide a robust definition that encompasses the holistic nature of CR. They explain that:

> Co-regulation is defined as warm and responsive interactions that provide the support, coaching, and modelling children need to understand, express and modulate their thoughts, feelings and behaviours.

Without CR, SR cannot develop – at least, not in ways that are healthy and growth promoting. Effective CR provides us with the theoretical and concrete understanding of how to handle overwhelming emotions and why this is fundamentally important to do. If provided consistently from birth, CR helps to build our tolerance of physical and emotional discomfort while building resilience. Shanker et al. (2015: 32) are unequivocal about the importance of CR in facilitating the development of SR, stating that *self-regulation is only made possible and proceeds from a strong relationship*.

Two key enablers of CR within the security of strong relationships are:

- The rich language used by the adult with the child

- Ample opportunities for play.

While it could be considered a fact belaboured far too frequently, play *is* the defining feature of human development and is hardwired into us. It is something that comes naturally, with psychological, emotional, social and physical problems manifesting in its absence (Porges, 2021; Gray, 2020a; Panksepp et al., 2017; Panksepp, 2012). It is during play/playful experiences that children are free to explore their fears and interests and express themselves in ways that are most comfortable to them – ways that do not carry the consequences of real life (Walker et al., 2011; Panksepp, 1998; Vygotsky, 1978; Bruner et al., 1976). This might look like a child expressing aggression or anger in ways that are playful, like acting out their feelings with puppets or toys, or a child engaging in messy play, like playing with sand, mud or paints. These are great ways for children to express feelings such as sadness, frustration or happiness. Ultimately, play builds brains – with dendritic length and complexity of neurons in the medial PFC being strengthened and refined by play, and it is vital for children's mental health. This is asserted by Gray (2011: 1), who highlights just a few benefits of play:

> Play functions as the major means by which children (1) develop intrinsic interests and competencies; (2) learn how to make decisions, solve problems, exert self-control, and follow rules; (3) learn to regulate their emotions; (4) make friends and learn to get along with others as equals; and (5) experience joy.

Note here the many benefits of play for a child's ability to self-regulate their thoughts, emotions and behaviour – all this becomes more likely when the adult is attuned to the child's current state and is adept at helping the child to navigate the exciting but sometimes challenging world of play. This is especially important for children who have been exposed to ACEs and trauma, as toxic stress has been shown to disrupt the development of executive functioning and the learning of prosocial behaviour (Anda et al., 2020; Burke Harris, 2018; Felitti et al., 1998). This is why the mutual joy in those co-regulatory serve and return interactions during play are so important for early brain development – because they help to regulate the body's stress response while enabling greater SR, building language and executive functioning skills. Creative and imaginative experiences such as painting, drawing, writing stories and making and playing with playdough with an adult's sensitive participation can all help to co-regulate a child's emotions and process their trauma safely, at their own pace and in their own ways.

The type of CR you provide will depend on a host of factors that you need to consider:

■ The process of CR is not static. It is ever evolving in line with the child's age and stage of understanding

■ CR is not a one-size-fits-all approach – what works with one child may not work with another

■ What works with one child on one occasion may not work with the same child the next time

■ The effectiveness of the CR you provide is heavily dependent on your emotional state and mental health at the time

■ CR is dependent on your knowledge of the child's (or young adult's) stressors and ability to minimize or prevent these from triggering them.

Theoretical Perspectives of Co-Regulation

Your personal views and preferred definitions of CR will depend on a range of factors. This might include your own upbringing and how you were supported to build resilience and independence, as well as your views on parenting and teaching – which will all inform how you view CR and your role as a co-regulator. Reflecting on CR, you may also feel naturally more drawn to some theoretical perspectives more than others, based on your personal and professional experiences. There exist various theoretical perspectives of CR, some of which are complementary and aligned with each other, whereas some could be considered divergent. It is also important to point out that much of the theories and supporting literature centred around concepts of SR are from a learning perspective, and hence many of the theoretical perspectives of CR are also centred around the adult's role in supporting self-regulated learning while barely addressing the fundamental importance of emotion regulation in both CR and SR (Hadwin et al., 2017; McCaslin and Burross, 2011).

Ultimately, however, while some do differ in their perspective of the adult's role, all underscore this role as critical to the development of SR. While this book does not provide an in-depth comprehensive examination of all the theories of CR, it does provide an overview of those most drawn upon across the education and care systems.

Broadly speaking, there exist three main perspectives of CR theory. These have been presented with the emotional – or attachment-based – perspective first, as effective CR is only possible in the safety of affectionate, responsive and stable relationships in which the child can expect to be supported to build their repertoire of emotional skills, such as

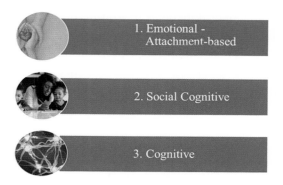

Figure 2.1 The Three Main Perspectives of Co-Regulation Theory

self-awareness, SR, resilience, responsible decision-making, social awareness and relationship skills. See Figure 2.1. As with brain development, once a healthy foundation is in place, the rest (that is, the more complex thought processes and ability to learn) will follow.

Emotional – Or Attachment-Based – Perspectives of Co-Regulation

Let us start at the beginning. Psychoanalyst, Erik Erikson's first of eight stages of psychosocial development is pertinent when exploring CR, because during this stage, trust versus mistrust in infancy, is where the roots of CR and SR begin. In the first year of life (or as Erikson sets out, from birth to approximately 18-months-old), the infant will develop a sense of trust – but only if the parent or caregiver is attuned, responsive and consistent in sensitively meeting the infant's essential physiological and emotional needs. Over time, this responsive care-giving helps to soothe a dysregulated nervous system, and as the infant grows, they will, as a result, be able to self-soothe, secure in the knowledge that their needs will be met, based on the consistent pattern of care received (Marazziti, 2009).

However, where such attentive care-giving and love are not provided in these early days of life, the infant will swiftly construct a view of the world that is harsh and uncaring – one in which they cannot expect to have their needs met for companionship and love, ultimately growing up with a sense of mistrust for people in the world. Erikson (1959: 1) reminds us:

> Life doesn't make any sense without interdependence. We need each other and the sooner we learn that, the better for us all.

Erikson is correct in his simple yet accurate observation – we do need each other. Humans are wired for social connection, with holistic wellbeing suffering in the absence of relationships and consequent difficulties in trusting others. Left unresolved, this can pave the way for unfulfilling adult relationships which are littered with mistrust, insecurity, anger and jealousy. This is reinforced by Bronson (2000: 164), who confirms what has long been well established by findings from neuroscience with regard to the impact of the adult's responses on early brain development and infants' emergent self-regulatory capacity, explaining that while:

> Responsiveness to biological rhythms and signals helps infants regulate biological and emotional systems, negative experiences have negative effects on brain development and control of behaviour and hinder healthy attachment to others.

In line with Erikson's views concerning the importance of this co-regulatory dyad, Bronson (2000: 164) goes on to state that early negative experiences (such as neglect, abuse and institutionalization) may predispose the individual to *respond with aggression or violence to stress or frustration.* Clearly this comes as little surprise given the necessity of co-regulatory responses to an emotionally labile infant – who, after all, is completely dependent on their primary carer to meet their needs. We do not enter this world equipped with the psychological, emotional, social or physical skills to withstand the adversities we encounter. While we each have the potential to, these need to be nurtured by adults who pay close attention to cues sent and respond consistently and sensitively with the right amount of support to enable children to understand that they can trust the adults in their world to care for them while helping them to overcome the challenges they encounter.

When we reflect on an infant's life during Erikson's first psychosocial stage, we know that brain development is occurring at an incredibly fast rate (as discussed in Chapter 3), and hence there exists a vast range of opportunities for personal and physical growth – but with these come challenges. These include communicating, building social skills, behaving in ways that are socially acceptable, potty training, self-feeding and navigating the world of play. Daily life for a toddler in an EY setting can thus be daunting as well as exciting – all of a sudden they have to share one main adult (teacher/practitioner) with as many as 30 other toddlers – each with their unique needs and interests that need to be accommodated by the adult, who also brings their own emotions, experiences and expectations. This is captured by Erikson (1987: 14–15), who posits:

> In the work of a teacher, relations are flexible. (S)he not only has to deal with affects in the children, the ultimate forms of which are not yet fully determined, but (s)he also cannot avoid registering her own affective response. Although (s)he is the object of transference, (s)he cannot avoid or eliminate her own personality, but must play a very personal part in the child's life. It is the x in the teacher's personality which influences the y in the child's development.

Here, Erikson captures the labile nature of young children's emotions while underscoring the impact of the adult's emotions in how they care for and respond to children. We have all been there – when we are feeling stressed, pressured or tired, we do not have the ability to be a calming, co-regulating presence for children. In fact, we tend to "add fuel to the fire." Over time, children will inevitably emulate the adult's behaviour – which, if we are not careful, can cause more harm than good.

Moving forward from Erikson's invaluable insights, we see that the research findings of Bowlby concerning the importance of healthy attachments and the safe base (1988, 1953) and Ainsworth's (1971) strange situation test and multiple attachments inform current policy and practice across the education and care systems, helping to change professionals' attitudes about the importance of children's attachments and your personal role in fostering babies' and children's self-confidence and self-esteem. More recently, the work of Porges (2021), Siegel et al. (2021), Tronick and Gold (2020), Music (2019), Zeegers et al. (2018), Cozolino (2013), Trevarthen and Delafield-Butt (2013) and Fonagy et al. (2004) continues to demonstrate how the attuned mind–mindedness of primary carers uniquely impacts the development of infants' physiological emotion regulation, with the implications of their work resonating clearly and consistently for professionals and primary carers alike across cultures. This is evident in the revised EYFS (2021), which emphasizes the centrality of children's personal, social and emotional development and the funds of knowledge each child brings to the setting. It is therefore critical to ensure that your provision (particularly your key person system) is designed to meet the unique and ever-changing needs of every child while keeping the child's voice at the centre of planning and provision.

Rewind. Reflect. Write!

1a In your own words, describe what co-regulation is.

1b Discuss its role in supporting infants'/children's ability to self-regulate.

2a Note down what you understand by the emotional perspective of co-regulation.

2b Discuss how far and in which ways this theoretical perspective explains co-regulation.

3 Discuss how, in your opinion, the EYFS embodies the emotional perspective of co-regulation. Try to include at least three practical ways.

4 Explain how the emotional perspective of CR takes into account early brain development.

Social Cognitive Perspectives of Co-Regulation

Developed by Bandura (1986) and originally referred to by him as social learning theory (1977, 1962), the social cognitive perspective of CR (DiDonato, 2013; Azevedo et al., 2012; Janssen et al., 2012; Whitebread et al., 2007; Schunk and Zimmerman, 1997) posits that SR and, indeed, all learning is situated socially, within a dynamic and reciprocal interaction between the individual, environment and behaviour. Within this dynamic, the role of the following are emphasized:

■ Observing adults (think of Bandura's classic Bobo doll experiment (1962))

■ Imitating adults

■ Using rewards and punishments to control behaviour.

Although Bandura considered the role of rewards and punishments in controlling behaviour, he built on these, acknowledging the role of the child's mental processes in four key ways:

■ Paying attention to the behaviour that is going to be imitated

■ Retaining the memory of the behaviour to be imitated

■ Reproducing/enacting the behaviour

■ Motivation/desire to enact the behaviour (which depends on how the child views any rewards and punishments).

This, which Bandura calls information-seeking behaviour (1992), highlights children's proficiency in seeking what they need in order to help them navigate their environment, those in it and their own behaviour, as opposed to behaviourist theories (Skinner, 1976; Thorndike, 1932), which advocate the use of rewards and punishments to either reinforce or extinguish certain behaviours that are desired by the adult or not. As Bandura (1991: 249) asserts:

> If human behaviour were regulated solely by external outcomes, people would behave like weathervanes, constantly shifting direction to conform to whatever momentary social influences happened to impinge upon them.

This is obvious given that we do not exist in a vacuum and that in all areas of our lives, we are surrounded and influenced by others – starting from our family in the home, to our teachers and peers at nursery and school (Cleary and Zimmerman, 2004; Kitsantas et al., 2000; Bronfenbrenner, 1979). This socio-cognitive perspective therefore also runs contrary to the cognitive perspective of CR (discussed in the following section), which underscores the role of the *individual* in building their capacity for SR via their own mental processes (Whitebread and Coltman, 2011; Yowell and Smylie, 1999). More recently, Bruner's concept of scaffolding is used to support and develop children's behaviour and learning in settings and classrooms, particularly across the United Kingdom and America today (Copple and Bredekamp, 2009). Yowell and Smylie (1999) rightly identify the need for intersubjectivity (Schore, 2021; Trevarthen and Aitken, 2001) as a solid foundation for scaffolding to take place, because without a reciprocal, respectful and trusting relationship, it will be very difficult to co-regulate a child whose nervous system has become dysregulated – let alone expect them to be effective learners. The idea of the scaffold is that it should provide a temporary support structure around the child's attempts to understand new ideas and complete new tasks (in this instance, to self-regulate). Once the child demonstrates ability independent of any adult intervention, the scaffold (support) is removed. Bruner provides a clear account of what scaffolding should look like in action:

> There is a vast amount of skilled activity required of a "teacher" to get a learner to discover on his own – scaffolding the task in a way that assures that only those parts of the task within the child's reach are left unresolved, and knowing what elements of a solution the child will recognize though he cannot yet perform them.
>
> (1977: xiv)

The adult's observations of the child's ability to self-regulate should guide how much they scaffold and what strategies they choose to use as part of this. Where the child is old enough and can understand and respond, it is important to ask them what they feel could best help them to process and manage their emotions in that moment. It might be that they want to do some mindful breathing or grounding techniques or solve a puzzle together. The more control they feel they have, the more swiftly they can return to a state of calm. After all, it is the perceived lack of control that can perpetuate feelings of powerlessness and panic. With this in mind, the purpose of the scaffold is to equip the child to reach higher levels of emotional and cognitive SR, which is achieved by the adult:

1   motivating and encouraging the child

2   giving models that can be imitated

3   simplifying the task or idea

4   highlighting "errors" or significant elements of the task.

You have been presented with some of the key theorists from the social cognitive perspective of CR theory; you may go on to further explore these in depth, as well as other perspectives. For now, have a go at answering the questions that follow.

Rewind. Reflect. Write!

1   Summarize the social cognitive perspectives of co-regulation.

2   Which do you find your views and practice most aligned to? Explain why.

3   Reflecting on Bandura's social cognitive perspective, note down some possible motivators for children concerning their ability to self-regulate within the social cognitive framework.

4a   Reflect on a time when you learned a behaviour from observing another person.

For example, you may have learned caring, co-regulating behaviour by observing a friend or colleague helping a distressed child to calm down.

Describe the behaviour you learned and how you learned it. Address whether your imitation of the behaviour was intentional, such as using specific techniques learned from observing the person help a child to calm down- or unintentional, such as behaving in a caring, co-regulating way because it "feels" right, but not necessarily to imitate the behaviour you observed.

4b   Explain how this fits into Bandura's four ways of information-seeking behaviour.

4c   How is this relevant to you in your daily practice when co-regulating children's emotional responses and behaviour?

Cognitive Perspectives of Co-Regulation

Partly born out of the dissatisfaction with behaviourist approaches and their simplistic emphasis on *external* behaviour rather than a child's *internal* processes that lie beneath this, cognitive perspectives of CR (Karpov and Haywood, 1998; Vygotsky, 1978; Piaget and Inhelder, 1972) underscore the significance of the mind as the information processor. At the risk of pointing out the obvious, it is important to flag here that a child's attention, perception and working memory (keeping information in mind while one is using it) are vital elements of information processing, but some children who have been exposed to ACEs find it difficult to listen, concentrate and follow instructions, due to key brain regions, including the PFC, hippocampus and limbic system, being compromised by the neurobiological impact of the ACEs (VanTieghem et al., 2021; Porges, 2017; Teicher and Samson, 2016; Siegel, 2012; Pechtel and Pizzagalli, 2011; Porges, 2003). It is therefore vital that you understand how to support children who struggle, to help them get the best out of experiences – which leads us neatly to Vygotsky's concept of the zone of proximal development (ZPD). This is widely referred to within cognitive perspectives of CR. As Vygotsky (1978: 52) explains:

> It is the distance between the actual developmental level as determined by independent problem-solving and the level of potential development as determined through problem solving under adult guidance or in collaboration with more capable peers.

McCaslin and Hickey (2001) theorized that CR is a manifestation of emergent (or unfolding) interaction in a ZPD, with teachers and children transitioning from co-regulating learning towards SR of behaviour and learning. The ZPD can thus be viewed as a prospective view of development, as it emphasizes the potential for development through learning – as opposed to a retrospective view which emphasizes the child's abilities, independent of any assistance. So the child's self-regulatory ability is determined by what they can achieve in collaboration with an adult or more competent peer, not by what they can achieve alone. This is helpful when we consider the many children who find it difficult to self-regulate as a result of any SEND, exposure to ACEs or the absence of healthy adult role models to show them how to self-regulate.

Aligned to his ZPD, Vygotsky's concept of mediation (1987, 1978) is integral to the cognitive perspective of CR. Vygotsky believed that there is a mediation process (the process through which the social and the individual mutually shape each other) that goes on between the child, the adult(s) and the environment (the third teacher) – and how, therefore, development is a mediated process. We can view mediation, then, as a three-way, inter-dependent relationship between the child, adult and environment. This is illustrated in Figure 2.2.

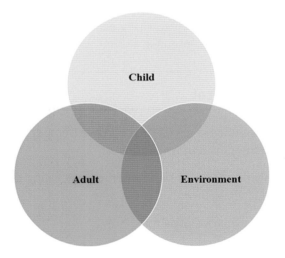

Figure 2.2 The Three-Way, Inter-Dependent Relationship Between the Child, Adult and Environment

(Note the similarity between Vygotsky's mediation and Bandura's emphasis on the interplay between the person, behaviour and environment.)

Central to Vygotsky's theory is that within the mediated process of children's development, *tools* are utilized to drive thinking, behaviour and learning. These are:

- Technical tools (such as computers or books), which change an external situation

- Psychological tools (language, thoughts and ideas), which direct the mind and guide the process of thinking. This is predominantly done through the child executing basic cognitive functions (such as memory, attention, perception and solving problems) within their social milieu — all of which, combined, influence behaviour and learning ability.

A fundamental premise here is that tools and symbols are first and foremost shared between individuals in society, and only then can they be internalized by children developing in society, as is reflected in this renowned quote:

> Every function in the child's cultural development appears twice: first, on the social level, and later on the individual level; first, between people (interpsychological), and then inside the child (intrapsychological). This applies equally to voluntary attention, to logical memory, and to the formation of concepts. All the higher functions originate as actual relations between human individuals.
>
> (Vygotsky, 1978: 57)

In conclusion, each of these theoretical perspectives of CR infuses daily provision and is applied in a variety of contexts, be these during the teaching/learning experiences you provide, the physical care routine or when comforting a distressed child. So it is important to hold in mind that there is no right or wrong perspective to draw on, as we will naturally behave and respond in ways that are informed by our personal experiences as well as the child's needs in-the-moment.

Rewind. Reflect. Write!

1   Note down your thoughts about the cognitive perspectives of co-regulation (including any strengths and limitations).

2   Explain what some mediators are when co-regulating children's emotions and behaviour.

3   List the mediators in your provision.

4   Now list some of the:

   a   Technical tools you use to co-regulate children's emotions and behaviour.

   b   Psychological tools you use to co-regulate children's emotions and behaviour.

Top Tips for Practice!

- Revisit your setting's policies concerning children's behaviour – reflect on ways they could be more reflective of children's agency in self-regulating

- Reflecting on all three perspectives of CR, think about how you and your team could improve your approach to co-regulating children's emotions and behaviour. Instigate some meetings with a view to implementing any points for action

- Note down some ways in which you and your team could give children further opportunities to collaborate and co-regulate each other's emotions and behaviour

- Create meaningful experiences/activities that give children the opportunity to apply and build on their SR skills through CR

- Provide tools for children to successfully self-regulate through your CR while encouraging their independent responsibility.

What Are Young Children's Co-Regulation Needs in Early Childhood?

Generally speaking, the younger the child, the greater the need to co-regulate their emotions and behaviour and as the child grows older, the less need for CR of their thoughts, emotions and behaviour – unless they have any SEND and struggle with self-regulating independently of external support. Remember: your three ultimate aims in co-regulating emotional responses, are to:

1 Reduce the child's stress levels

2 Help the child return to a state of calm

3 Model and provide SR strategies for them to use in-the-moment and in the future.

As mentioned, the type, intensity and duration of the CR you provide will depend on diverse factors, one of which is the age and stage of understanding of the child. The following is a broad outline of the CR needed by young children in different phases of early childhood, starting with infancy (adapted from Murray et al., 2015).

In infancy, children need you to:

- Provide affectionate and nurturing relationships

- *Anticipate* needs and swiftly respond to cues for engagement

- Provide structure and consistent routine (while allowing for flexibility as necessary)

- Provide swift physical and emotional comfort when a child is distressed or dysregulated; speak calmly, softly and give affection

- Adapt the environment to decrease demands and stress.

In toddlerhood, in addition to the previous, you also need to:

- Teach age-appropriate rules and expectations

- Support children to label and express their emotions ("name it to tame it")

- Model waiting and self-calming strategies (those outlined in this book will be useful)

- Redirect the child's attention to help regulate their behaviour (you will become adept at doing this with whatever resources you have around at the time).

In preschool-aged children, in addition to the previous, you need to:

■ Coach children through identification of solutions to simple problems

■ Acknowledge the efforts made by children when trying to self-regulate. Labelling exactly what they did can be very powerful in helping them to remember and use the strategies in a range of contexts in the future

■ Coach/break down rule-following and task completion, using your knowledge of the individual child and their dispositions to help you. Remember, a one-size-fits-all approach will not work and will only lead to frustration for you and the child

■ Model, prompt and reinforce self-calming strategies like taking deep breaths, doing some simple stretches or mindfulness activities – strategies that can be effectively used in-the-moment

■ Provide external structures for calming down, including cosy or calm-down spaces or designated outdoor areas and resources (examples are provided further on in this chapter).

Now that you have read about some of the co-regulatory strategies across the age ranges, have a go at answering the following questions.

Rewind. Reflect. Write!

1   Reflecting on all the previous co-regulatory strategies, note down any that are not listed.

2   Explain at least two key differences in the adult's co-regulatory behaviours between infancy to pre-school aged children.

3   Carefully read through each aspect of co-regulation.

    a Note down the aspects of co-regulation that you and your team are doing successfully.

    b Now note down those you need to work on and how you intend to do this.

4   What are the possible consequences if co-regulation is not provided in ways that are age and stage appropriate?

When it comes to co-regulating children's emotions and behaviour, there exist many varied approaches to our co-regulatory relationships, the resources we choose to use and the environments that we choose to provide. To make it a little easier to reflect on some of these, this book refers to Murray et al. (2015), who indicate three main approaches to achieving CR with babies, children and young adults. This is illustrated in Figure 2.3. These are:

1   The provision of warm and responsive relationships

2   Through the teaching and modelling of SR skills

3   The structure of the indoor and outdoor environments.

Each approach will mean something different to everyone, depending on influences including (but not exclusive to):

■ The type of setting

■ The structure of the indoor and outdoor environments

■ The age of children cared for

■ The adults' temperament

■ The children's temperament

■ The level of CR they receive from their primary carers

■ The presence of any SEND

■ The emotional availability of the adults at the time.

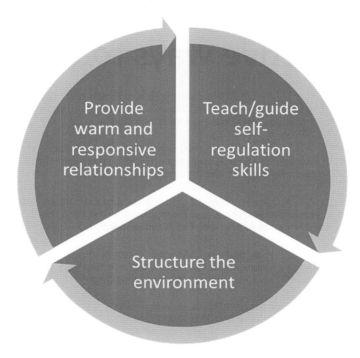

Figure 2.3 The Three Approaches to Achieving Co-Regulation

It is also important to bear in mind that even genetic differences in, for example, emotional reactivity are influenced by nature and nurture, with caregiver and environmental differences playing an integral role in nurturing the child's emergent self-regulatory abilities (Sroufe, 1995).

Each of the three approaches will now be examined in turn.

I The Provision of Warm and Responsive Relationships

You set the foundations for SR to be possible, and while each of the three approaches is equally important, getting those warm and responsive relationships in place as *the* foundation of your ever-evolving, co-regulatory support is vital. The main aim of co-regulating a child's thoughts, feelings and behaviour is to equip them to move from a state of dependency to independence – that is, to master the ability to self-regulate. This is highlighted in Figure 2.4.

We cannot hope to co-regulate others when they become dysregulated if we do not make every effort to connect with them in ways that are authentic. This is particularly important to hold in mind with children who are hypervigilant and find it difficult to trust due to exposure to ACEs and trauma. Responding swiftly and sensitively is

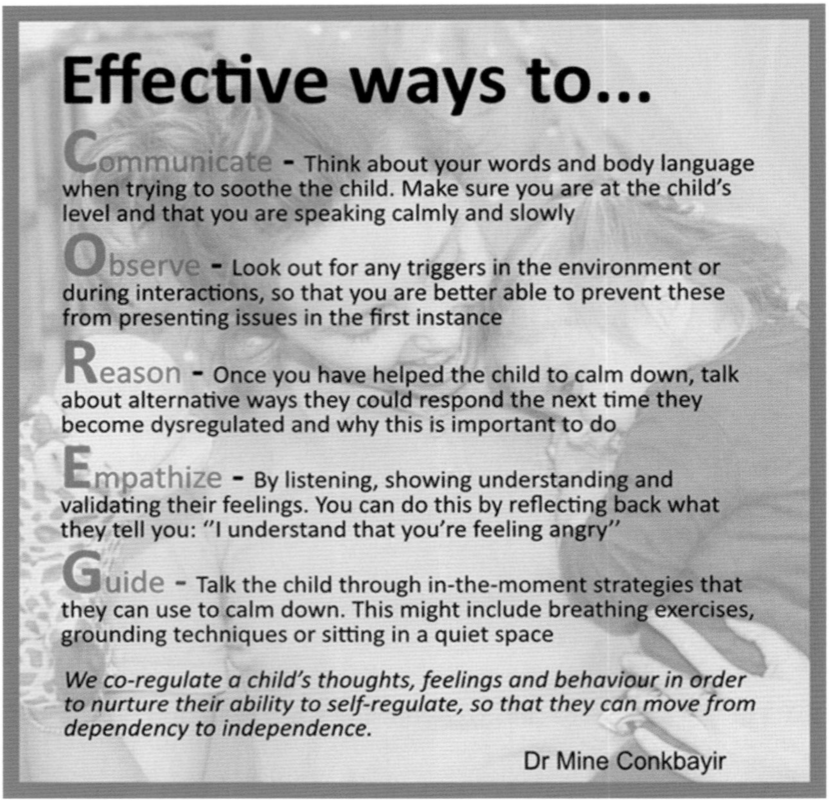

Effective ways to...

Communicate - Think about your words and body language when trying to soothe the child. Make sure you are at the child's level and that you are speaking calmly and slowly

Observe - Look out for any triggers in the environment or during interactions, so that you are better able to prevent these from presenting issues in the first instance

Reason - Once you have helped the child to calm down, talk about alternative ways they could respond the next time they become dysregulated and why this is important to do

Empathize - By listening, showing understanding and validating their feelings. You can do this by reflecting back what they tell you: "I understand that you're feeling angry"

Guide - Talk the child through in-the-moment strategies that they can use to calm down. This might include breathing exercises, grounding techniques or sitting in a quiet space

We co-regulate a child's thoughts, feelings and behaviour in order to nurture their ability to self-regulate, so that they can move from dependency to independence.

Dr Mine Conkbayir

Figure 2.4 The CO-REG Acronym

vital because this (as the acronym suggests) can immediately diffuse the intensity and duration of the feelings of dysregulation. So influencing factors that we do not often consider, such as our verbal and non-verbal communication, our positioning when we communicate and the tone we adopt, alongside the effort we make to identify any triggers and offer practical support, all count when it comes to CR. Although it takes time and effort to co-regulate, as opposed to issuing threats and punishments to signs of emotional dysregulation, it is time and resources well spent because all this enables practitioners and primary carers alike to move away from counter-productive behaviour management approaches and instead move closer to relational ways of supporting children to better manage *their own* emotions (Delahooke, 2019). After all, if we fail to nurture this essential set of life skills in children from the outset, we will only ever keep falling back on futile behaviour management strategies, because we never instilled the ability to reflect and *choose* to respond differently to stressors. This is the essential difference between SR and behaviour management: *SR equips children with the skills to manage their own dysregulation, whereas behaviour management removes all agency from the child.* Dysregulated behaviour is instead criticized and punished while doing nothing to equip children to better regulate their emotions and behaviour – which is what we need to support from birth. Behaviour management is discussed further in Chapter 5.

From birth, we all need to experience warm and responsive relationships in which we can swiftly come to understand that our needs will be met by adults who are attuned to our personality, needs and desires. In this regard, providing CR should not only take place during times of a child's dysregulation but instead infuse all interactions between adults and babies and children as much as possible. That is not to say we must co-regulate all the time but that we must endeavour to, as regularly and consistently as is possible. Babies are highly perceptive and emotionally aware. They can recognize and are comforted by their mother's scent, her voice and her touch. Babies are by nature primed for affectionate care and stimulation to help ensure healthy brain development, even from before birth (DeCasper and Prescott, 2009; DeCasper and Spence, 1986). Trevarthen and Delafield-Butt (2013: 5) explain:

> A new-born infant's movements are especially sensitive to sight, hearing and touch of an attentive mother in face-to-face engagement and they can take a creative part in a shared narrative of expressive action.

The "shared narrative of expressive action" can be observed taking place within hours of birth, through babies demonstrating their readiness and ability to communicate (Trevarthen, 2011b) with their primary caregivers through protoconversations – which, put simply, are interactions between the caregiver and baby which include words, sounds and gestures that convey meaning, before the onset of language in the child. This might look like a father picking up his four-month-old daughter who is crying and holding her close to him as he looks into her eyes, smiling, as he gently tells her "I know you're upset right now, but daddy's here and you're going to be OK," to which his daughter responds by gazing into his eyes, listening to him and then smiling as she gradually stops crying.

It is important to note that an infant's temperament and responsiveness to their parents' attempts at comfort also contribute to and shape processes of attachment and CR. According to Bates et al. (2012: 1), a child's temperament is defined as *biologically based differences in reactivity and self-regulation*, with infants who are receptive, relaxed and cheerful reportedly receiving more affectionate care than infants who are viewed by their parents as difficult to engage and soothe (Carrasco et al., 2020; Delgado et al., 2018; Schermerhorn et al., 2013; Bates et al., 2012). Aligned to this, studies have shown that children with self-regulatory difficulties can be more challenging to parent (Bates et al., 2012), which is likely to exacerbate the child's difficulty in self-regulating while perpetuating feelings of frustration and disconnect in parents. This bi-directional relationship between temperament-related behaviour and parenting behaviour and how each influences the other needs to be reflected on honestly by all primary carers and those working with infants and young children. This can help to ensure that all infants and children receive the due care and co-regulatory support they deserve and need – particularly those most vulnerable to self-regulatory difficulties. This is because CR and SR cannot occur where infants and young children feel – or are – unsafe.

The language we use should be carefully considered so that we build emotional vocabulary from the start, which children can extend as they get older. This is particularly important with children who have communication difficulties and SEND and babies, who, although do not have the necessary expressive language to tell us how they are feeling, have enough receptive language (understanding of language) to comprehend, or at least begin to comprehend, what we are talking about. Children who are capable of using expressive language will swiftly learn the meaning of words and incorporate these into their vocabulary. This in turn could help diffuse the intensity of those more overwhelming emotions like anger, agitation and anxiety, as children will be able to articulate how they are feeling and what they need to process and overcome the emotion. It is therefore important to use the correct terms for such emotions while describing their impact on the brain and body, so that from the youngest age, children can develop the competence to identify them and receive the CR they need to reach a state of calm. When they are adept or old enough, they will eventually be able to self-regulate in times of need.

In this regard, the quantity and quality of the language young children are exposed to early in life can predict their later linguistic and cognitive skills (Hirsh-Pasek et al., 2015; Weisleder and Fernald, 2013; Rowe, 2012; Rodriguez and Tamis-LeMonda, 2011). This has implications for the impact of co-regulatory support and ultimately for early brain development. Where adults consistently co-regulate children's emotions and behaviour through the use of context-specific language, gestures and strategies that reassure and calm, they communicate that the emotional distress is manageable. This soothes the young child while building and strengthening neural connections associated with emotion regulation and language, thereby helping to positively inform their future responses to stressors.

One influential study (Romeo et al., 2018) confirmed that merely talking at infants and young children is not enough to stimulate brain development and language. Their study of 40 children aged between four- and six-years-old tracked the quality and quantity of communication using child-worn language recorders and brain imaging techniques. They demonstrated that the amount of adult speech directed at young children was not significant enough to cause neuroanatomical changes or promote language development but that the back-and-forth verbal and non-verbal exchanges rewired the brain and advanced maturation of the language pathways important for language processing. Their findings showed increased activation in the frontal lobe (cortical, or "upstairs," brain) and increased Broca's activation (the brain region responsible for expressing language) as a result of the back-and-forth interactions between parents and their children in the study. These two key brain regions are highlighted in Figure 2.5.

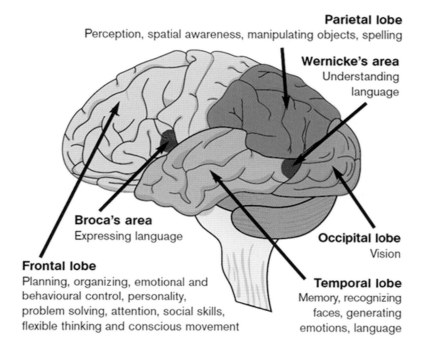

Parietal lobe
Perception, spatial awareness, manipulating objects, spelling

Wernicke's area
Understanding language

Broca's area
Expressing language

Occipital lobe
Vision

Frontal lobe
Planning, organizing, emotional and behavioural control, personality, problem solving, attention, social skills, flexible thinking and conscious movement

Temporal lobe
Memory, recognizing faces, generating emotions, language

Figure 2.5 Key Brain Regions Associated With Language

Romeo et al. (2018: 7876) explain:

> Functional findings indicate that children's language exposure is related to activation specifically in left prefrontal cortical regions and Broca's area and adjacent pathways which are particularly sensitive to early linguistic input, especially dialogic conversation.

The "dialogic conversation" referred to, is simply a conversation in which two or more individuals explore the meaning of something – and in the context of CR, it would be open questions that the adult asks the child to encourage discussion, express safely how they are feeling and ultimately help them calm down. This is explored as part of Emotion Coaching further on in this chapter.

Opening statements based on the observed behaviours of the child might include:

- *I can see you look very upset. Do you want to tell me what happened?*

- *I understand that made you feel angry. I would feel angry too.*

- *I noticed you got cross when you had to come in after outdoor play.*

- *It's OK to feel frustrated, but it's not OK to hit or shout at our friends.*

■ *What could you do the next time you feel frustrated?*

■ *What can I do to help you feel better?*

When used in ways that are appropriate to the child's stage of understanding, such dialogic conversations can be effective in not only developing their prosocial understanding and skills but also in building their ability to discuss, reason and solve problems – all of which advance higher-order thinking while building self-regulatory ability. As demonstrated by Romeo et al. (2018), such regular interactions also play a key role in advancing early brain development, particularly in the brain regions responsible for higher-order thinking and language – which are fundamentally important in equipping children to articulate how they are feeling and why.

A key recommendation from this study is to raise parental awareness of the importance of reciprocal interactions in which the child is actively engaged in language, as children's conversational exposure provides an excellent way to capitalize on the early neural plasticity which underpins cognitive development.

Read and respond to the following reflective questions.

Rewind. Reflect. Write!

1 Explain what co-regulation is.

2 Discuss at least two factors that you need to consider when co-regulating children's emotions and behaviour.

3a Reflecting on the CO-REG acronym, which aspects do you feel you need to improve and why?

3b Outline two ways you will do this.

4 Do the three approaches to achieving CR differ for small and large groups of children? Explain your answer.

5a Explain what a dialogic conversation is.

5b Why are these important for early brain development?

5c Discuss the brain regions particularly activated during a dialogic conversation.

6 Give three examples of dialogic questions that you use with a child to explore their emotional wellbeing.

7 Could dialogic conversations be improved in your setting/home? Discuss how.

8 Discuss three ways you could further raise parental awareness of the importance of reciprocal interactions in supporting language development.

9 Discuss the relationship between language skills and the ability to self-regulate.

The following case study outlines how one father's inclusion of emotional vocabulary within the security of a warm and responsive relationship made a positive difference to his 18-month-old son, who started to show signs of anxiety following the third lockdown in the United Kingdom as a result of the coronavirus pandemic. Read it and answer the questions that follow.

Josh is our first son – he is generally a very contented child and naturally curious, enjoying exploring his environment and meeting new children at playgroups, but he is a sensitive soul, and recently he has been at home with his mum for most of the three lockdowns, so he has not had the exposure to lots of other places and people that he would have normally. He seems to have developed a fear of new people and groups, staying close to his mum or me and crying when other people are close to him. I didn't want to focus on it too much, as I was a shy child too, and it got reinforced the more people told me I was shy. I wanted to avoid telling him not to be shy, but I wanted to help him overcome it too.

I decided to speak to a colleague, who gave me some sound advice about how I might be able to help him, and so far, it is working!

My wife and I now take the time to actually observe Josh, which helps us to understand when he starts getting anxious and why. We get to his level and do a lot of acknowledging and reassuring. Typically, it's when we are getting ready to go to the local playgroup sessions, so I ask him, "Are you feeling scared?" He usually replies, "Yes," which leads me to ask why. He will then say "stay home" or "want mummy." We give him lots of reassurance and tell him that we understand and that sometimes we feel scared – or anxious. We then try to reassure him that it is OK to feel anxious but that when he sees the staff and other children at playgroup (naming them), he always has fun. This always works! I also asked him if taking his small panda bear toy in his coat pocket would help him to feel OK if he missed being at home. He now takes his soft toy with him, which also helps him to separate from us. It's a process, but it is definitely working. Using the words to help him understand and describe how he is feeling is helping him – and us – so much.

> ## Read. Reflect. Write!
>
> **1a** Reflecting on the case study, what emotions was Josh displaying?
>
> **1b** How did his parents co-regulate these emotions and his behaviours?
>
> **2a** How would you support Josh in the setting? Discuss.
>
> **2b** How would you support his parents and why? Discuss.

The Three Rs

As discussed in Chapter 1, the brain is a social organ, primed for connection with responsive adults from birth. The infant brain grows at an exponential rate during early childhood, with brain regions and neural networks associated with language being most flexible in the first few years of life (Tronick and Gold, 2020; Romeo et al., 2018; Lieberman, 2015), when the brain is much more sensitive to experience than in later years. As Tierney and Nelson (2009: 5) explain:

> Although development continues into early adult years, early childhood represents a period particularly important to development of a healthy brain. The foundations of sensory and perceptual systems that are critical to language, social behaviour and emotion are formed in the early years and are strongly influenced by experiences during this time. This is not to say that later development cannot affect these behaviours, but experiences in the early years of childhood affect the development of brain architecture in a way that later experiences do not.

When reflecting on this sensitive period of brain growth and development regarding our role as co-regulators, it might be helpful to consider the three Rs (respectful and responsive relationships). The three Rs enable infants and children to learn about their world and their place in it through first-hand experience of reciprocal interactions which require them to use their emergent cognitive, physical, language, social and emotional skills as they engage with a responsive adult. This adult observes their cues and engages with and responds to them in ways that are timely, authentic and useful in identifying their emotions and helping them to begin to self-regulate. Also integral to achieving the three Rs are:

- Involving young children in decisions that affect them

- Validating their emotions

- Explaining what you are doing and why

■ Adjusting your tone of voice and pace to their level

■ Taking the time to read their cues and responding in ways that ensure that they feel listened to and valued.

Underpinning the three Rs is intersubjectivity. Even though this may not be a term that is readily used in your daily work with babies and young children, it is something you likely achieve with them on a daily basis. Intersubjectivity is the way a person understands and relates to another. It is how we share our focus and experiences with one another and can be defined as the close relationship between two individuals which is characterized by joint attention in which the movements, non–verbal gestures like eye contact, hand gestures, facial expressions and language are in complete harmony – as in the phrase "being in synch with each other." Although intersubjectivity tends to be discussed in the context of the mother and infant dyad, it is present in all close relationships, be these between romantic partners, colleagues, friends or relatives. Hughes and Baylin (2012: 103) define intersubjectivity as:

> The reciprocal relationship between a parent and child. Within this mind–to–mind rapport, both the parent and child are open to one another, receptive to and sharing each other's experience of self, other and the world.

The following example provides an example of intersubjectivity between a young child and her nanny. Read it and answer the questions that follow.

While playing in the garden with her nanny, two-year-old Tammy falls over while running and starts to cry. Her nanny offers her a cuddle and picks her up, reassuring her as she takes her into the kitchen, before helping her to sit down on a chair. She takes a look at Tammy's knee and wipes it clean before applying a plaster. As she does so, she starts singing Tammy's favourite song. Hearing this, Tammy smiles, wiping her tears. She then joins in, and they look at each other, smiling, before they sing the chorus of the song together.

Rewind. Reflect. Write!

1   What enabled this intersubjective exchange to take place? Explain.

2   Identify the features of this exchange which made it intersubjective.

3   How did the nanny co-regulate Tammy's emotional responses and behaviour?

4   Explain why intersubjectivity plays an important role in co-regulation.

The Magic Number Is 10!

Shanker et al. (2017) propose 10 easy-to-follow steps when co-regulating children's emergent ability to self-regulate. It is effective because it considers the realities of CR – that on some occasions, it will work, and on others, it might not go to plan. This can be a result of the child's level of distress and how hyper- or hypo-aroused they are at the time. CR can also be affected by the adult's mood and resilience in the moment, as well as their levels of tiredness and irritability. Although it can feel disappointing when your intervention does not have the desired impact, you need not get despondent, because it is a journey – as long as you continually reflect on and revise your approaches to co-regulating babies' and children's emotions and behaviour, you will find the best approaches that meet their current individual needs. Take a look at the following list.

1 Spot the patterns in the child's behaviour

2 Seek to strengthen children's SR skills, as opposed to trying to control their behaviour

3 Do not expect instant change – change happens gradually (this goes for your practice and its impact)

4 Celebrate each child's attempts to self-regulate! Don't forget to share with their primary carers

5 Expect it to go wrong – SR does not always happen (we can vouch for that as adults!)

6 Make sure the children understand the terms you use (like "self-regulate" and "calm")

7 Communicate at each child's unique level – particularly during times of their dysregulation

8 Better late than never! It is never too late to start self-regulating – this applies to you and children

9 Reframe those behaviours that you tend to view as "challenging" and instead question why the behaviour is occurring

10 Be that positive SR model! How you self-regulate is perhaps the most significant SR lesson of all.

Rewind. Reflect. Write!

1 Explain how you currently put the three Rs into action as part of your interactions with:

  a Babies

  b Children.

2   Which aspects of your interactions do you think could be improved and why?

3   Describe the characteristics of intersubjectivity.

4   Consider the co-regulation in your setting for promoting:

   a   Babies' self-regulatory skills

   b   Children's self-regulatory skills.

5a   How do you currently support primary carers to understand the importance of the three Rs with their children?

5b   How might this be developed and why?

Top Tips for Practice!

- Hold regular staff meetings to share knowledge about the babies and children in order to further enhance support for parents in promoting their baby's learning in the home

- Support parents/primary carers by sharing with them any signs in their child's behaviour that indicate they are becoming dysregulated – and how to support them

- Ensure staff undertake regular training in SR, which is targeted on updating knowledge on children's triggers and how to identify and minimize these

- Make language accessible for all children from infancy by ensuring they are not merely talked at but that you are actively promoting their receptive language.

2   Teaching and Modelling of Self-Regulation Skills

Put simply, you cannot co-regulate if you cannot self-regulate. Children and young adults *need* the presence of an adult who can "hold space" (be physically, mentally and emotionally present) with them during times of need – as well as provide a positive role model for companionship in general. Although realistically, none of us are calm and emotionally present all of the time, providing a foundation of love and responsive care that is generally consistent and predictable is vital in equipping children with the practical in-the-moment strategies to use when they are feeling dysregulated. As the child grows older and matures intellectually, these strategies will develop with them.

Where children enjoy those warm and responsive relationships, they are more likely to be receptive to learning SR skills through the adult's role modelling, instruction and opportunities for practice – which includes opportunity to get it "wrong" in a non-judgmental climate of safety and trust. Teaching and modelling SR also requires the adult to observe children's attempts at self-regulating in order to offer prompts, scaffolding as necessary. The more consistently and readily the child can self-regulate, the less need for teaching, modelling and scaffolding.

Co-regulating the emotions and behaviour of children and young adults is no easy task. Children with SEND are likely to be triggered frequently on a daily basis (across those five domains of SR) and will need adults who can identify and minimize the presence of these triggers while being confident in co-regulating them when they do become dysregulated. (CR and SEND are examined in Chapter 4.) It is also important to hold in mind that children who have been exposed to ACEs may also find it difficult to self-regulate. This is often due to not having been provided with a healthy role model for SR by their primary carers and being in a state of chronic hyper-arousal as a result of the exposure to the toxic stressors in their lives. Rollins and Crandall (2021: 2) highlight the negative impact of ACEs on key brain regions responsible for SR and executive functioning:

> Brain imaging studies indicate that ACEs may negatively affect the development and structure of the prefrontal cortex, hippocampus, amygdala, and other parts of the brain that are important to self-regulation and emotion, whereas nurturing experiences, such as positive parenting, promote more normative brain development even in the face of ACEs.

Early childhood presents a unique and unparalleled developmental phase during which secure attachments and consistent, attuned co-regulatory support ground young children while boosting their self-confidence and consequent self-efficacy over time. Given that our brains are regulated by others (Perry, 2021; Maté, 2019; Porges, 2017; Siegel and Bryson, 2015), CR can be an immediately effective strategy that enables the child to learn new ways of responding and behaving that are socially acceptable and growth promoting. CR ultimately triggers new neural connections which strengthen with repetition and reinforcement of experiences, leading to adaptive ways of behaving and responding to triggers – as opposed to being stuck in maladaptive ways of behaving and managing trauma. Put simply – human connections build neural connections, and *we* need to make each one count.

The process of CR is therefore also beneficial for the adult, as they too will model and feel the physiological and behavioural effects of self-regulating – as opposed to issuing futile yet harmful punishments that are (mis)guided by behaviour management approaches. As Cozolino (2013: 265) reminds us:

> As human beings, we need to connect with our children as much as they need to connect with us.

With this mutual dependence in mind, CR can be particularly helpful for adults who did not experience co-regulating relationships in their childhoods and hence might be easily triggered by children's dysregulated behaviours. This is captured by Hughes and Baylin (2012: 12), who acknowledge the potentially devasting impact on a child if their parents are generally emotionally unavailable and unable to enjoy the relationship with them:

> When there is a lack of reciprocal positive experience in the parent-child relationship for a given period of time . . . parents must rely heavily on whatever executive powers of self-control they can summon to keep from becoming blatantly abusive or neglectful.

Thus, their teaching and modelling of SR skills will support the development of their own capacity to self-regulate (Hughes and Baylin, 2012; Marrazziti, 2009; Mennin, 2006). On which note, before we examine some tried and tested CR strategies, let us focus on *you*. Read on to see how you fare when it comes to self-regulating your emotions and behaviour during emotionally charged or difficult times.

The following points for practice have been provided by the head teacher of a pupil referral unit (PRU) who always prioritizes SR and CR in all he and his team do at the centre.

We always try to have a calm sense of self before engaging with pupils, making sure we are in check with our own emotions beforehand. We always address Maslow's hierarchy of needs in the first instance, making sure the pupils' basic needs are/have been met, always being consistent when talking to our younger pupils, including calm, reassuring voices; validating their emotions; and also supportive silence if required. As part of our approach to co-regulating children's emotions and behaviour, we do the following:

- Breathing techniques to help calm
- Reflecting back to the child what they say, to acknowledge their anxiety, using a calm tone of voice
- Allowing them space
- Allowing them to leave the class when necessary (while still observing them)
- Swapping staff so that the pupil gets a change of face

- Offering a warm and sympathetic approach can work

- Changing tone of voice, depending on the activity

- Child-led but with boundaries and rules (discussed between us and agreed)

- Turn-taking

- Role modelling appropriate language (manners – "please" and "thank you")

- Distraction

- Non-verbal cues

- When a pupil is dysregulated, I often take them outside to play throw and catch. This repetitive action, talking in a calm voice and distracting them to focus on catching the ball always works well.

Self-Regulation – Do You Sink or Swim?

This is a question I often ask practitioners and primary carers, and in most instances, it does tend to elicit some awkward responses, as if struggling with SR is something to be ashamed of – which of course is not the case. Inviting adults to reflect on how effectively they can manage their own thoughts, feelings and behaviour and how they overcome stressors in their lives can provide some insight into how adept they are at co-regulating others, so it is a dialogue we should all be encouraging and engaging in honestly. While we all have "off-days," with minimum capacity to stay calm and support others, if this is our norm, we will not be best positioned to co-regulate babies' and children's emotions and behaviours. Moreover, left unresolved, poor SR *will* have a long-term negative impact on psychological and physiological health, with a potentially compromised ability to build and maintain personal and professional relationships and dependence on alcohol, cigarettes and recreational drugs to self-soothe in the absence of self-regulatory capacity.

So how do *you* fare when it comes to self-regulating – particularly during stressful moments? This leads us to your journey along the *Stream of Self-Regulation*.

The Stream of Self-Regulation

This Stream of Self-Regulation (Figure 2.6) provides a quick and easy way for you to identify how effectively you self-regulate your emotions and behaviour. The Stream helps to raise your *self-awareness* and ability to *reflect* on any areas that you might need to work on, without the inclusion of numbers and scales, so as to remove any pressure of scoring points. It is a simple tool with recommended strategies to help you easily navigate your way through your personal self-regulation journey. (One of the strategies referred to, the *Keep Your Cool Toolbox*, is a free SR app that I designed. Its website address can be found in the Bibliography.)

Take a look and answer the questions that follow.

The Stream of Self-Regulation

When it comes to self-regulating your emotions and behaviour, do you feel like you are sinking or swimming?
This Stream of Self-Regulation provides an easy way for you to identify how effectively you self-regulate. It helps to raise your self-awareness and ability to reflect on any areas that you might need to work on, so that you can stay calm during emotionally charged situations. Practical strategies are provided to help you navigate your self-regulation journey.

Practice guided meditation

I view difficult situations as opportunities to nurture children's self-regulation skills

Enjoy daily exercise

Try grounding exercises, e.g. The 5,4,3,2,1 technique

I always manage to stay calm during emotionally charged situations

I view difficult situations as opportunities to practice my self-regulation skills

Practice positive affirmations

Listen to soothing music

I'm good at maintaining open communication with others even when I feel upset or angry

I'm generally flexible and can adapt to situations when necessary

I often find it difficult to be emotionally present for others during emotionally charged situations

Practice journaling

Avoid recreational drugs

I am often involved in conflict in relationships

I rely on smoking and/or alcohol to calm me down

Try the Keep Your Cool Toolbox app

I always end up showing my anger and tend to shout in times of personal stress

Consider therapy (Seek advice from your GP)

I often cause co-dysregulation during emotionally charged situations

Take deep breaths

Figure 2.6 The Stream of Self-Regulation

Rewind. Reflect. Write!

1 Read through the Stream of Self-Regulation and reflect honestly about your general ability to self-regulate in challenging situations.

1a Select two statements from the Stream that resonate most with you and explain why.

1b Are there strategies on the list that you have not tried? Note these down with a view to trying them.

2 What do you understand about the impact of ACEs on a child's ability to self-regulate? Discuss.

3a How do you tend to "hold space" for a dysregulated child?

3b Have there been occasions when you have not managed to do this and co-regulate a child? What were the reasons for this?

3c What was the outcome? Discuss.

4 Reflecting on the head teacher's list of co-regulatory strategies, were there any that you have not yet tried? Note these down and take back to your team to try.

5 In your experience, what are the key characteristics of effective co-regulation and why?

We will now shift our attention to the evidence-based approach of Emotion Coaching, which is used globally to help co-regulate children's thoughts, feelings and behaviour.

Emotion Coaching as a Co-Regulation Tool

Emotion Coaching (EC) is a globally adopted relational approach (which means it is dependent on relationships) to supporting children's behaviour. It is based on the work of John Gottman and his colleagues in America, who emphasize the process of emotion regulation rather than behaviour modification – in other words, a focus on the emotions and desires which ultimately drive the behaviour, as opposed to focusing on the behaviour only. As Gottman and DeClaire (1997: 2) explain:

> Emotion coaching is about helping children to understand the different emotions they experience, why they occur, and how to handle them.

The emphasis on supporting children to understand their emotions and equipping them to choose different, healthier ways to respond to triggers is fundamental to effective CR. It is what sets it apart from the more traditional behavioural strategies to supporting behaviour, which advocate a one-size-fits-all, punitive approach. An EC approach also means that the adult is:

- Aware of their own emotions

- Aware of the child's emotions.

EC consists of two key elements:

1   Empathy (tuning into young children's thoughts and feelings)

2   Guidance.

These two elements guide the adult's approach whenever emotionally charged moments occur. Emotional empathy involves recognizing, labelling and validating a child's emotions, regardless of their behaviour, in order to promote self-awareness of their emotions – and how to better manage them. The circumstances might also require setting limits on appropriate behaviour (such as stating clearly what is acceptable behaviour and what is not) and possible consequential action – but key to this process is guidance: engaging with the child in seeking solutions, in order to support their ability to learn to self-regulate and to seek alternative ways of responding during times of upset, anger or frustration.

EC helps to create nurturing relationships that support (or scaffold) effective stress management skills, which promote emotional and behavioural SR. It provides practitioners with a valuable tool for supporting children's behaviour while nurturing the wellbeing of both adults and children.

EC consists of three steps, as outlined by its founders, Rose et al. (2015: 23):

1   Recognizing, empathizing, validating and labelling feelings

2   Setting limits on behaviour

3   Problem-solving with the child/young person.

EC reminds us and children that all emotions are acceptable, but not all behaviour.

It is important to understand that EC is not a one-size-fits-all approach – what works with one child might not work with another. Nor is it a "quick fix" solution. It will take time and trial and error to find out what works best with each individual child – it is also worth bearing in mind that what works with one child one day might not work the next day.

How Emotion Coaching Can Support Practice in an Early Years Setting

Children in an emotional state need to be returned to a relaxed, calm state before we can reason with them (remember – it is all about first calming the emotionally reactive "downstairs" brain before we can engage the thinking "upstairs" brain). Gottman and DeClaire (1997) believe that if we offer solutions before we empathize, it is the equivalent to trying to build a house before a firm foundation has been laid. What children need when they are angry or sad, no matter how "challenging" their behaviour, is emotional first aid. Practitioners need to get in sync with the child by recognizing and then acknowledging the existence of their feelings. Empathy from the practitioner helps the child to calm down, providing a safe haven of acceptance that builds a strong bond between the practitioner and child. Once the child has calmed, she/he is more open and able to reason and the practitioner can work with the child to create effective neural connections to the rational (thinking) parts of the brain. This enables the child to become better at managing their emotions and behaviour.

EC also enables practitioners to take advantage of key moments to teach appropriate behaviour in the moment that it occurs – instead of reprimanding (telling off or punishing) the child. In essence, EC provides the practitioner with an effective strategy which helps children learn to self-regulate their emotions and consequently their behaviour by:

- Triggering a calmer response through empathetic support

- Assisting/co-regulating children to self-soothe and increase their awareness of their own emotional state

- Using the emotional moment as an opportunity to scaffold children's self-management of their emotions and behaviour.

How Emotion Coaching Works in Practice

EC is beneficial to all children, but particularly supports children with SEND. This includes children who have conduct difficulties and those exposed to violent environments, including inter-parental violence, maltreatment and community violence.

Also, recent research in the United Kingdom has evaluated the impact of using EC techniques in professional practice, particularly during behavioural incidents (Rose et al., 2015; Gilbert et al., 2015). Practitioners and parents were trained and supported to help embed EC into practice, with findings demonstrating that EC:

- Helps children to regulate, improve and take ownership of their behaviour

- Helps children to calm down and better understand their emotions

■ Helps practitioners to be more sensitive to children's needs

■ Helps create more consistent responses to children's behaviour

■ Helps practitioners to feel more in control during incidents

■ Helps to promote positive relationships.

EC promotes young children's self-awareness and SR of their behaviour and generates more nurturing relationships. In nurturing relationships, young children can feel protected, comforted and secure within a context of caring and trustworthy adults, who can support them in their journey to achieving SR. As one practitioner put it:

> It makes the children feel more secure and gives them a vocabulary to talk about how they are feeling instead of just acting out. This helps them to be more positive and happier.

And one parent commented:

> My boys seem to calm down a lot quicker than before and my daughter is understanding that she's not on her own with her emotions. Their confidence is improving and they know it's normal to have all these feelings.

Ultimately, EC works. It works to not only improve children's behaviour, but Gottman et al.'s research has shown that emotion-coached children:

■ Are more emotionally stable – because they have the skills to calm themselves down when they need to

■ Are more resilient – because they are more confident in handling life's ups and downs

■ Achieve more academically in school – because they are able to self-regulate and therefore ready and able to learn

■ Are more popular – because they do not "flip their lid" and can make and maintain friendships

■ Have fewer behavioural problems – because they can regulate their emotional responses and behaviour

■ Have fewer infectious illnesses – because they can regulate their fight or flight response, which, if constantly activated, compromises immunity.

The following real-life scenarios and accompanying questions are designed to encourage you to reflect on your emotions during a child's dysregulation and your responses to the child. Read and respond to the three scenarios and the questions in Table 2.1. (It will be useful to grab a notebook at this point!)

Table 2.1 Emotion Coaching Scenarios

Scenario	Emotions You Might Experience	Emotions You Think the Child Is Feeling	What You Would Do	Aspects of Emotion Coaching You Would Use in That Moment	Impact on Baby/Child
Two-year-old child very upset and throwing Lego bricks, not wanting adults to approach her.					
Three-year-old boy refusing to put his shoes on because he doesn't want to leave the house.					
Twelve-month-old doesn't want his mother to leave him in the morning – he is crying as he clings onto her and screams when you try to touch him.					

Rewind. Reflect. Write!

1   What type of approach is Emotion Coaching?

2   Look back at the three steps of Emotion Coaching.

   a Do you think the first step is important?

   b Explain the reasons why.

3   Explain how Emotion Coaching can benefit:

   a The adult

   b The child.

4 Now that you have an insight into Emotion Coaching as a strategy for supporting children's behaviour and wellbeing, how might it be implemented in your own working practice?

5 What could be the challenges for you in using Emotion Coaching in your setting?

6 Imagine you use Emotion Coaching successfully with one child, only for it not to be as effective the next day with the same child.

   a Why might this be?

   b What might you do differently?

7 Discuss your thoughts on traditional behaviourist approaches to behaviour, compared to relational approaches. Which do you find more effective? Explain.

Top Tips for Practice!

- Encourage your team and primary carers to understand what SR is – and that SR skills develop over a lifetime, with you all playing a key role in nurturing them

- Share your strategies for co-regulating with primary carers

- Practice Emotion Coaching with children and encourage primary carers to try this

- Create growth-promoting environments that facilitate co-regulation of emotions and behaviour

- Use your key person system to create and maintain supportive, reliable relationships

- Make sure your team is adept at identifying and understanding each child's cues when they begin to feel dysregulated

- Remember that some staff members find it more difficult to self-regulate than others

- Have meaningful supports in place to nurture the wellbeing of all your team

- Promote critical thinking by creating an environment where children feel safe to explore and are comforted if they feel scared or confused.

3 The Structure of the Indoor and Outdoor Environments

Co-regulating children's – and indeed, your colleagues' – emotions and behaviour cannot be compartmentalized into one specific aspect of your role. CR needs to be an underpinning and all-encompassing core feature of your provision. Children, staff and primary carers alike need to know and feel that they are psychologically safe, no matter how tough it gets – and let's be honest, life in EY settings and schools can get stressful! Your provision will make all the difference to a child's ability to self-regulate – or not. It is therefore important to hold in mind that your setting in general needs to be SR ready. For example, having a SR space in a setting that is otherwise cluttered and disorganized will undermine your efforts to co-regulate children and send the wrong messages to them – and their families. You also need to ensure that your setting is well resourced to support children's SR skills, not least because these resources will further enhance the work you already do to co-regulate through your responsive relationships, modelling and the set-up of your environments. Your resources will show the children and their primary carers that you care about their mental health and that you are making the effort to prioritize this alongside academic outcomes. Most resources to support SR can be used both indoors and outdoors, and, as discussed, being outdoors in nature can do wonders for everyone's mental health, so the more frequently you can use the resources outdoors – do so!

How do you make sure your environments are comfortable and comforting places to learn and thrive in? The following are a few tips to help you when thinking about the type of SR space you want to create:

■ The SR space must be separate to other cosy spaces, such as dens and story areas

■ It should include a neutral-coloured rug and cushions

■ Some soft toys for children to cuddle (which must be cleaned regularly)

■ A blanket

■ Communication aids that enable a child to identify and express their feelings in-the-moment. For example, break cards. These enable a child to identify and express their feelings while giving them the option of having a break to self-regulate before they return to the day's routine

■ Sensory bottles (or similar resources), which could be made with the children

■ Laminated breathing stars, which staff would model for and with the children

■ Family photographs

■ Ear defenders

■ Squeezy objects (such as stress balls)

■ Fidget toys

■ Stories about feelings.

The following section is very practical in nature, consisting mainly of real-life case studies and photographs which evidence high-quality, effective indoor and outdoor environments and the resources used to facilitate CR and SR.

Creating a Co-Regulating Indoor Environment

It does not have to be costly to create and maintain an indoor environment that enables CR. Don't forget – this should be predominantly achieved through the emotional climate that you create. After all, a well-resourced environment means nothing if the staff in it do not build authentic and co-regulating relationships with children and their families. This is particularly important for children from families experiencing relationship difficulties or mental health issues, who are more likely to develop difficulties with their own mental health and emotional and social wellbeing. It is also important to include children in the designing and resourcing of the (indoor and outdoor) SR spaces, as this lends itself to increased understanding of SR and a sense of ownership, agency and pride in what they have helped to create.

The following case study was provided by the head of Early Years at Thrive Childcare and Education. She outlines the inception of their indoor and outdoor SR spaces (which are also presented further on in this chapter).

The SR spaces, both indoor and outdoor, were created as an acknowledgement that there was nowhere for babies and children to go when they needed to be alone or a space of calm, away from the stimulating room. We acknowledged that having 20 or 30 children in a room is actually not conducive to developing SR nor is it natural. At home, you would not have this many children! So our SR spaces started indoors – as a safe place to get away from the busyness of the daily routine. Regarding our outdoor SR spaces, it was one of the forest school managers who initiated the outdoor SR spaces, again, in recognition of the big, loud noises and that children would benefit from some time away from this – and a rest if they needed it. Staff created these spaces using the SR Guidance that we designed, taking into consideration the resources (such as relevant story books and breathing stars) and furnishings to create a cosy and calming space. This is all done as part of a continual cycle of reflection and development, based on staff observations of the children's needs at the time – particularly those children who have SEND or if they had a child who had a SR Support form – this identifies specific objectives or requirements. Where children would previously become stressed and "lash out," they are now able to identify the onset of overwhelming feelings and take themselves off to the SR space until they felt calm again. The children absolutely love these spaces and visibly benefit from them. That said, we do have a few nurseries that do not yet have an outdoor SR space but this is mainly due to the characteristics of their outdoor space. For example, some have trees and a shaded area, which organically became used as a SR space by the children. This is always so reassuring to see, because it shows us that they know they are starting to feel dysregulated and know what they can do to help themselves in ways that are safe and useful.

The following photograph is of a toddler, aged 18-months-old. She was settling in and was struggling with separation anxiety. She would, however, head to this SR space, which always helped to regulate her. She often loved to snuggle up and lie down, observing the children playing. Her Key Person would stay nearby until she was ready for a cuddle and start engaging in her own time.

This SR space is nice and simple and the children love sitting and lying down here. You will notice that the colours are pastel shades, to prevent any hyper-sensitive children from becoming triggered. To the left, there are three types of resources which the children also make use of, these being a basket of the laminated breathing stars, books about emotions and feelings cards, to help children identify and talk about how they are feeling. This is a quick and effective way to build emotional vocabulary, which ultimately helps to diffuse the intensity of those more overwhelming feelings. On the right is a basket which is usually full of sensory objects, including balls and fidget toys. The children are also welcome to bring their own fidget toys from home, which they use in the SR space.

This photograph shows a range of resources which reside in a large basket on the floor in the SR space in one of our settings. This makes it accessible for babies too. Babies and children alike enjoy exploring the wooden sensory cubes, which are filled with objects that make different sounds when shaken. Children love looking inside them and observing the little objects move, which they find calming. The books are often read by children independently, but where asked for, or when the practitioner thinks it would be particularly helpful (for example, having calmed a child down following dysregulation), they are read together.

Rewind. Reflect. Write!

Ia In your opinion, what are the key elements of an effective self-regulation space?

Ib Would you say that your setting is generally conducive to facilitating self-regulation? Discuss.

2 Revisit the section on the type of self-regulation space you want to create.

   a Which criteria do you meet?

   b Which do you need to build on?

   c Make a plan of action.

The following case study was provided by the head teacher of the PRU, the New Leaf Inclusion Centre. Here, he briefly outlines some of the resources that the children most like to use when they feel disregulated.

I'm currently working on developing our collection of sensory resources, as they are so popular with all the children, particularly when they are feeling angry, stressed or hypo-aroused. During these moments, children mostly engage in:

- Sand play

- Water play

- Lego play

- Various sensory toys – I have some water beads which children often choose to explore when they become dysregulated. We often blow up balloons and then fill them with water beads, which we play tennis with, while we are talking about why they are feeling a certain way. It is a non-pressurizing way for them to express themselves and one which they always respond to.

Children also have free access to our dark room or sensory tent, where they go to and snuggle up in when they feel tired, need some alone time or if they feel too angry to be around anybody. When they feel ready, they come out and we talk about what is bothering them.

Now that you have read the case study, respond to the following questions.

Rewind. Reflect. Write!

I   What are your thoughts about this head teacher's approach to co-regulating children during times of dysregulation? Discuss.

2a Does he use resources that you might not have previously considered regulating? What are these? Discuss.

2b Does he use resources that you would consider trying in your indoor environment? Outline what these are.

3   At New Leaf, children are never reprimanded – even when they become aggressive. What do you think about this relational approach?

Specialist support practitioner for children and young people Amanda Peddle (2019) works in diverse schools across the United Kingdom, supporting children in small groups and on a one-to-one basis. Here she outlines the nature of her role and how she teaches (younger and older) children about the brain and the body and how these are impacted by stress. She also details how she co-regulates children and how this positively influences their capacity to self-regulate.

As a practitioner promoting the development of co- and self-regulation in a multitude of settings, I am often faced with situations where I am able to use the skills of co-regulation to model to other staff how effective this can be. I have found this to be the best way to make the concept relevant to staff within the educational setting especially. The top-down narrative of behaviour and discipline policies can often seem at odds with an individual, person-centred interaction – and the development path for staff rarely includes development in areas of self-regulation.

One particular occasion provided me with an impromptu teachable moment and this has stayed with me, due to the impact on one of the staff members, in particular.

A SEND coordinator in a local secondary school approached me, asking if I would assist with a child who was completely "defiant" and "refusing" to move, engage or respond. When I arrived, there were a number of staff attempting to engage him – a young teenage boy, small in stature, stood in a hallway with his head bowed and hands around his face crossed, so his face could not be seen.

There were a number of commands being issued at him at varying levels of volume – some more nurturing in tone, but still offering a choice of outcomes (all punitive and of varying degrees of seriousness). I asked all staff to leave the area and they moved away into classrooms and corridors around – some to observe from a distance.

I sat on the floor at his feet but a small amount of space still between us. I said nothing to start with, I slowly began to explain that staff had moved away, that he did not need to move, speak, look or interact at all until he was ready and that I would wait for him – all the time, edging slightly closer.

After a few minutes he started to look down under his arms and then at me and made some eye contact, and after chatting for a while, he sat next to me and after some time he moved away with myself and the SEND coordinator, to a safe area to have some time to settle.

Staff had been trying for over an hour and he was in a complete frozen state. He needed to feel safe and non-threatened, and his response to a self-regulated adult was a great example to show staff on the frontline how that may look. The whole interaction took around 12 minutes.

While the interaction for the child was clearly of benefit and allowed him to have a positive experience, the larger benefit was that my relationship with the SEND coordinator changed dramatically. We had differed in opinion on many students and she had been sceptical of my approaches, but the professional relationship that has grown since then and the reflective discussions concerning self-regulation have been enlightened and exciting. This also filters down to her advocacy of my skillset to other staff and professionals and has created a wider conversation about the future role of self- and co-regulation in the school.

I have done some of my best work sat on floors, on staircases, under trees – in diverse settings and in all weathers, being the calm that is needed to promote the stillness in the child/young person/parent. The impact is huge and I am still approached by men and women who tell me how important "that" moment was to them as a child.

The resources I use do not tend to focus on providing labelled emotions, as I want this to come organically from the child, where possible. I instead focus on teaching children about their emotional responses and how this impacts on a physiological level. The following photograph shows just a few of the soft toys that are always a success in teaching children about how their emotions such as anger, fear and sadness can affect how they feel physically.

The yellow soft toy resembles the stomach, the red soft toy in the centre represents the heart, while the blue soft toy represents one lung (of a pair). You will also see in the background a book. This is a book I wrote, *TAM'S Journey*, which is a children's book about a young boy, called TAM, who goes on the adventure of a lifetime, learning about his brain and emotions. This page of the book is all about fight or flight and how it impacts the body. The children visibly enjoy talking about this when reading and using the soft toys, because they can so easily relate to what is being described. This knowledge stays with them and the next time they feel angry or upset, they find ways to self-regulate that are healthy and useful.

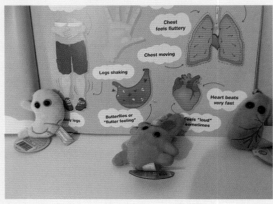

Now that you have read the case study, take a few moments to reflect on its main messages and answer the following questions.

Rewind. Reflect. Write!

I   What are the key messages from this case study for you?

2a Identify the strategies Amanda draws on to co-regulate children.

2b In which ways do you think they are effective? Discuss.

2c What other co-regulatory strategies might you draw on to support a child who has anger issues?

3   In the case study, Amanda alluded to having experienced difficulties in encouraging staff to work in relation ways, until they saw her in action. How would you encourage sceptical staff "to get on board" and use more relational ways to support children's behaviour?

Let us now focus our attention on the indoor environment of EY settings and some of the resources used to promote children's and their families' understanding of SR and CR. The following case study outlines how staff at Thrive Childcare and Education nurseries build understanding and instigate conversations on these subjects on a regular basis. These conversations enable families to share with practitioners their CR and SR successes and any personal difficulties that they might be experiencing which inhibit them from emotionally connecting with their child. This can be invaluable in working out how best to support the unique child in ways that are aligned to their temperament and preoccupations at the time.

We have been on our self-regulation journey for three years now and the deeper we go, the more we realise the importance of spreading the word to all our families as much as we can, so that they are equipped to co-regulate their children's emotions and behaviour. It isn't about a one-off coffee morning or a letter home, but findings ways of building in practical ways to get the conversation underway.

At the entrance in our nursery, we have a permanent self-regulation station, as part of our open-door policy. The station consists of a large wicker basket containing parents' leaflets about the basics of self-regulation and co-regulation and large laminated cut-out breathing stars with instructions, which parents take home to use with their children.

Recently, one boy (four-years-old), noticed that his mum was getting stressed, so he offered her a breathing star from the basket, saying, "Mummy, I think you need a breathing star," which his mum affectionately smiled at and replied, "You're right! Thank you." We thought it was brilliant that he was able to initially identify the signs of stress in his mother *and* be able to offer her a tool to help her overcome those feelings. This led her to tell us about what has been going on at home and that she was getting increasingly more stressed and therefore "snappy" with her child. We had a few more conversations and offered some suggestions as to how she could overcome these feelings and why this was important in terms of her ability to co-regulate her son's behaviour.

Much of our conversations with most families revolve around those simple but important aspects of co-regulation, like being aware of our tone of voice, body language and smiling – especially when we find the behaviour frustrating, as this is when our children need us to be patient – as opposed to telling them off.

The following case study is provided by one of the setting managers at Thrive. She explains how she and her team are developing SR areas and the resources for their setting. It is an honest account of how her initial reflections concerning the current approach to supporting children to process their emotions did not seem quite "right" – and how they set about improving it.

Every term as manager, I undertake a quality practice review, gathering information from supervisions, tracking and assessments and quality audits. Last term, I noted that the book areas/quiet areas were becoming slightly lost and confusing. Areas designed to look at books and be quiet were enhanced with puppets and small word resources. The impact of this was not one of calm and tranquillity, but more excitement and stimulation and I think that is often the most common misconception. We celebrate book areas and make them aesthetically pleasing and engaging with cushions and props. We talk about having somewhere to be quiet and snuggle down, but not all books are quiet snuggly books. Some are about dragons and knights and adventures and promote awe and wonder, but not calm and inner peace. On reflection, there were clearly mixed messages being given. We had other areas in the rooms, affectionately called "Thinking Areas" where children were encouraged to think about their actions and give literacy to some of the emotions they may have been feeling, including sad, tired or worried. (To be clear – these were not behaviour correction areas.)

We added emotional literacy resources and some tokenistic items that supported this, but we still were not getting it right. We have a positive behaviour policy and I am the named positive behaviour coordinator and I genuinely feel passionate about giving children opportunities to regulate their feelings and become literate with emotional terminology. Our nursery is peppered with positive reinforcements of understanding and supporting children. As a SENDCo and a mum to children who haven't trod the easiest of paths in terms of emotional development, I regularly share and support staff in their knowledge and understanding of the emotional challenges and struggles children face.

So when a copy of the Thrive "Promoting Children's Self-Regulation" Policy landed on my desk, it immediately struck a chord. Yes we had the same ethos and beliefs, yes we were passionate about supporting children to feel safe, secure and motivated, but we needed to reflect on *how* we were doing this in terms of our physical environment and provision. The self-regulation area concept was clear. It's not a book area, it's not a thinking area (although a lot of thinking and possibly exploring books as a coping mechanism/strategy does take place), it's a small place where we can be small, where we can provide calm, peace and the ability to re-energize, fidget, rest, cry, be reassured and focus.

It's a place where that "tummy ache" can be given a name such as frustration, worry or fear. It's a place where we can count to 10, take deep breaths and have a drink of water. We developed a "calm down and focus kit" which contains a variety of sensory items for children to explore and we've added photo albums of the children's family and friends and special people. We have created an area where we can just be!

We added bags in the 2–3's area (which a colleague kindly drew the distinctly coloured monsters, because if I'd been left to do it, the emotion would certainly have been one of confusion!) We filled the bags with appropriate contents to enable focus. We've ensured that the visual impact is neutral, calm and inviting. I've carried out staff training and children are being introduced to these areas either on a one-to-one basis or in small groups. It is important that children know what these are for and see them as somewhere that is accessible. We now have separate book areas which are more clearly defined. There is no confusion. I feel like we are now more equipped and unified in our approach to understanding not only what our role is as adults and facilitators, but the role of the environment in such an important part of child development. I hope that this has provided an insight into our rationale and my starting point for developing our approach and resources. We are grateful to Mine and Ursula for the inspiration.

The following are just two examples of the bags and their resources made by one of the practitioners at the setting. You will see that the resources are coloured to "match" their emotion. Depicted in the following is the set of red resources to help a child process feelings of "anger."

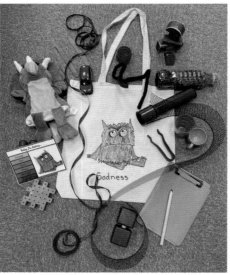

Depicted in the above photograph is the set of blue resources to help a child process feelings of sadness. Effective in their simplicity, these resources not only familiarize children with the associated language concerning feeling sad but encourage them to express themselves with the mark-making materials included.

Rewind. Reflect. Write!

1   What are your thoughts about a permanent self-regulation station as part of the indoor environment?

2   Is this something you would consider incorporating into your setting? Discuss.

3a How might you adapt your current indoor environment to be more conducive to encouraging co-regulation take place between adults and children?

3b What resources would you need? Make a plan of implementation to share with your team (including the leadership team).

4   What more might be needed to encourage co-regulation to take place among families in the home? Discuss.

Top Tips for Practice!

- Use the following criteria to create an audit of your current environment and resources, with a view to instigating any necessary changes to make these more SR ready:

  - Do children have freedom of movement between areas?

  - Are there enough resources that can be shared among a few children?

  - Are resources well stocked and well cared for by staff? (For example, are the pencils sharpened? Is there a variety of paper? Are the books in good repair? Do jigsaws have all their pieces?)

  - Do resources support children's current interests?

  - Is there a wide range of open–ended resources?

  - Are there designated spaces of calm/SR spaces?

  - Are there spaces of interest and stimulation?

  - Do images and resources represent all children and families who attend the setting?

  - Do activities allow children to sit/stand/lie/kneel/stand in ways that are most comfortable to them?

  - Are there sufficient experiences and areas which promote whole body movement?

  - Is there regular access to the outdoors?

  - Do children have free access to fresh drinking water throughout the day?

Creating a Co-Regulating Outdoor Environment

There is something particularly liberating about being outdoors, especially in nature. We immediately feel grounded, calmer and more able to think "clearly." Time outdoors generally means time away from tech devices, which is ultimately a positive thing when we consider that we are rapidly losing our connection to nature and that children, particularly in the United States and United Kingdom, spend half as much time outdoors than their parents did (Williams, 2018: 8). Studies continue to demonstrate that even briefly glancing out of the window at green, leafy areas relieves and relaxes us in stressful situations (Arvay, 2018; Kaplan, 2001), though, of course, nothing beats being outside in nature and where possible; we should all be getting our daily dose of Vitamin D! As Williams (2018: 10) alerts us:

> Scientists are quantifying nature's effects not only on mood and wellbeing, but also on our ability to think – to remember things, to plan, to create, to daydream and to focus.

Reflect on this with regard to those children who do find it difficult to self-regulate and all this entails, like focusing their attention on their work and teacher and trying to follow multiple instructions while sat down in a cluttered, restrictive classroom. A growing number of studies demonstrate that taking the learning outdoors, or at least affording children daily, frequent opportunities to be outdoors for much-needed breaks from lessons, can exert a positive impact on mental health, holistic wellbeing and behaviour, particularly on those children who get dysregulated easily (Raney et al., 2019; Weeland et al., 2019; White et al., 2019). This is highlighted by Weeland et al., (2019: 2) who conducted two meta-analyses on the effects of exposure to nature on the SR of school children. They concluded that:

> Exposure to nature may thus be a promising tool for stimulating self-regulation and preventing child psychopathology. Moreover, nature may also have important advantages over other prevention and intervention efforts. First of all, it can be easily implemented in different domains of children's environment, such as in schools and school yards, sports clubs and residential areas. Second, exposure to nature is afford-able, accessible and safe. Exposing children to nature might also have spill-over effects: through additional beneficial effects on children's physical health (e.g. exercise); by positively affecting the physical and mental health of their accompanying parents, caregivers and teachers.

The following case studies were provided by the head teacher of New Leaf Inclusion Centre, who, along with his team and the children, created a welcoming outdoor space at the Centre. This has proven an invaluable resource that immediately helps to instil a sense of calm, enabling children to self-regulate and learn in ways that are not so linear and prescriptive, to embrace challenge, communicate efficiently and work collaboratively. As the head teacher told me:

> You don't have to be sat at a desk to learn maths, science and physical education. Get the children outdoors! It does wonders for their social, emotional, physical and intellectual development.

One pupil was struggling in the classroom following a difficult weekend at home, causing significant anxiety about being brought into school. The member of staff was able to take him out of the classroom and work on their planters – a calm and purposeful activity. Discussions took place with the pupil in a relaxed environment, whereby we were able to identify issues that were disclosed and follow up through our safeguarding protocols. There would be no room for this type of conversation and disclosure in a busy classroom – and more importantly, the child would have not been feeling as calm as he was outdoors.

On this particular day, the pupil in this photograph found the classroom environment very oppressive. She refused to work and didn't take long to disengage – this quickly escalated to the point of dysregulation. Staff spotted the signs early and were able to move to a different environment (outside), where the pupil quickly settled. Further, the

pupil was supported to identify her emotions, enabling earlier intervention should she become as dysregulated again in the future.

The following is just one example of a nursery chain setting's outdoor SR space, replete with scented plants and herbs, alongside windchimes, story books and sensory objects. The nursery is one of many of the Thrive Childcare and Education group, which embeds the principles of SR in all they do. One manager explains:

This outdoor self-regulation space was designed and built with the children, which made it all the more appealing to them – not only during times of need, but also when they just wanted some "quiet time" away from the hustle and bustle of the daily routine at the nursery. Even if we are inside and the child wants to use this space, we always allow them to – regardless of weather conditions. In fact, the rain also helps to instil calm!

Now that you have read both case studies, have a go at answering the questions that follow.

Rewind. Reflect. Write!

1a What strikes you about the outdoor space used by the teachers at the PRU? Discuss.

1b What are the advantages of using the outdoor space in this way?

2 Compare and contrast the outdoor spaces used at the PRU with the designated space at the EY setting (depicted above).

3 Reflecting on the layout of your outdoor environment (if you have one), how could you transform this into a designated space for calm/a self-regulation space? Make a plan to share with your team.

As demonstrated in the previous case studies, sometimes, just being outside in nature can be enough to help calm dysregulated children (or, indeed, adults), before they feel ready to regroup. Access to the outdoors should never be restricted, rigidly set at certain times or used as a bargaining tool, for children "if they behave" or "when they have finished their work." The more children are trusted to exercise control and choice in how they choose to self-regulate, the greater their capacity to trust themselves and develop the self-efficacy to help themselves when they start to feel dysregulated.

Top Tips for Practice!

- Safety first! Carry out a risk assessment on the area to help you identify and minimize potential risks. This might include adding fencing to a low wall, to make sure that the children cannot climb over it, or putting up a curved mirror, to enable staff to see into one corner which would otherwise be hidden from view

- Decide who will be responsible for the maintenance of this space

- Avoid disorganization and clutter – an untidy and cluttered space will further dysregulate the child(ren)

- Decide how many children should use the space at one time. Think about whether you will set a limit on this and what you will base this decision on as a team

- Think about the type of shelter you will use and its durability

- What resources? – Draw on nature as much as possible for your outdoor co-regulatory space and the resources you choose with the children. Think about the soothing herbs and flowers that you could plant together to use in this space

- Select resources that stimulate the eight senses

- Think about storage – where will you keep the resources so that they remain intact?

- Think about how often you will rotate (change) the resources so that the children do not lose interest in the space and its resources

- Make sure your whole team is familiar with your self-regulation–informed approach so that they know how to support children to access and use this space for its intended purpose.

Concluding Thoughts

This chapter has presented you with diverse issues to reflect on concerning the importance of CR for babies and children. Theoretical approaches were explored as part of this, alongside the three main approaches to CR (Murray et al., 2015) and the fundamentally important role of the adult's own ability to self-regulate. While obstacles are expected when challenging and changing existing practice, your knowledge and conviction will be vital in getting your team and families on board when it comes to creating co-regulating environments as a core part of your SR-informed provision.

Further Reading

- Gilbert, L., Gus, L. and Rose, J. (2021). *Emotion Coaching with Children and Young People in Schools: Promoting Positive Behaviour, Wellbeing and Resilience.* London: Jessica Kingsley Publishers.

  This book includes simple descriptions and practical tips, with signposting to resources, case studies and vignettes to illustrate its practical application in homes and educational settings. It supports adults to promote empathic responses to "challenging" behaviours and situations, helping children and young people to understand their emotions and learn to manage them and their behaviour in the longer term.

- Murphy, L. K. (2021). *Co-Regulation Handbook: Creating Competent, Authentic Roles for Kids With Social Learning Differences, So We All Stay Positively Connected Through the Ups and Downs of Learning.* Kindle.

  This book is a useful resource for parents, as well as teachers and therapists across disciplines. It provides a practical guide for how you could move away from constantly prompting children towards building more authentic connections – and through this greater competence in supporting self-regulation. In this book, you will learn how to create a positive learning environment for everyone and, as a result, feel more empowered in your role as co-regulator.

- Rose, J., Gilbert, L. and Richards, V. (2015). *Health and Wellbeing in Early Childhood.* London: Sage Publishing.

  This comprehensive and accessible book provides contemporary scientific insights into children's holistic wellbeing from biopsychological, psychoneurobiological and ecological systems models. Mindful Moments and case studies are woven into each of the chapters to help contextualize them, and there is a chapter dedicated to the theory and implementation of Emotion Coaching.

3 The Developing Brain
A Whistle-Stop Tour

How often do you pause to think about the wonders of your brain? Marcus and Freeman (2015: 217) offer a fascinating and all-encompassing entry to this infinitely captivating organ:

> As the most complex system in the known universe, the human brain would merit study even if there were no immediate practical significance; the fact that a three-pound piece of meat can perform many intellectual feats that still surpass our greatest computers naturally makes the brain an object of wonder.

What to Expect in This Chapter

This chapter will introduce the reader to the developing brain, from conception to early childhood. As part of the discussions concerning the brain, we take a look at the nervous system and its two sub-divisions. A timeline of brain growth and development is also included, followed by a closer look at specific brain regions and their respective functions.

The concept of the "upstairs" and "downstairs" brain will also be introduced in this chapter and revisited throughout the book. Attention will be paid to the fundamental importance of experiences and relationships in shaping early brain development, as it is during this period that a child's brain develops exponentially more than at any other time in life. Consideration will be given to the way forward for neuroscience in providing greater insights into the human brain, while some practical ideas are provided towards the end of the chapter to help teach children about their brain. Questions are included to help consolidate the reader's understanding and to help the reader to challenge particular arguments that have been presented. A Further Reading section ends the chapter.

DOI: 10.4324/9781003327479-3

By the End of This Chapter, You Will Be Able to:

- Define and describe what the nervous system does

- Define and describe what the central nervous system (CNS) and the peripheral nervous system (PNS) do

- Explain what the brain is and its functions

- Summarize the timeline of brain development

- Explain the what the limbic system is and its functions

- Explain and model the "upstairs" and "downstairs" brain

- Explain the function of neurons

- Discuss the role of synapses and synaptogenesis in brain growth and development

- Explain the significance of myelination in brain growth and development

- Discuss the future of neuroscience in providing insights into the brain

- Suggest activities that promote children's understanding of the brain.

An Introduction to Your Nervous System

Before we go on a whistle-stop tour of the developing brain, let us begin by exploring some of the key components of the nervous system in detail. Understanding the different parts of the nervous system and how it works will help you to better understand child development and your role in supporting the healthy holistic wellbeing and development of children.

The human nervous system includes:

- The brain

- The spinal cord

- A complex network of nerve fibres that connect the brain to all other parts of the body.

These incredible components enable us – amongst many other things – to breathe, think, feel pain and emotions, speak, move our body and make sense of the world around us.

There are two parts to the nervous system – the CNS and the peripheral (or outer) nervous system. See Figure 3.1.

The central nervous system includes the brain and spinal cord. The brain is the body's "control centre." It receives information from our eyes (sight), ears (sound), nose

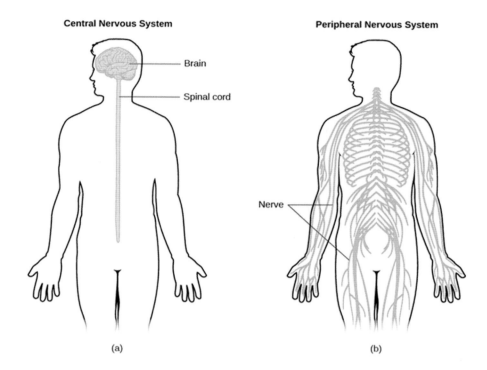

Central Nervous System

Brain

Spinal cord

(a)

Peripheral Nervous System

Nerve

(b)

Figure 3.1 The Central and Peripheral Nervous Systems

(smell), tongue (taste) and skin (touch). It makes sense of the messages it receives and decides on the appropriate response or action. The spinal cord connects to the brain and runs down the backbone. It is sometimes described as the "motorway" of the nervous system. Electrical currents travel up and down the spinal cord and across nerves, sending messages to and from the brain and the rest of the body. The peripheral nervous system is made up of nerve fibres that branch out from the CNS to every other part of the body, including organs, muscles and glands.

The Sympathetic and Parasympathetic Nervous Systems

The nervous system can be further divided into two other systems – the sympathetic and parasympathetic nervous systems. *Knowing more about these two systems is extremely important if you support young children.* One controls our stress response; the other helps us to relax and resist stress. These two systems are illustrated in Figure 3.2.

The sympathetic nervous system (SNS) controls our response to a perceived threat or danger and prepares us to take action. This is known as our fight or flight – or stress – response. When the brain perceives danger, it sends warning messages down the spinal cord and into nerve fibres that connect to glands and organs. Stress hormones like cortisol and adrenaline are then released into the brain and bloodstream. These trigger other physical reactions – for example, our heart pumps faster and the pupils in our

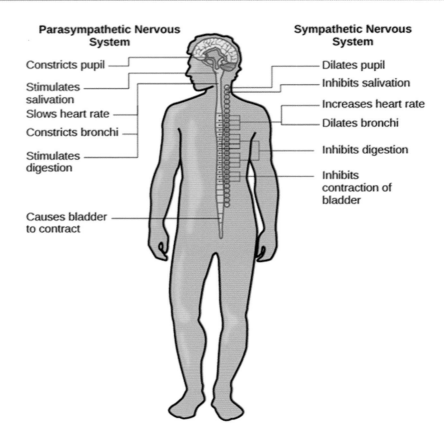

Figure 3.2 The Sympathetic and Parasympathetic Nervous Systems

eyes expand (dilate). Sometimes, these changes are helpful. They make us alert and give us the energy to tackle (fight) or escape from (take flight) a dangerous situation, but repeated stressful experiences are not good for the mind or body, especially for young children – being exposed to stress or trauma can disrupt the healthy development of a child's brain.

The parasympathetic nervous system (PNS) works in the opposite way. It calms the body by slowing down our heart rate and breathing. This, in turn, calms the muscles in our digestive system and enables us to rest and regain our energy after a stressful event (hence, it is sometimes referred to as the rest and digest response). In short, the PNS helps the mind and body to resist or recover from the negative effects caused by the sympathetic system.

The sympathetic and the parasympathetic systems tend to work in opposition to each other. Think of it like a car – the sympathetic system acts like the accelerator pedal, and the parasympathetic system acts like the brake. The stress response, activated by the sympathetic nervous system, can help to explain certain responses in children, such as anxious behaviour and sudden outbursts of anger.

The good news is that EY practitioners, teachers and parents can help children to cope better with stressful situations by teaching them how to develop their rest and digest response – in other words, by stimulating the PNS. For example, if a child can learn to slow down their breathing when they feel stressed, angry or anxious, the parasympathetic system "tells" the brain that they are not in any danger. As a result, the child's heart rate slows down and they are much less likely to enter a state of fight or flight.

Calming children down – or equipping them to calm themselves down (self-regulate) when they are stressed and upset – activates their PNS. The co-regulating, calming techniques that you learned about in Chapter 2 are useful here.

Rewind. Reflect. Write!

1a Outline the structure of the nervous system.

1b Discuss the function of the nervous system.

2 What are the two major divisions of the nervous system?

3 Based upon what you have learned so far about the sympathetic nervous system and the parasympathetic nervous system place the signs and indicators (listed below) into the correct column in a table. (You will need to draw your own table, but one has been started for you at the bottom of this box):

Heart beats in slow, rhythmic pattern

Heart beats fast

Blood pressure lowers

Breathing is fast and shallow

Pupils of the eyes expand (can make you sensitive to light)

Breathing is full and slow

Pupils of the eyes shrink

Gut is active (helping you to digest and absorb the nutrients from food)

Gut becomes sensitive (making it difficult to digest)

Blood rushes to your skeletal muscles and away from your brain (making it hard to think clearly)

Increased blood flow to gut, lungs and brain

Stress hormones rush through the body (making you feel anxious)

Inhibits saliva production (causing the mouth to feel dry and the throat to feel tight)

Increases energy

Restricts production of stress hormones (e.g. adrenaline and cortisol)

Conserves energy

Sympathetic Nervous System	Parasympathetic Nervous System

Brain Growth and Development During Pregnancy

We can use our knowledge of the nervous system to understand how the brain develops during pregnancy. The growth and development of the human brain begin very soon after conception. This development is as incredible as it is rapid, and approximately four weeks after conception, the foetus's brain begins to form even before a mother may become aware that she is pregnant. However, many factors can impact the essential process of brain growth and development, including the mother's physical and emotional health and her lifestyle. Pregnancy usually lasts for nine months (40 weeks). These nine months are broken into three trimesters, and each trimester is three months long.

First Trimester

During the first trimester, the basic brain shape begins to form. After just a few weeks, the embryo forms something called the neural plate. This is the foundation of the nervous system. As this grows, it becomes longer, folding in on itself to become the neural tube. The bulge of the tube eventually becomes the brain, while the rest of the tube stretches into a spinal cord and eventually develops into the rest of the nervous system.

Roughly halfway through the first trimester, the neural tube closes and the brain separates into three parts: the forebrain, midbrain and hindbrain (see Figure 3.3; at five weeks). The forebrain will become part of the cerebrum (the outer layer of the brain), the midbrain will form part of the brain stem and the hindbrain will become the cerebellum.

During the first trimester, the brain develops rapidly and makes up nearly half of the foetus's weight (the embryo is called the foetus at about week eight). For comparison, by the time the baby is born, the brain is only 10% of their body weight.

Even though specific areas of the brain are starting to develop, it is not until week six or seven that the first electrical brain activity begins to occur. This activity represents the foetus's first synapses – the connections between the neurons (brain cells). As you will cover in more detail later, synapses enable neurons to communicate with each other. From the time the neural tube closes, the brain will grow at a rate of 250,000 neurons per minute for the next 21 weeks.

Ultrasounds can reveal the foetus moving as early as eight weeks into pregnancy. The communication between neurons is what helps the foetus to learn to move. The mother will probably not feel any movement during the first trimester. Figure 3.3 illustrates brain growth in the first trimester of pregnancy.

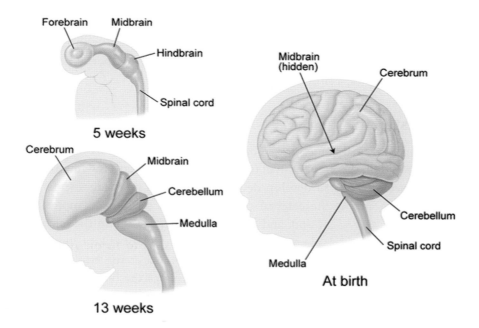

Figure 3.3 Foetal Brain Development

Source: Jonathan Dimes for Baby Centre (2020).

Second Trimester

During the second trimester, the baby's brain directs the diaphragm and chest muscles to contract. These are sometimes called "practice breaths." The baby also learns its first sucking and swallowing reflexes. At 21 weeks, the baby's swallowing reflexes allow several ounces of amniotic fluid (the fluid surrounding a foetus within the amniotic sac) to be swallowed every day. This means that the baby is tasting every time swallowing happens.

By the end of the second trimester, the brain stem is almost entirely developed, and the development of neurons and synapses enables the foetus to make its first voluntary (deliberate) movements. This is when the mother is likely to feel the baby's first kicks. The brain's development is further accelerated by this sensory input. From brain imaging, we now know that touch (even in the womb) stimulates brain development.

Of particular importance at this time is the beginning of a key process called myelination. This is the coating of neurons with a fatty sheath, which enables faster information processing. This process continues into adolescence. Babies and young children often lack sufficient myelin. It is believed that myelination is affected by the mother's physical and emotional wellbeing.

By the end of the second trimester, the nervous system will also have developed enough to enable the baby to detect loud noises from outside. In fact, the mother may feel the baby startle when there is a loud noise outside the womb. The baby will start to identify the sound of their mother's voice, and they may even turn their head towards the sound. Many neuroscientists argue that it is important for mothers and close family members to talk to or read to the foetus in the womb, as this sensory input will accelerate neural development. This process will also help the mother to build that all-important and all-encompassing bond with her baby.

Third Trimester

During the third and final trimester, the baby's brain almost triples in weight. There is further rapid growth in the number of neurons and their connections with one another. The cerebral cortex begins to develop deep grooves (gyri) and ridges (sulci), which increase the surface area of the cerebral cortex so that it can process more information, and the cerebrum separates into the left and right hemispheres. At this point, it looks like a "typical" brain.

The cerebellum (the area at the base of the brain) is the fastest growing part of the brain in the third trimester. This is the part responsible for motor control, so the baby will begin to move more, wiggle its fingers and toes, stretch and kick.

The NHS website has some useful information that explains what is happening in a baby's development week by week:

www.nhs.uk/start4life/pregnancy/week-by-week

Table 3.1 provides a summary of how the baby's brain grows and develops during pregnancy.

Table 3.1 Brain Growth and Development During Pregnancy

Weeks Pregnant	Brain Growth and Development
4 weeks	The neural plate forms and starts to curl into a tube.
6 weeks	The neural tube is closed at both ends. The baby's brain is now made up of three areas (forebrain, midbrain and hindbrain), and the ventricles have formed.
8 weeks	A network of nerves starts to extend throughout the baby's body.
12 weeks	The baby's key reflexes are in place.
20 weeks	Myelin starts to develop along some of the baby's nerve networks.
28 weeks	The baby's senses of hearing, smell, sight and touch are working.
28 to 39 weeks	The baby's brain triples in weight. Deep grooves form in the cerebral cortex to allow more surface area for neurons.

During their time in the womb, the baby produces new neurons and connections between these neurons at an astonishing rate. Almost all of the 86 billion neurons that make up the adult brain are formed during this time.

Rewind. Reflect. Write!

1 The mother's health during pregnancy is incredibly important in terms of ensuring her baby's healthy brain development. List at least 10 recommendations to support good maternal health during pregnancy.

2 Do some research into the possible harmful effects that the following can have on the developing foetus. Make a note of your findings.

- Poor diet
- Smoking nicotine
- Recreational drug use.

3a Describe the process of myelination.

3b Explain its importance. (You may wish to do some online research to support your answer.)

4 In your own words, write a brief overview of brain growth and development during the:

a First trimester of pregnancy

b Second trimester of pregnancy

c Third trimester of pregnancy.

5   Supposing a parent was worried about her stress levels affecting her unborn baby. What advice would you give her and why?

Know Your Neurons!

Although the number of neurons does not change much throughout life, the number of synaptic connections between them does. Synapses will be discussed further on. For now, we will return to those billions of neurons.

Neurons are often called brain cells because this is ultimately where all neurons report to, but they are found throughout the nervous system (in the brain, the spinal cord and the nerves that extend throughout our body). Neurons are information messengers. They use electrical impulses and chemical signals to transmit information between different areas of the brain and between the brain and the rest of the nervous system. Everything we think, feel and do would be impossible without the work of neurons and their support cells – they are like the building blocks of the brain and the nervous system.

There are many different types of neurons, each shaped differently, depending on their function in the brain and the body. You might be accustomed to seeing images of the *interneuron*, which is the most common neuron. There are approximately 20 billion interneurons (also known as association neurons), and they are only found in the central nervous system (the brain and the spinal cord). The interneuron is shown in Figure 3.4.

The Structure of a Neuron

As stated, not all neurons look the same – this depends on their function. However, as you can see in Figure 3.4, most neurons consist of three main parts: a cell body and two different extensions – dendrites (branch-like extensions) and an axon (a long tail-like structure).

■ The cell body (also known as the soma) contains the nucleus. This is the "brain" within the brain cell. It controls the cell's activities and contains the cell's genetic material

■ Dendrites look like the branches of a tree and *receive messages* from other cells in neighbouring neurons into the cell body

■ The axon looks like a long tail and transmits messages from the cell body to other cells via this tail-like structure. Axons *take information away* from the cell body towards the *axon terminals*, where synapses (connections) link with neighbouring neurons.

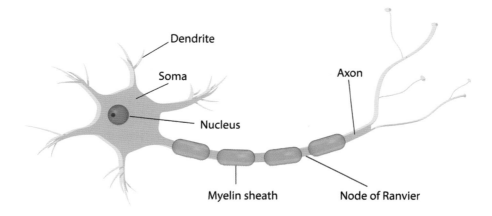

Figure 3.4 The Interneuron

As their name suggests, interneurons interlink with the other types of neurons, which means that they pass signals between sensory neurons, motor neurons and other interneurons. Often, they form complex paths that help us to react to external stimuli. Say, for example, you touch a hot iron – the signal from the sensory neurons in your fingertips travels to interneurons in your spinal cord. Interneurons would transmit the signal up the spinal cord to neurons in the brain, where the heat sensation would be perceived as pain. Interneurons would then send a signal to the motor neurons controlling your finger muscles (causing you to move your hand away from the iron quickly).

By no means is the brain fully developed at birth – it is the only organ that does most of its developing post-birth. Those 86 billion neurons are present, but they are poorly connected to each other. It is the infant's environment, experiences and interactions with those around them that will strengthen these neural connections and help the brain to become more organized. In addition, remember that each neuron will form many connections with target neurons. As a general rule, 86 trillion bits of information move around your brain every second! Take a look at the following numbers:

Know the Numbers!

Here's the maths (Azevedo et al., 2009; Herculano-Houzel, 2009)*:*

86 billion neurons

×

10 action potentials per second (2 to 200 Hz range)

×

100 synapses for each axon (estimate)

=

86,000,000,000,000 bits of information transmitted per second!

Super Synapses – The Brain's Superhighways

Neurons would not be able to do their jobs without another amazing piece of brain equipment – the synapse. For humans to be able to develop specific skills and abilities, neurons must join together and communicate effectively, but they cannot do this without the help of synapses. A synapse is the tiny gap where two neurons make contact – specifically, between the presynaptic axon and postsynaptic area (this could be the dendrite, the cell body or the axon of the postsynaptic neuron). Usually, the terms presynaptic and postsynaptic are used to specify two neurons that are connected. If one neuron fires (the presynaptic cell), it can chemically activate another cell on which it synapses, as shown in Figure 3.5. Interestingly, psychologist Donald Hebb's globally renowned maxim, *neurons that fire together, wire together* (1949: 66), from all those decades ago remains just as pertinent today.

As explained, when a neuron is sufficiently excited, it produces an electrical signal which travels from the junction between the cell body and axon to the axon terminals.

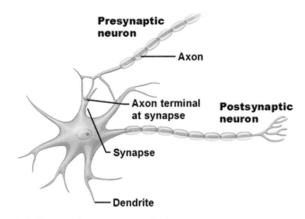

Synapse – Where Two Neurons Communicate in One Direction

(a) Two neurons connected by synapses

Figure 3.5 A Synapse Connecting Two Neurons

This electrical signal is often referred to as a nerve impulse but is more correctly known as an action potential. Action potentials enable signals to travel very rapidly along the neuron (LeDoux, 2002). Once the action potential reaches the axon terminals, it cannot travel any further because of the synapse, or gap, between the neighbouring neurons. However, like people, neurons need to communicate with each other, so they get round this block to the electrical signal by releasing special chemical signals called neurotransmitters. These travel across the synapse to affect another (target) neuron. The target neuron then converts the message back to an electrical impulse to continue the process. Imagine that an electrical message is sent from one neuron to another. The message leaves the cell body of the sending neuron and then travels down its axon. Once it gets to the end of the axon (the axon terminal), there is a small gap (called a synaptic cleft). The message has to cross this gap to reach the receiving neuron. The synapse is the point where the message can cross the gap.

Synaptogenesis

Synaptogenesis is a scientific term that means the creation or formation of new connections (synapses) between neurons. Each neuron can have thousands of connections with other neurons. At birth, each neuron has approximately 2,500 synapses. By three-years-old, the number of synapses is approximately 15,000 per neuron – roughly twice that of the average adult brain! Never again in the life course does the brain make so many connections, and everything you do builds brains, which becomes the child's internal voice from the outset.

Although we are capable of learning all our lives, at five-years-old, brain regions responsible for language, emotional, physical and social development begin to close down as the brain becomes more organized and, as a result, less malleable and more adult-like.

The Process of Synaptogenesis

Synaptogenesis is not just about creating synapses, vital though this is in building up a healthy network of neurons. It is a fairly lengthy process and involves:

- Synapse creation

- Synapse maintenance (or stabilization)

- Consolidation or elimination of the synapse. (Consolidation means establishing a neural pathway.) If a synaptic connection is not needed or used often enough, it gets eliminated – also referred to as being pruned. The phrase *use it or lose it* is relevant here, as connections that are used regularly get stronger and those that are not used eventually weaken and die.

Synaptogenesis occurs throughout life, but there are at least two periods when it happens at a much faster rate: infancy and adolescence. As you can see from the collection of brain imaging scans in Figure 3.6, synaptic density increases exponentially in the early years and is at its greatest at just two-years-old. The implications that this holds for us as parents, primary carers and professionals cannot be overestimated.

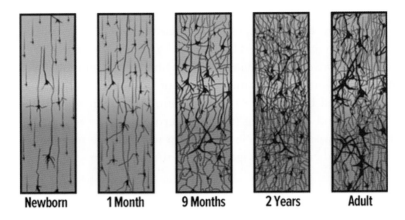

Newborn   1 Month   9 Months   2 Years   Adult

Figure 3.6 Synaptic Density Development, From Birth to Adulthood

Source: Corel, J. L. (1975). *The Postnatal Development of the Human Cerebral Cortex*. Cambridge, MA: Harvard University Press.

Factors That Influence Synaptogenesis

Parents, EY practitioners and teachers can support the creation of synapses and strengthen neural pathways in the brain in a number of ways. Two key factors stand out here – providing appropriate learning experiences and repetition.

Experiences

The process of synaptogenesis depends on the stimulation of new learning and experiences and frequent opportunities for repetition and extension of these learning experiences. These are the building blocks of brain development. Every conversation and every interaction with their environment encourages more synaptic connections to be created in a child's brain. If the complexity of these experiences is gradually increased, this creates even more connections. All these experiences directly affect the brain's growth and structure, especially during early childhood. Unfortunately, the opposite is also true. The brain of a child deprived of learning opportunities and experiences will not be able to create the same amount of synaptic connections as the brain of a child provided with abundant opportunities.

In the first three years of life, a child can develop an understanding of themselves, their key relationships and their surroundings. They can also develop an ability to pay attention and manage stress. However, all these abilities are dependent on the child having the opportunity to experience them. In other words, they are experience dependent. Conversely, experience-expectant processes are those which are vital to development and indeed life itself – the brain expects and is primed to be exposed to (for example) visual, auditory, linguistic and kinaesthetic input in order to ensure its healthy development across the life trajectory.

Repetition

Experiences need to be repeated if the developing brain is to retain their value. Having the opportunity to regularly practise skills such as language, movement, exploration and solving problems enables an infant to build familiarity, self-confidence and competence. For this reason, repetition is considered one of the essential influences in promoting neural growth and learning. Quite simply, the more something is done, the stronger the connection and pathway that is laid down. Think of a child learning to ride a bike – the more they practise, the stronger these connections in their brain become, and the better they become at riding the bike. Conversely, if the child does not regularly practise riding their bike, these synaptic connections will remain weak, and they will find riding a bike more difficult.

Synaptic Pruning

Repetition brings us to another important feature of synaptogenesis, which was mentioned earlier – pruning. As you now know, there is an explosive creation of new synapses during those early years of life. In fact, with more than one million synaptic connections being created every second, there is an over-production, and many are simply not needed. During this sensitive period of brain development, the brain eliminates the synapses that are not strong enough or are not being used. This is called synaptic pruning. Picture yourself pruning a bush. You cut the old, dead leaves away to keep the bush growing healthily. Synaptic pruning has the same effect – it improves (streamlines) children's brain function, making the remaining networks work more quickly and efficiently. Constant stimulation causes synapses to grow and become permanent, whereas if a child receives little stimulation, the brain will keep fewer of those connections. Synaptic pruning is an essential part of brain development. As the child learns and masters important new skills, pruning helps their brain to make room for these vital new connections between neurons. Scientists believe that without synaptic pruning, children would not be able to walk, talk or even see properly.

Sensitive Periods

The concept of sensitive periods refers to distinct phases when the brain is best able to receive and use information gained from experiences in order to learn specific skills. The period of birth to five years represents one sensitive period, as it is a time of prolific neural growth and development. The teenage years are another sensitive period. Outside these periods, learning specific skills still occurs, but the brain is less malleable – less adaptive to change – as the neural networks become more established over time. When EY practitioners and teachers understand the crucial role of sensitive periods in supporting early brain development, they can think more critically about how they plan and organize their learning environments and what changes can be made to maximize each child's learning experience.

Myelination

As previously mentioned, myelination is a process where the axons of neurons become covered in a white fatty substance (in the form of a sheath) that helps conduction of the action potential. Myelin is made in the Schwann cells, which wrap around axons of motor and sensory neurons to form the myelin sheath (a bit like the casing of a sausage). Areas with lots of myelination (the term given for this white covering) are therefore called white matter, while areas lacking myelin, normally consisting of the dendrites and cell bodies, make up the grey matter. This distinction is very clearly seen in the cross-section of the brain shown in Figure 3.7.

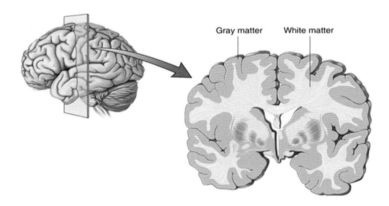

Figure 3.7 White and Grey Matter in the Brain

Like changes in synapses, myelination is an important developmental process and one that continues into our 20s (Williamson and Lyons, 2018; Almeida and Lyons, 2017; Fields, 2008), with myelinated neural circuits conducting information much faster than unmyelinated circuits. This improves the speed of information processing, which ultimately makes for more effective learning. Humans are born with a virtually unmyelinated CNS, and this prolonged period of myelination indicates that, like synaptic changes, it might be experience-dependent. Neuroscientists now have imaging techniques that allow them to examine myelin and have indeed found that myelin can change in responses to environmental experiences. Much of the direct evidence comes from work in animals, but there is also correlative evidence from humans, showing that myelination correlates with learning, development of skills and memory (Fields, 2008). Indeed, one study shows that the amount of myelination in a structure increased proportionately to the number of hours a person had practiced playing a musical instrument (Bengtsson et al., 2005). For further information concerning this study, please refer to the Bibliography.

Now that you have read about some basics of the brain and its development, have a go at answering the following questions.

Rewind. Reflect. Write!

1 In your own words, explain what a neuron is.

2 How many neurons are we born with?

3 Write the following four terms in the correct places on the interneuron:

■ Cell body

■ Dendrites

■ Axon

■ Myelin sheath

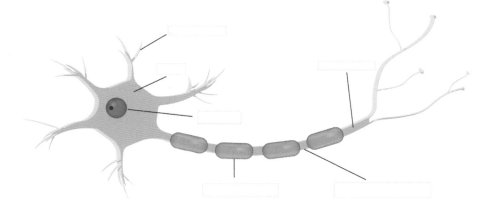

4 Do some online research and find out the following:

   a Name three other types of neurons

   b Outline where in the body they are found

   c Describe the function of each type of neuron.

5a In your own words, explain what a synapse is.

5b Discuss the role of synaptogenesis in early brain development.

Welcome to Your Brilliant Brain!

It weighs approximately 3.3 pounds (generally a little less for female adult brains), is pinkish-brown in colour, has the texture of a firm jelly and resides in your skull – welcome to your brilliant brain! It might not sound so awe inspiring in that brief description, but the human brain holds the key to consciousness, intelligence and creativity – and we may never get to fully understand this astonishing organ and the secrets it holds. At birth, a baby's brain weighs approximately 350 to 400 grams (three-quarters of a pound) and (as aforementioned) contains roughly 86 billion neurons – that is almost as many as there are stars in the Milky Way galaxy! It is thought that roughly 16 billion of these neurons are located in the cerebral cortex.

The Process of Early Brain Development From Birth to Seven Years

Although a baby's brain looks like that of an adult, it is far from being fully developed. From birth to seven years in particular, the brain continues to grow and vital new connections and pathways are being made all the time.

Growth in Brain Size

At birth, the average baby's brain is about a quarter of the size of the average adult brain. Incredibly, it doubles in size in the first year of life. From there, the brain continues to grow rapidly. By the age of three, it is about 80% of an adult brain, and by five-years-old, it is 90% – nearly fully grown.

Growth in the Number of Connections Between Brain Cells

Although most of the neurons we need as an adult are formed in the womb, the synapses that enable these cells to communicate with each other are not – as stated earlier, they are largely created in the first three year of life. As these connections link up different parts of the brain, they effectively enable us to move, think, communicate and do just about everything else!

As you will explore in more detail in the next section, the brain actually creates many more synaptic connections than it needs – at age two or three, the brain has up to twice as many synapses as it will have in adulthood. These surplus connections are gradually eliminated throughout early childhood and adolescence as the brain makes space for new connections and those it uses regularly. This process is known as "blooming and pruning."

Strengthening of Neural Pathways

A neural pathway is a series of connected neurons that send signals from one part of the brain to another. Think of a physical pathway – if you keep using the same route, you can remember it almost automatically. Neural pathways work in this way. The more something is done, the better neurons in different parts of the brain become at remembering what to do and anticipating what will happen next.

Early childhood is a critical time to lay down these neural pathways. However, not all pathways are beneficial. Unfortunately, due to negative experiences, some pathways that are laid down in this period are unhealthy, and these negatively impact a child's understanding of the world around them. For example, being regularly ignored, humiliated or even reprimanded when in distress can make a child fearful and distrustful of others.

Cognitive Changes

As the connections and pathways in the brain become stronger, so a child's range of skills and abilities should gradually improve. One such area of improvement is cognition.

Cognition refers to the mental processes used when gaining knowledge and understanding. These skills and abilities include thinking, remembering, perception, planning and language. For example, during the second year of life, there is a dramatic increase in the number of connections in the brain's language areas. These changes correspond to the sudden spike in children's language abilities – sometimes called the "vocabulary explosion" (McMurray, 2007) – which typically occurs during this period. Often, a child's vocabulary will quadruple between their first and second birthday.

The period from birth to seven represents the best opportunity for a child's brain to develop the cognitive abilities they need to become capable and confident learners, and although the brain continues to develop and change into adulthood, the first seven years are critical in building a strong, healthy foundation in all areas of life. This brings to mind the famous quote by the ancient philosopher Aristotle, who proclaimed: "give me a child until he is seven and I will show you the man" (Bambrough, 2011: 27).

Let us take a closer look at the brain itself. Figure 3.8 is an easy way to remember some of the key structures of the brain.

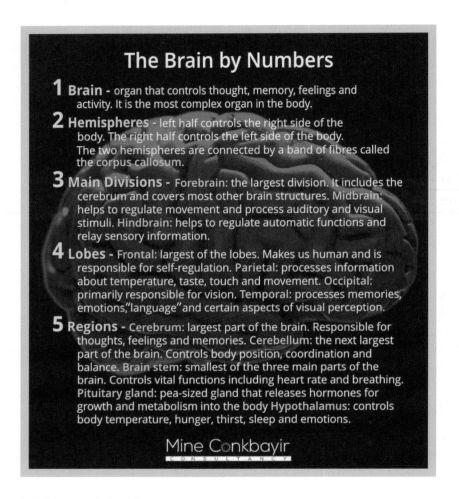

Figure 3.8 The Brain by Numbers

We will now unpack the information a little further. As we know, the brain controls everything we think, feel and do. It is the seat of rationality, creativity and imagination and, along with other key organs, it keeps us alive. The human brain is symmetrical, split down the middle: the right cerebral hemisphere receives sensory input from and directs movement on the left side of the body, while the left hemisphere governs corresponding functions for the right side.

You may have even been asked whether you consider yourself "left-brained" or "right-brained" depending on how, for example, creative or logical you deem yourself. This is due to the brain containing two hemispheres – the left and right. Each hemisphere is primarily responsible for different functions, as outlined in Table 3.2.

Table 3.2 Left and Right Hemispheric Brain Functions

Left Hemispheric Functions	Right Hemispheric Functions
Motor control of the right side of the body	Motor control of the left side of the body
Right hand control	Left hand control
Analytic thought	Emotion
Logic	Imagination
Reasoning	Creativity
Security	Risk-taking
Language (written and verbal)	Intuition
Maths/number skills	Art
Science	Music
Objectivity	Subjectivity

The distinction between the functionality of the two hemispheres is predominantly a result of the ground-breaking research of Sperry (1982; 1965) and Gazzaniga et al. (1965) and consequent left brain and right brain theory. However, the left and right brain debate does not stand up to any scientific scrutiny, having been debunked by various researchers over the decades – and is in fact a myth (Lincoln, 2020; McGilchrist, 2019; Nielson et al., 2013; Lindell and Kidd, 2011; Howard-Jones, 2009). As renowned psychiatrist and author McGilchrist (2019: xiv) contends:

> Trawl the internet and you will find all kinds of misinformation. . . . One of my favourites is a list "left brain functions and right brain functions" which I sometimes use in lectures with the health warning in the title: "Right and WRONG!" The left and the right halves of the brain do function differently in some ways, but these differences are more subtle than is popularly believed. . . . The real story of hemisphere difference is a complex one – but it is one that is entirely coherent.

Essentially, the two sides of the brain are complementary in their functioning and we must therefore hold in mind that integration is critical. As Allen and van der Zwan (2019: 196) recommend:

> The myth of left- or right-brain dominance is problematically enduring. Parents and educators should be extremely cautious when approaching educational programs, interventions, phone apps, or books that claim to stimulate one hemisphere in preference to the other (e.g. right-brain approaches).

The Corpus Callosum – Bridging the Left and Right

The two hemispheres are connected by a thick bundle of fibres called the corpus callosum (the largest white matter fibre bundle in the brain), as identified by the red arrow in Figure 3.9.

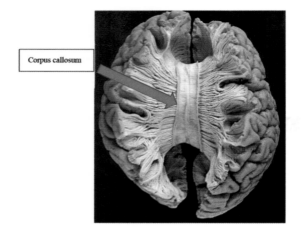

Figure 3.9 The Corpus Callosum

So the two hemispheres are not truly separate, because communication between them is essential – and enabled by the corpus callosum (and other smaller fibres) through which a constant traffic of neural messages pass from side to side, but this process can be seriously derailed. The corpus callosum of some individuals who have experienced post-traumatic stress disorder (PTSD) as a result of abuse undergoes structural changes, with a significant decrease in volume and poorer integration of the two hemispheres (Graziano et al., 2019; Siehl et al., 2018; Liberzon and Abelson, 2016; Kennis et al., 2015; Fani et al., 2012). This has implications for holistic wellbeing and learning ability and should therefore be considered when caring for and educating children who have experienced trauma.

Sitting on top of the brain stem is the cerebrum – the largest and most prominent part of the brain, and, as mentioned, this is divided into the left and right hemispheres. The visible surface layer of the cerebrum is called the cerebral cortex (cortex comes from the Latin word for "bark"). Although it is only about three millimetres in thickness, the cerebral cortex is responsible for many higher-order brain functions, such as planning, perception, memory, interpreting visual information and speech, and, as mentioned earlier, the cortex is covered in gyri and sulci, which makes it look a little like a walnut. These increase the size of the cortex, making more room for neurons. Situated underneath the cerebrum, at the back of the head, is the cerebellum (or "little brain"). This is responsible for balance and muscle coordination.

As you can see in Figure 3.10, the cortex is divided into four lobes, each of which has specialized functions.

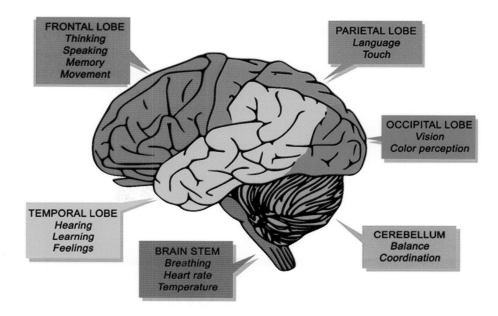

Figure 3.10 The Four Lobes of the Brain

■ The frontal lobe – this is where higher executive functions, including planning and prioritizing, organization, reasoning, attention and working memory occur. Frequently mentioned in this book is the PFC – a key brain region in the frontal lobe, responsible for these (and more) executive functioning skills. Vital though this area is, it develops very slowly. In fact, neuroscientists believe that it does not fully mature until we reach our mid-20s! This is highly significant when we consider what adults sometimes expect of young children in terms of their ability to self-regulate

■ The parietal lobe – residing behind the frontal lobe, this plays a key role in integrating information from different sensory systems, including temperature, smell, touch, pain and proprioception. Both hemispheres of the parietal lobes work together with other lobes to help the CNS process language

■ The temporal lobe – with one temporal lobe located in each brain hemisphere, this is a sensory brain region, responsible for hearing, understanding language, creating and preserving memory, face and object recognition, perception and processing auditory information

■ The occipital lobe – this major visual processing centre in the brain resides across both hemispheres and is located at the very back of the brain. It contains the primary visual cortex, which is responsible for processing incoming visual information and then passing onto other brain regions. Synaesthesia (mentioned in Chapter 4) is related to this lobe.

While these and other brain regions have been highlighted throughout this book, it is important to remember that the brain is not modular (Genon et al., 2018). Although it is organized into distinct areas that are integrated into vast and intricate networks, it does not carry out its functions in tidy little compartments which do not depend on or interact with other areas. Take the amygdala, for example. While it is referred to as the "brain's panic button," this book reveals the interplay between the amygdala as part of the limbic system and the frontal lobe, particularly during times of stress. Our neurons are always interconnected and never stop firing.

Figure 3.11 summarizes just a few key facts that have been presented about the brain thus far.

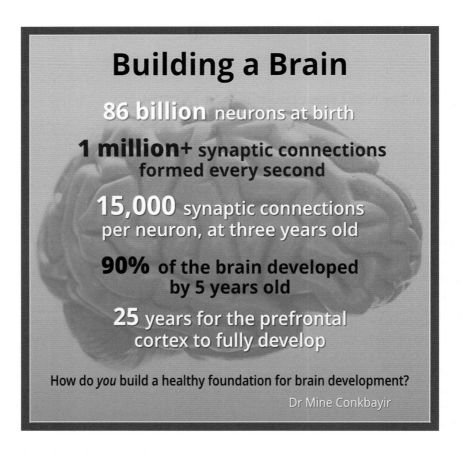

Figure 3.11 Building a Brain

Rewind. Reflect. Write!

1a What is the role of the corpus callosum?

1b How is the corpus callosum impacted by toxic stress?

2a Do some research on the two hemispheres of the brain and write at least two paragraphs about these – including the myth of the "left" and "right brain."

2b What are your thoughts about this being a myth?

3 Identify the four lobes of the brain and write a brief description of each.

4 Outline the five brain regions and the function of each one.

5 Discuss the role of the prefrontal cortex in:

    a Learning

    b Self-regulation.

We are now going to delve deeper into the brain and its structure to find out why some children can find it difficult to regulate (manage) their emotions and behaviour.

The Brain's Emotion Centre – The Limbic System

If you were to look underneath the cerebrum to the centre of the brain, you would find the limbic system. The limbic system is a collection of structures that are heavily involved in triggering our emotional and behavioural responses. Powerful emotions such as anger, sadness, envy and joy are all activated in this region of the brain. It also plays an important role in regulating our mood and levels of motivation. For these reasons, the limbic system is sometimes called the "emotional brain." Our limbic system is mainly involuntary (unconscious), often causing us to act before we are able to think. This is because a great deal of sensory information (what we can see, smell and hear) passes through the limbic system first before being processed in the decision-making areas of the brain (the frontal lobes). If this sensory information is deemed a threat or too overwhelming, the limbic system activates the body's fight or flight response. For young children, a "threat" might simply be something like not wanting to share a toy.

The limbic system performs many vital functions. Part of the limbic system helps the brain to process and store memories, which means that it aids our ability to retain and recall information (which is key to learning). Our stress response (how we respond to potential or perceived threats and stressful situations) also begins in the limbic system. It helps us to survive by regulating several essential physiological functions, such as our breathing, heart rate and appetite. Illustrated in Figure 3.12, you can see some of the key components of the limbic system.

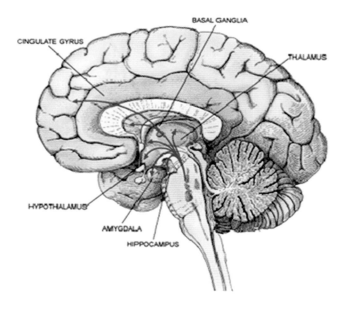

Figure 3.12 The Limbic System

- **The amygdala** – (pronounced uh–mig–duh–luh), this plays a central role in our emotional responses. It also acts like the brain's panic button. It is activated when we feel frightened, angry or anxious, automatically triggering our fight or flight response by sending out signals to other parts of the limbic system to release stress hormones that prepare the body to fight or run away

- **The hippocampus** – looking a little bit like a seahorse, this structure is the memory centre – or filing cabinet – of the brain. It forms, organizes and stores new memories. It also helps us to associate memories with various senses. For example, the smell of gingerbread might remind some people of Christmas. The hippocampus would process this memory and store it deep in the brain

- **The thalamus** – this acts as a kind of "pit stop" for motor and sensory information. For example, sensory impulses travel from the surface of the body towards the thalamus, which receives them as sensations. These sensations are then passed to the surface of the brain for interpretation

- **The hypothalamus** – it works with the adjoining pituitary gland to produce several important hormones (chemical messengers) and to release these into the brain and bloodstream. For example, the hormone cortisol is produced by the hypothalamus in response to physical and emotional stress. The hypothalamus also helps to maintain our body's internal balance by regulating our blood pressure and heart rate, as well as our breathing, body temperature, appetite, thirst and sleep cycles.

The "Upstairs" and "Downstairs" Brain

The concept of the "upstairs" and "downstairs" brain was developed by the American neuroscientist Dr Dan Siegel (Siegel and Bryson, 2011) as part of his hand model of the brain. Although it may sound simplistic, it is a very effective way of understanding the relationship between the cerebral cortex (the surface layer of the brain) and the limbic system and how the two work together (or not) in young children.

Imagine your brain is a two-storey house. The "upstairs" brain comprises the four lobes you looked at earlier – the frontal, temporal, parietal and occipital lobes – and the thin cerebral cortex that covers each of these. Of particular importance is the frontal lobe, specifically its PFC (the brain region just behind our forehead). As stated, this brain region is responsible for our executive functioning skills – our ability to focus, plan, prioritize, reason and make rational decisions. It also helps us to become more self-aware and aware of others.

The "downstairs" brain is the lower regions of the brain, including the limbic system. As you learned earlier, the limbic system is responsible for some critical functions that keep us alive (like breathing and regulating our heart rate) as well as our impulses and emotions. Between the "upstairs" and "downstairs" brains is a connecting "staircase." This is the network of neurons and synapses that carry information up and down, to and from the different parts of the brain. Both areas of our brain need to work together for us to function well. However, young children's "upstairs" and "downstairs" brains often struggle to work together.

What Causes This?

1   On the one hand, the executive functions of the "upstairs" brain draws upon a particular set of skills (including the ability to focus, plan, prioritize, reason and make rational decisions), which takes many years to fully develop. On the other hand, the limbic system of the downstairs brain develops much more quickly. Therefore, when a child perceives a threat or becomes angry, the "upstairs" part of the brain, which should help them to stay calm, has not yet developed enough to understand and restrain the powerful emotional reactions created in the "downstairs" brain – or limbic system

2   The stress hormones (primarily cortisol and adrenaline) that are released in the "downstairs" brain during the fight or flight response often stop messages from getting through to the "upstairs brain." In other words, the staircase becomes

cluttered. This happens in adults too. Put simply, the stress hormones can prevent us from accessing our "upstairs" brain, which is key in helping us to think clearly and rationally. More on this shortly.

Both of these factors may cause children to become dysregulated (in other words, become deeply upset or angry or have a marked change in mood) and show behaviours that may challenge others while overwhelming themselves.

Dr Dan Siegel uses another concept as part of the "upstairs" and "downstairs" brain to explain what happens when the reasoning part of the brain (the PFC) is unable to control the powerful emotions coming from down below in the limbic system. He calls this "flipping the lid," and it is an idea that is becoming more widely used in the training of EY practitioners. It is also a useful way of helping children to understand why they get angry (for example) and perhaps react in ways that further dysregulate them.

The "lid flips" when the amygdala (the brain's "panic button") is activated, and a child's upstairs brain loses all control of the "downstairs brain." This can happen in just a few seconds and can be due to a range of reasons: a child might have had a disagreement with their friend, be feeling sad or be feeling angry at being told off for not paying attention in class. When this happens, the child metaphorically "flips their lid," and there is an explosion of emotion (which then directs their behaviour).

There are various YouTube clips available where you can watch Dan Siegel explaining his hand model of the brain in more detail. Here are some examples:

Dr Daniel Siegel's hand model of the brain (www.youtube.com/watch?v=f-m2YcdMdFw)

Dr Daniel Siegel – "'Flipping Your Lid:' A Scientific Explanation" (www.youtube.com/watch?v=G0T_2NNoC68)

Adults can also "flip their lid," so the same model can also be applied to parenting and coping with stress in the workplace, for example:

Dr Daniel Siegel's hand model of the brain (www.youtube.com/watch?v=qFTljLo1bK8)

When a child "flips their lid," their behaviour is often mislabelled by adults "naughty" or "challenging," and the child may be reprimanded or punished in some way (told to take a "time out," for example). However, this is a missed opportunity and is psychologically damaging to the child (Kohn, 2018). What the child really needs in this moment is CR from an adult to help them return to a safe psychological state while enabling them to learn from the experience. This will also teach them how to manage in similar situations in the future – ultimately, to self-regulate. The "flipping lid" concept and the hand model of the brain help to explain why a child who feels threatened or anxious can find it incredibly difficult to regulate their emotions and subsequent behaviour. Parents, primary carers, EY practitioners and teachers are incredibly important during this process. They can help children to become more aware of their emotions and teach them strategies that help them to remain calm while their "upstairs" brain catches up and, to use another analogy, "comes back online."

Rewind. Reflect. Write!

1 In your own words, explain Siegel's hand model of the brain (including the names of the key brain regions involved).

2 To demonstrate the "flipping lid" and the relationship between the "upstairs" and "downstairs" brain, Siegel devised his hand model of the brain. Try modelling it using these instructions:

Hold one of your hands in the air, tuck your thumb into the palm of your hand and then bring your fingers down over the top of your thumb. You have now formed the rudimentary structure of the brain. When powerful emotions coming from the limbic system (the thumb in this model) become too great, the PFC (the fingers that wrap around it) is not strong enough to hold the emotions back. At this point, a child "flips their lid" and there is a strong, sometimes explosive, emotional reaction.

3 Revisit Siegel's hand model of the brain. Your task is to:

a Share this model (regularly) with the children in your setting. Consider how you will share it with them (individually, as a group, at points in the week and whenever needed).

b Think about and note down how you will record the impact teaching the children about this will have on children's behaviour.

c Note down and discuss with your team, whom you will enlist to support embedding this into your practice.

d Consider whether you need to develop a new policy to inform your delivery or whether you have an existing policy that you could update to include your setting's teaching about the brain to children and the rationale behind this.

4 Explain why it is important to engage the "downstairs" brain before we can expect children to think rationally (engage their "upstairs" brain).

Top Tips for Practice!

■ Visit the website Neuroscience for Kids at: https://faculty.washington.edu/chudler/outside.html – it is full of fun and practical ways to introduce the nervous system to young children. The outdoor game "synaptic tag" is a particularly fun and imaginative way to teach young children about their brains!

■ Gather some of your favourite facts from your reading so far and make a plan of how you will cascade your learning to your team

■ Design a quiz to ascertain what they have learned – make this as interactive as possible! Polls and multiple choice are good options here.

Back to the Future – Moving Forward With Neuroscientific Understanding of the Brain

Findings from neuroscience continue to advance at an ever-rapid rate, with insights concerning the very essence of what it means to be human – down to the substrate of the individual neuron (Elam et al., 2021; Seung, 2013). Yet such incredible advances are firmly rooted in the history of neuroscience. The following section provides an overview of some of these key advances in neuroscientific research.

The Human Connectome

Take, for example, the human connectome (or wiring diagram of the nervous system) – this was first achieved by Ramón y Cajal, who, during the last decade of

19th century, proposed that the brain consisted of a vast number of individual neurons that communicated with each other through junctions called synapses – as opposed to viewing the human nervous system as one large entity. His beautiful illustrations, still globally renowned and relevant today, paved the way for current connectome projects (which will be discussed later). Figure 3.13 is just one example of Cajal's intricate illustrations (1899) of the brain's structure down to its finest detail.

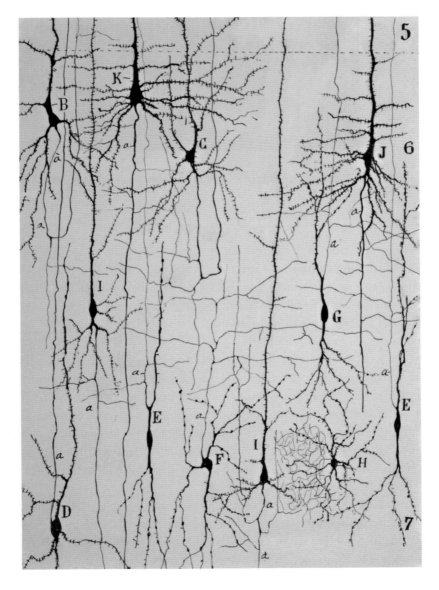

Figure 3.13 Microscopic Brain Structure

At its simplest, a connectome is the complete map of the billions of neurons and trillions of neural connections in the brain. It is sometimes referred to as a neural map or, as aforementioned, a wiring diagram of neurons, their various components and the vast connections between these billions of neurons. Think of it like a highly detailed street map, with every road, street, lane and roundabouts all identified. Figure 3.14 shows the connectome of a section of the human brain.

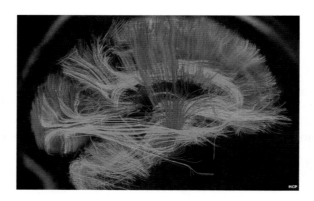

Figure 3.14 A Side View of the Brain's Left Hemisphere, Including the Cerebrum and Cerebellum

Source: Human Connectome Project (2013).

Connectomes are not exclusive to human beings – flies, mice, cats and whales (and so on) each have connectomes – connectomes thus come in different shapes and sizes. We can also speak of connectomes of specific brain regions, such as hippocampal connectomes, thalamic connectomes, cortical connectomes – or cerebellar connectomes (like the one in Figure 3.14), which, due to their specificity and smaller size than an entire brain, take less time to complete.

Fisher (2013: 149) highlights the seemingly infinite possibilities of our species to create fascinating approaches that help us to understand the very core of human nature while simultaneously remaining unenlightened about how best to utilize this information – partly due to limitations of neuroimaging equipment and techniques but also limitations in neuroscientists' level of knowledge and understanding. After all, we cannot know what we do not know. Perhaps, as the science continues to advance, so too will our knowledge and understanding of how best to utilize results from studies:

> We are privileged to be the only organism on Earth capable of directly reading our own genetic makeup, not only documenting that of the species as a whole, but also able to catalogue the myriad variations in each individual member. At the same time, we remain woefully ignorant of what all this means for neurons, the brain, human cognition and behaviour. This, then, could be a key challenge laid down for future generations of neuroscientists.

The Human Connectome Project

All our genes together are known as our genome, and the most extraordinary and revealing investigation which examined our genome was the Human Genome Project (HGP), which began in 1990 and was completed in 2003. This incredible feat resulted in the complete mapping and understanding of the structure, organization and function of all the genes of human beings. Three billion letters that have various functions, including the encoding of our genes, our hereditary information and those that contain instructions concerning how cells can use the genes, have all been mapped. What could be greater than this endeavour? Well, in short, the Human Connectome Project! First coined by two professors simultaneously but independently (Hagmann, 2005; Sporns et al., 2005), the term connectome refers to the complete mapping of the human brain's 86 billion neurons and the structure and functionality of their trillions of synaptic connections. Numerous connectome (or connectivity) studies have been conducted, including the Human Connectome Project, which ran from 2009 to 2014. Yet when we consider that at present the only *complete* connectome is that of a type of roundworm (Cook et al., 2019), as well as an almost complete connectome of the fruit fly (Scheffer et al., 2020), which has a brain the size of a poppyseed – we can appreciate the magnitude of the undertaking. As Seung (2013) brings to our attention – unlike our genome, our connectome changes throughout life and has a million times more connections than our genome has letters! While some studies have found that innovations in post-mortem human brain reconstructions may help to advance attempts at completing the human connectome (Yendiki et al., 2021; Schmitz et al., 2018), at present, a complete connectome of the whole human brain with findings that are applicable outside the laboratory will take decades to accomplish.

If you're wondering how any of this is relevant to the daily context of life, the human connectome has important implications for understanding the basic wiring that underlies day-to-day brain function, such as feeling, moving, thinking, believing, remembering and processing sensory information and translating this into appropriate action. Not only will it reveal all this basic functionality, but also disease-related conditions which might be attributable to the brain's wiring – as opposed to chemical imbalances, which is what are currently thought of as the (partial) cause of conditions like depression and schizophrenia. This is recognized by Tozzi et al. (2020: 1), who explain:

> A human connectome could reveal the basic wiring that underlies thinking, remembering, reacting, moving, believing and feeling. With more and more evidence that conditions such as autism and schizophrenia are caused by brain miswiring rather than, say, imbalances of neurochemicals, many neuroscientists believe mapping the connectome is more important than ever. Given the pressing public health need, we must increase our understanding of how connectome dysfunctions give rise to different mental states. Mental conditions arising from

high levels of negative emotion or from the loss of positive emotional experience affect over 400 million people globally.

An immediately relatable concept born out of the human connectome is provided by Seung (2013), a professor of computational neuroscience. He defines the four Rs of connectome change as:

1 **Reweighting** – which refers to the connections between neurons weakening or strengthening, depending on experience. This means that neurons reweight or *change* based on the reduction or increase in weight

2 **Reconnection** – this is where neurons reconnect with each other by creating and eliminating synapses

3 **Rewiring** – this refers to neurons' ability to rewire by growing and withdrawing their branches. Think back to the image of an individual neuron with its dendrites branching out to connect with other neurons and its axon: these are what grow and withdraw (or reduce), depending on a host of factors (Alberts et al., 2014)

4 **Regeneration** – this refers to how new neurons are created and existing ones are eliminated through the process of regeneration (or renewal).

Seung asserts that while genetics plays a role in influencing these four Rs, there is good evidence that they are also significantly influenced by our experiences – which is particularly true for the first few years of life, when the brain is wiring itself up and becoming more organized during infancy and early childhood. This brings us to the age-old debate that seems to have finally been put to rest by another development in neuroscience – epigenetics.

Epigenetics – Nature Versus Nurture No Longer Exists

Continuing with our "back to the future" theme, let us now turn our attention to epigenetics. Four decades on from Cajal's discoveries, the world was introduced to the concept of epigenetics by embryologist Conrad Waddington in 1942. So where epigenetics is presented as cutting-edge neuroscience, this too is actually decades old but continually being refined in line with technological advances and consequent developments in thinking.

Although the term has various interpretations, Waddington's concept of epigenetics remains widely used to describe the existence of mechanisms of inheritance in addition to genetics (Bard, 2008). Put simply, epigenetics is concerned with how environmental influences directly impact the expression of our genes. Ultimately, this means that the old idea that genes are set in stone has been disproven and that energy and resources are better focused on further examining the complex interrelationship between genes (nature) and the environment (nurture).

How Is Epigenetics Useful to You?

This exciting branch of neuroscience gives us evidence regarding the pivotal role of external factors that can influence gene expression and ultimately human development. As stated, factors such as lifestyle choices, the environment, the presence of prolonged stress and maternal health each play a role in determining gene expression and brain architecture (Cazaly et al., 2019; Dhana et al., 2018; McCartney et al., 2018). In your work with families and young children, being well versed in the factors which can influence gene expression and offering sensitive, timely and continued practical support can help prospective parents to think about their current lifestyles and make any beneficial changes. Providing practical advice to help families cope with any long-term stress or trauma or accessing early intervention during pregnancy can help to minimize the possibility of detrimental gene activity occurring in response to toxic environmental influences.

The Role of Epigenetics and Neuroscience in Explaining Early Brain Growth

As previously discussed, although the brain contains approximately 86 billion neurons at birth, the greater part of neural development actually occurs during the prenatal period and dies off soon after birth, which makes prenatal brain development a critical time. Factors such as poor nutrition; drug and or alcohol abuse; disease; dependency on prescription drugs; and chronic, toxic maternal stress can consequently impede brain growth and development even before the child is born. We therefore cannot underestimate the importance of the prenatal period in terms of its influence on brain development (Fox and Shonkoff, 2011), as the two are inextricably linked. Rose and Abi-Rached (2013: 194) identify:

> It seems obvious that intensive intervention on early parenting is the path required to break the cycle of antisocial and violent conduct that destroys lives and costs our societies so dearly.

Some of the most influential studies concerning epigenetics originate from neuroscience research. One example is Meany's persuasive research study (2001), which demonstrated the influence of maternal behaviours on neural growth. Meany's study showed that there is a direct link between maternal care and handling of pups by rat mothers (licking and affection given to her pups) which leads to alteration in the sculpting of neural circuits, especially in the sensitive period of plasticity. As Weaver et al. (2004: 847) explain, this affirmative maternal behaviour towards her pups exerted a positive influence on the pups' gene expression, which consequently improved their response to stress, which they say:

> Altered the offspring DNA methylation patterns in the hippocampus, thus affecting the development of hypothalamic-pituitary-adrenal responses to stress through tissue-specific effects on gene expression.

Crucially, similar conclusions were reached in human studies carried out on post-mortem brain tissue of individuals who died by suicide who had a history of childhood abuse (McGowan et al., 2009; Szyf et al., 2008). If you would like further details about this interesting study, please refer to the Bibliography, but the important take-home message from their study is that they concluded that early life adversity does play a critical role in altering DNA methylation patterns and hence neural develop-ment, which leaves a legacy on the brain long into adulthood. McGowan et al. (2009: 346) determined that:

> Early life events can alter the epigenetic state of relevant genomic regions, the expression of which may contribute to individual differences in the risk for psychopathology.

The plethora of books, articles and reports concerning early brain development gen-erally expound the importance of building a healthy brain from birth. Yet it is far more useful to start from preconception and conception. Professionals in the field now refer to this crucial developmental phase as the first 1001 days – the time from the start of pregnancy to a child's second birthday. This is due to research consistently showing the impact of children's early experiences on their adult emotional and mental health as well as their educational and employment opportunities (Asmussen et al., 2020; Bellis et al., 2019; Barker, 1995). The highly publicized *A Vision for the 1001 Critical Days* (Reed and Parish, 2021; Wave Trust, 2014; Barker, 1995) highlights the import-ance of the in-utero environment with regard to growth and development, from conception to a child's second birthday. Evidence cited by Asmussen et al. (2020: 70) further emphasizes its importance in terms of influencing health and development in the longer term:

> Exposure to abuse and neglect in childhood may impact children's development in the following ways: (1) stress-related increases in cortisol, which exert wear and tear on the nervous and autoimmune systems, weakening children's resilience to disease over time; (2) the recalibration of different brain systems following exposure to abuse and neglect, which may increase children's vulnerability to later mental health problems; and (3) changes in epigenetic modulation associated with low nurturing childhood environments.

Ultimately, epigenetics demonstrates that even our genetic "blueprint" is not, as we once thought, permanent. Just like the brain's lifelong malleability, epigenetic discoveries have been found in, for example, addiction, early life stress, PTSD and depression. As these become even further refined, so too can the interventions and treatments for them – as neuroscientists are drawing ever closer to developing epigenetics biomarkers (these measure disease-associated and drug-associated epigenetic changes), it may not be too far away. As identified by Cazaly et al. (2019: 11):

> The fact that epigenetic profiles are plastic and reversible holds great promise for developing epigenetic biomarkers and drug targets. Furthermore, epigenetics captures the spatial and temporal variation on top of each individual's unique genome and thus better informs the decision-making in personalized medicine.

Spiking Neural Network Architecture

In 2018, the world's largest neuromorphic supercomputer (the use of very large computers and software which mimic neurobiological architectures) was launched. The first version of it is shown in Figure 3.15.

The Spiking Neural Network Architecture (SpiNNaker) computer (and its various iterations), which, put very simply, works like a brain and models the connectivity of the brain, is revolutionary – modelling up to a billion neurons and their trillions of synaptic connections in biological real time (Begley, 2020; Sen-Bhattacharya et al., 2017). However, when we delve a little deeper, we will see that, again, the origins of something so seemingly unknowable are firmly rooted in the extraordinary work of the early computer pioneers. One of the initiators was the fêted Alan Turing, who designed

Figure 3.15 The 500,000-Core SpiNNaker Human Brain Project Platform

the eponymous Turing machine in 1936 at Bletchley Park in the United Kingdom. The first recognizable electric computer, however, was developed by English engineer Tommy Flowers in 1943 and was called the Colossus, as depicted in Figure 3.16.

Figure 3.16 The First Electric Programmable Computer

Look back at both giant computers – they are very similar in appearance and size, despite the decades of innovation which separate them. One could be forgiven for thinking that hardly any progress had been made at all. Given that the awe-inspiring and mystical brain has taken billions of years to evolve and computers have only been in existence for less than a century, we have a very long way to go in completely unravelling its intricacies and mysteries. While giant leaps have irrefutably been made in technological advancements and computing, it may prove impossible to completely map and replicate the entire human brain. The enormity of this endeavour is captured by van Albada et al. (2018: 2), who explain:

> Today's supercomputers require tens of minutes to simulate one second of biological time and consume megawatts of power. This means that any studies on processes like plasticity, learning, and development exhibited over hours and days of biological time are outside our reach.

But, there is good news – although it is out of reach for now and there is some way to go, Professor Steve Furber (Arm Research, 2022), who was instrumental in the launch of SpiNNaker, is unequivocal about the potential of SpiNNaker to achieve its goal, stating that while they continue to upscale it, part of this actually involves downsizing the enormous machine, stating that: "we may well soon have a computer with the processing power of the human brain – inside a desktop machine." A far cry from computer technology when Turing laid the groundwork for Flowers' Colossus in 1943 – and so the quest continues . . .

Rewind. Reflect. Write!

1a In your own words, what are the ambitious goals of the Human Connectome Project?

1b What are the implications of this project in terms of understanding the human brain?

2a In your own words, explain what epigenetics is.

2b What is its significance to wellbeing and mental health in early childhood?

3 Conduct some desk-based research and answer the following questions:

   a Identify at least two advantages of SpiNNaker technology in unravelling the mysteries of the human brain.

   b Now discuss at least two limitations of SpiNNaker technology in unravelling the mysteries of the human brain.

   c Could these limitations be overcome? Discuss.

4a In your opinion (and based on your research), do you think that the very essence of the entire human brain will ever be revealed by the neurosciences?

4b Do you think this is important to do? Explain your answer.

5 In your opinion, what are the three major goals of future neuroscientific research? Provide a clear rationale for your choices.

Teaching Children About Their Brains – It's Not Rocket Science. It's Neuroscience!

Let's face it, the brain is a fascinating organ (as demonstrated throughout this book). It is the source of infinite curiosity of diverse professionals, but its functionality is not only relevant to them – it is relevant to each and every one of us. Given that we demand so much of children's brains, it makes sense to also teach them about this extraordinary organ! This can help to build their understanding of the connection between emotions and learning (which you could teach via the hand brain model and the "upstairs" and "downstairs" brain), the basic functions of the brain and what they can do to better regulate their emotional responses and behaviour – both in the setting and at home. (Revisit Chapter 2 for some in-the-moment strategies.)

To ensure you engage every child so that the information resonates with them, make sure you present the information in ways that are:

■ Easy to understand (this goes for parents as well as children)

■ In manageable "chunks"

■ Fun and exciting

■ Hands-on

■ Interactive (engaging all the senses).

Getting parents on board will add to the effectiveness of this teaching, as they too can benefit from the information, especially concerning "flipping one's lid," as this is an emotion that is familiar to us all in times of stress or frustration. If we can give parents the tools to manage those big, overwhelming feelings, this can only positively impact their children. It does not need to be complex information – just enough to help children (and their parents) understand why we, for example, can overreact to some situations and how we can *choose* to respond differently.

This section mainly consists of practical prompts, questions and ideas for you to take into your practice. Doing some extra reading around the topics presented will help to inspire your suggestions for change to your provision.

Try It!

Read the three titles and their accompanying explanations, below.

Your Brilliant Brain! – Include facts such as its weight, size and texture – you could make this all the more fun by modelling brains out of dough or even a vegan jelly, which would encompass scientific concepts like changes of state, when the jelly cools and sets. You could also make a model of the brain with your group using a cauliflower (Nitty Gritty Science, 2021) and paint (or food colouring, which is effectively absorbed by cauliflower) and cutting it down the middle to enable the children to label some key regions and learn about these. Allowing the children to eat their edible models also means minimizing waste, so it also works as a valuable lesson in sustainability. This excellent video (just 30 seconds in duration) available on YouTube will guide you: "Cauliflower Brain – Make a Brain Model Using Entire Head of Cauliflower and Label Functions," at: www.youtube.com/watch?v=MIhfstdnxLY.

You may already be familiar with the **Brain Hemisphere Hat**. This is a wonderful, hands-on resource that you could make with the children to teach them about their brains. Do not be put off by the complex terms – use your creativity and initiative and just focus on one or two brain regions at a time to talk through with children, or make one of your own with the children! Figure 3.17 shows a child in a Montessori setting learning about the brain, using a range of resources, including the Hat. It could be designed as an independent activity or one that children could do in small groups – which will likely be more engaging and enjoyable. Have a go and see!

Figure 3.17 The Brain Hemisphere Hat

Source: Living Montessori Now. (2018).

The Free Printable Brain Hemisphere Hat (2021) can be downloaded at: https://ellenjmchenry.com/store/wp-content/uploads/2016/04/Brain-Hat-2.0-download.pdf.

Your emotions – Take the children's lead here and talk about how they sometimes feel and why. You could also explore how others' emotions affect them while using/introducing the appropriate emotional vocabulary, such as "anger," "fear," "anxiety," "sadness," "empathy" and "happiness." All this would be linked to the relevant brain regions and the impact on the body, say, for example, when we are feeling angry and how this feels physically. Figure 3.18 is one way in which the chief executive of a chain of nurseries built the young children's understanding of their emotions and how they feel when they "flip their lid."

You will notice that there is an upstairs and downstairs section to this model representing the brain – each with some small world figures. Upstairs, one of the figures is looking through a telescope to keep watch of what happens downstairs. Having demonstrated the hand model of the brain to the children and encouraging them to join in, the children spoke about how they felt when they (for example) became angry. They shook the whole model up and down and displaced the small figures – so that those upstairs fell downstairs and vice versa. This represented the limbic system temporarily taking over during times of anger and upset.

How to help your brain grow – Here, you could explore good nutrition, getting the recommended amount of exercise and sleep and how learning helps the brain to "grow" and remain "plastic." Where appropriate for the children's stage of understanding,

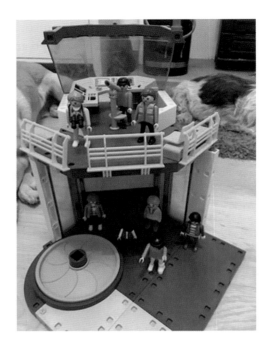

Figure 3.18 The "Upstairs" and "Downstairs" Brain

you could even use key terms like "synapses." You could have a lot of fun to represent the brain's growth and its synaptic connections by using a range of resources like a balloon to represent the growing brain and coloured strings or large elastic to represent the synapses connecting each time a child learns a new skill.

Pipe cleaners are also an easy, hands-on and fun way to learn about synapses! Figure 3.19 is made from three different-coloured pipe cleaners, each representing different parts of the neuron.

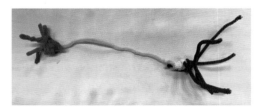

Figure 3.19 An Individual Neuron Made From Pipe Cleaners

The book *Fantastic Elastic Brain* by JoAnn Deak is an excellent, highly informative and engaging book full of easily accessible information about the brain for parents, teachers and children alike. Where possible, keeping one or two copies in your classroom/setting will prove useful, as well as recommending it to families.

Using each of these three titles, create a plan of how you and your team will teach/talk to children about each topic. Your learning as a result of reading this book and its suggested resources, combined with some online research, will prove sufficient in teaching children the "brain basics"!

■   For each experience, think about what content you will include

■   How you will present it

■   What you want the children to learn from the experience

■   How you could involve parents (and any resources needed to make this happen, like developing simple leaflets which contain simple activity ideas to try at home with their children).

Now let us look at one example of good practice in building children's understanding of the brain in closer detail. The case study that follows was provided by the area manager of Portico Nursery Group in the United Kingdom, which has six nurseries. The case study might give you further ideas concerning how to teach young children about their brains, how to self-regulate and why this is important for us all to do.

At Portico Lodge, we currently have 40 children enrolled, aged birth to five. Our nursery is registered for 32 children.

Our vision

Since staff received in-house training from the area manager, our vision has been to support children's emotional development, so they can better manage their feelings and emotions – to self-regulate. We have done this by putting our "promoting positive behaviour policy" in the bin and writing a new policy – a self-regulation policy. At Portico Lodge, our most recent initiative has been to encourage all children to confidently use our self-regulation area without any prompts and have a good understanding of their feelings and behaviours.

Our role as practitioners

Our role as practitioners has been to find and demonstrate coping strategies for children to use when stressed, upset, over-stimulated, angry or scared. We do this by building good relationships with children and adopting a positive attitude. We use these strategies during our daily interactions and routine with the children, so that they can confidently draw on the tools in their "toolkit" to ultimately help themselves and become more independent.

We ensure that all resources are age appropriate and children have structure to their day. We do like to add some challenging activities to support children's ability to solve problems and critical thinking processes, and to encourage children to explore new experiences by having a go. We would also map the room out to reduce and avoid over-simulation by making sure that children have opportunities in the room to self-regulate when needed, by having quiet zones, relaxing areas and a self-regulation area.

What we did

During an activity we started introducing vocabulary such as "let me think about that" while pointing to our heads. We then received a comment from a child aged four: "your brain is working in your head isn't it?" This sparked a discussion about the brain. We extended the children's learning by explaining some things about the brain to the children who showed an interest at the time. We used relatable language by explaining that the brain had an "upstairs" (cerebral cortex) where all our thinking is done and a "downstairs" (limbic system) where our feelings live. This is where we spoke about the times our feelings stopped us from solving problems, persevering and being creative. I spoke to the children about teamwork and asked them who knew what it meant. One child answered "it's about working together" and another answered "helping our friends." I explained to the group that the "upstairs" brain and "downstairs" brain need to work together as a team in order to make good choices, self-regulate, make relationships, play games and take on challenges.

We spoke about how sometimes we can get angry, frustrated, scared and upset, at which point I explained to the children that it is OK and it just meant that our "downstairs" brain was working a little harder than the "upstairs" brain and introduced here the concept of "flipping our lids."

I asked a question about how it feels when they have these feelings. I received responses such as:

■ Scared – *It feels bad and makes me shake. I'm scared of the dark, but daddy tells me monsters are only in books* (girl, aged three)

- Sad – *I cry when I'm sad. It makes tears come out and I get sleepy. It makes me sad when somebody is mean to me* (boy, aged three)

- Happy – *It makes me happy when my mummy tickles me. I laugh so much* (girl, aged three)

- Happy – *When I'm happy I smile. It feels good. It makes me happy when I'm playing with my friends and family* (girl, aged three)

- Angry – *When I'm angry it gives me headache and I get a grumpy face. I get angry when I'm tired* (boy, aged three).

When we spoke about the staircase, we explained to the children that this is in between the "downstairs" and "upstairs" brain and that it allows information to be passed between the two levels. We discussed that we need to engage the "upstairs" brain and not make the "downstairs" brain any more stressed, frustrated or angry.

We have created a self-regulation area where the children can use different breathing techniques by simply breathing in and out slowly, blowing bubbles or blowing into windmills. We have added fidget toys, bean bags, puzzles, blocks and books to help and encourage both levels of the brain to work together.

We received in-house training from our area manager on early brain development and emotional wellbeing. Since then, staff have been encouraged to use strategies such as the HighScope conflict resolution method to co-regulate with the children. We have created quiet zones and safe spaces for children and introduced various breathing apps. Staff receive regular training concerning the brain, nutrition, neurodiversity and mental health.

When assessing and observing children, we focus on the Characteristics of Effective Learning of the EYFS, while looking at children's behaviours and how effective the learning is. In order for children to use what is learnt in new situations, we understand that children need to be given lots of opportunities to be curious and enthusiastic. Our display includes information about mindfulness and how we can redirect our emotions by using lots of different techniques to focus on what is happening in-the-moment.

How we got parents/families involved

We send out a weekly newsletter with information about what is happening or upcoming in the setting. We have provided lots of ideas and suggestions when it comes to self-regulation and sent posters about the "upstairs"/"downstairs" brain. Parents with children with "challenging" behaviour have been invited into nursery to speak about techniques and advice on how to deal with this and we show them some of the strategies that we have put in place, like the calming water bottles, tissue boxes, windmills and how to use the HighScope technique (which is based on active learning, positive adult-child interactions, a child-friendly learning environment and a consistent daily routine). We focus on promoting mental health and offer plenty of support for both children, parents and staff.

The impact

Parents have commented to staff that since their child has attended our setting, their behaviour and approach to situations has improved, while others comment on how well the strategies given to them by staff have worked at home; that they do not get as stressed and that their own mental health is improving.

The impact on the preschool children here at Portico Lodge has been very positive. We have noticed the children beginning to self-regulate without staff having to intervene; children are exploring more confidently and having a go at new and exciting activities. Pre-school children are also encouraging each other to self-regulate and talk about how they are feeling. The children will often take themselves into the self-regulation area if they feel like they need to have alone time or if they are upset or angry – and they can come and go as often as they need.

Parents using some of the self-regulation strategies at home frequently tell us that they are really helping. What is heartening is that a couple who have just had another baby told staff that they use a naughty step! We told them to get rid of it, and they did – they have created a quiet area instead, which is working really well. One little girl told her mum and dad that she needed a happy and sad place – they have since made an area under her bed and called it her "happy and sad zone."

One child who has special needs often takes himself to the self-regulation area when he is feeling over-stimulated and likes to spin the windmills and play with the fidget toys, as this calms him down. When he is ready, he leaves the area and goes off to explore somewhere else in the room. Another child who has delayed speech tends to get frustrated easily. He has found his voice by using the emotion cards/spoons and likes to use the resources in the area to release frustration. School transitions have been a lot smoother as children have been able to talk about their worries and have supported each other through school visits and leaving nursery, while the younger children moving up to preschool from 2–3s have been observing their peers and mirroring some of the strategies that the other children have been using in the last year. Basically, a lot of co-regulation is happening!

One little boy's parents have made his reading area into somewhere he can go when he feels anxious or stressed. He gets stressed coming into nursery, and one morning, his dad watched the manager (Charlotte) use the breathing techniques to help calm him. While collecting him, his dad told her, "I watched what you did with him – it was amazing." His mum is a high school teacher. During a parents' meeting, Charlotte spoke to his mum about the "upstairs" and "downstairs" brain. She told Charlotte that she loved the concept and will share it with her high school students – how wonderful!

As a result of the pandemic, teaching the children about their "upstairs" and "downstairs" brain and self-regulation has been important for their mental health and wellbeing. We have seen children who were unsure, nervous, confused and very unsettled, but upon their return to nursery, are able to calm themselves down and recall the techniques we taught them to encourage their "upstairs" and "downstairs" brain to work as a team.

We are so delighted with the impact of introducing the brain and self-regulation to the children, staff and parents and we are looking forward to building on the work that we are all doing together.

The following display shows some of the pictures that the children drew of their "upstairs" and "downstairs" brain.

Figure 3.20 Children's Pictures of the "Downstairs" and "Upstairs" Brain

Figure 3.21 Self-Regulation Area

Figure 3.21 depicts part of the wider space, which includes the SR area which was mentioned in the case study. If you look closely, you will see the children's pictures of the "upstairs" and "downstairs" brain are displayed here, along with a wide range of resources included to help the children to identify and express their emotions.

Now have a go at answering the questions that follow.

Rewind. Reflect. Write!

I Reflecting on the final section, "Teaching Children About Their Brains," answer the following questions:

   a Outline three key areas of learning that stood out for you, briefly explaining your choices.

   b Do you currently teach children about their brains and emotions? Discuss.

   c Reflecting on the work done by the nursery in the case study, make a plan of action (with your team) to embed teaching about the brain, emotions and wellbeing – with lots of strategies that children can do independently and in-the-moment to self-regulate.

   d How will you get parents on board and encourage them to continue the learning and self-regulation and co-regulation strategies at home? Make a plan for implementation.

2 How might this nursery extend their collaboration with parents/families concerning their teaching about the brain? Note down some suggestions.

3 Outline the aspects of their practice that you thought were effective in promoting children's self-regulation and co-regulation skills.

Concluding Thoughts

This chapter introduced you to the neuroscience of the developing brain and the interactive influences of genes and experience which shape the developing brain. Contemporary key concepts concerning SR and CR were also examined in order to equip you with simple yet effective ways to teach children about the impact of emotions on the brain, body and behaviour. Just as we teach young children about the various parts of the human body and their functions, we must get used to doing likewise about the brain. However, similar to the EY workforce in recent years, there tends to be a reticence concerning grappling with this knowledge and imparting it to children and their families – as if it is too scientific or specialist. Learning how the brain works helps children to regulate their bodies and their brains when they experience strong or uncomfortable feelings, while developing their emotional vocabulary. It lays the basis for self-awareness and self-regulatory capacities which will stay – and evolve with them across the life course.

Further Reading

■ Eagleman, D. (2015). *The Brain: The Story of You*. London: Canongate Books Ltd.

You may already be familiar with the televised documentary, *The Brain With David Eagleman*, in which he engages and entertains viewers about the wonders and mysteries of the human brain. This book is no different. In its six chapters, he takes us on a fascinating journey of the brain and how it constructs reality and controls behaviour. Drawing on the latest discoveries, he asks pertinent questions about our future while demonstrating how understanding neuroscience can enhance our wellbeing, boost our cognitive skills and even create a more just society and ultimately a better future for everyone.

■ Marcus, G. and Freeman, J. (2015). *The Future of the Brain: Essays by the World's Leading Neuroscientists*. Princeton and Oxford: Princeton University Press.

This book takes readers to the absolute frontiers of science. It includes original essays by leading researchers, such as Olaf Sporns (discussed in this chapter concerning his key role in the Human Connectome Project), who describe the incredible technological advances that will (one day) enable us to map all the neurons in the brain and the challenges that lie ahead. A must-read for anyone wanting to delve deeper into the brain and the implications of neuroscience for understanding the very essence of what it means to be human.

■ Tranter, M. (2021). *A Million Things to Ask a Neuroscientist: The Brain Made Easy*. London: Mike Tranter.

In this engaging and humorous book, the author answers a range of questions submitted by the public while revealing extraordinary insights about the brain in the process. Similar to the other books recommended, this includes a chapter which takes a behind-the-scenes look at how cutting-edge neuroscience research is changing – and will continue to change the future.

4 Sensory Integration – Too Much or Not Enough

How to Get Your Provision Just Right

Children instinctively know what they need in order to move from a state of discomfort to comfort. It is not the role of parents or teachers to try to restrain or reprimand their efforts – efforts which are beautifully exemplified by the wonderful occupational therapist and neuropsychologist, Ayres (2005: 8):

> A human being is designed to enjoy things that promote the development of his brain and therefore we naturally seek sensations that help organize our brain. This is one of the reasons why children love to be picked up, rocked and hugged and why they love to run and jump. They want to move because the sensations of movement nourish their brains.

What to Expect in This Chapter

In this chapter, some of the more common SEND will be explored, with accessible definitions and explanations of their origins. Emphasis will be on sensory integration (SI) difficulties and how these manifest, including discussion on hyper- and hypo-sensitivities in children with SEND, including autism and ADHD. Potential triggers will be explored in relation to Dr Shanker's five domains of stressors – both in and out of the setting. Diverse in-the-moment strategies are suggested to help nurture self-regulation in children who have SEND – while involving their primary carers in this essential process. Reflective questions are included to help consolidate the reader's understanding, and a Further Reading list ends the chapter.

By the End of This Chapter, You Will Be Able to:

■ Identify and explain the function of all eight senses

■ Define sensory integration

DOI: 10.4324/9781003327479-4

- Explain the integral role of primitive reflexes in achieving sensory integration

- Discuss the importance of healthy gross motor development in acquiring hand-writing skills

- Define sensory overload

- Define sensory processing difficulties (which although is more commonly known as sensory processing disorder (SPD), the term disorder will be avoided)

- Differentiate between sensory overload and sensory processing difficulties

- Describe the signs of hyper- and hypo-sensitivity

- Describe what it means to up-regulate and down-regulate a child

- Outline activities to up-regulate and down-regulate a child

- Identify the stressors which influence the ability of a child with SEND to self-regulate

- Discuss how these stressors influence the ability of a child with SEND to self-regulate

- Understand some of the neurobiological causes of autism

- Outline some practical ways to build autistic children's self-regulation skills

- Understand some of the neurobiological causes of ADHD

- Outline some practical ways to build self-regulation skills in children who have ADHD.

Making Sense of the Eight Senses

Contrary to the long-held belief that humans have five senses, we actually have eight senses. The five more common senses are vision (sight), auditory (hearing), gustatory (taste), tactile (touch) – from the body's largest sense organ, the skin – and olfactory (smell). The other three senses are perhaps not so obvious, as they are concerned with the inside of the body – they are internal. These are:

- Interoception

- Proprioception

- Vestibular.

A corresponding cortical area exists in the brain (sensory cortex) for each of the senses, these being the visual cortex, somatosensory cortex, auditory cortex, olfactory cortex and gustatory cortex. Table 4.1 outlines the main functions of our eight senses.

Table 4.1 The Eight Senses

Sense	Function	Location in the Brain
Vision	Our brain interprets the signals it receives from the eyeballs and tells us what we are looking at. This sense is also important for us to make sense of non-verbal cues and track movement with our eyes to ensure we move safely.	The occipital lobe (at the back of the head) is the primary visual area of the brain.
Auditory	We receive auditory input through our ears. Once received, we gauge whether it is important or just background noise, where it comes from, how close it is and whether we have heard it before.	The primary auditory cortex is located in the superior temporal gyrus of the brain (positioned horizontally to the head, above the ear).
Olfactory	The sensory receptors in our nose pick up information about the odours around us. They pass this information along a channel of nerves to the brain. Remember – smell is strongly linked to emotion and memory and can hence trigger unexpected trauma reactions in some individuals.	There are two olfactory bulbs on the bottom side of the brain, one above each nasal cavity. These receive information about smells from the nose and send it to the brain.
Tactile	This helps us to understand the important sensations of pressure, texture, pain, hot and cold – as well as how to discriminate between them all. Note that touch also plays an integral role in bonding and relationships.	The primary somatosensory cortex is the primary receptive area for touch sensations. This is located in the lateral postcentral gyrus – a prominent structure in the parietal lobe of the human brain (near the back and top of the head).
Gustatory	Located in the mouth, tongue and throat, our taste cells react to food and drinks. They tell us about flavours, texture and temperature.	The gustatory cortex is located in cerebral cortex (the outer part of the brain).
Interoception	This sense helps us to be aware of what is happening inside our body. For example, knowing when we feel hot, cold, tired, hungry or afraid.	The brain region which controls interoception is the insula cortex, which is located deep within the cerebral cortex.
Proprioception	This sense enables you to tell where your body parts are, relative to other body parts. This includes walking without looking at your feet and knowing how hard to press on a pen when writing.	Proprioceptive and visual information of one's own body is integrated in the parietal lobe in the brain (near the back and top of the head).
Vestibular	This sense helps us to maintain balance and body posture.	The major sensory organs of the vestibular system are located in the inner ear, next to the cochlea.

The main function of our senses is to inform our CNS about any factors that might influence our environment – be this internally (within our body) or externally (in our environment). The CNS receives stimuli from our senses and then integrates all the information, enabling us to respond to our environment – which ultimately helps us to function optimally in all areas of our lives. Our senses enable us to identify how hot or cold it is, to feel pain and to sense how our body is positioned. Each of these senses has its own system for detecting the environment that must send signals to the correct brain regions. The sense of balance comes from the vestibular organs in the inner ear, which can tell when our body is tilted in different directions, while proprioception tells us what position our body is in, where the different parts of our body are, how they move and how much strength our muscles need to use. Critically, our senses are closely connected to our emotions and memories, which means that they can significantly impact how we feel – so if even one of our senses is off kilter or not integrated, this can diminish our experience of life itself – this will become apparent in the case studies that are presented in this chapter. Figure 4.1 provides an overview of the senses, which is used by occupational therapists (OTs) globally to understand the interrelated nature of our senses.

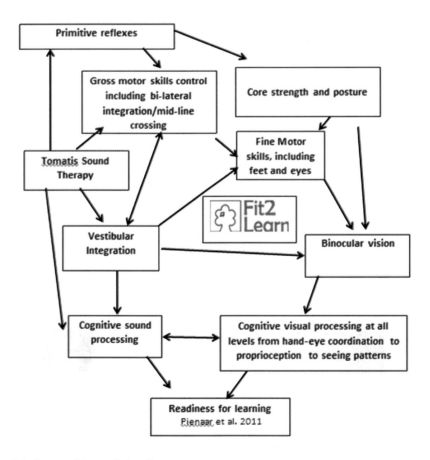

Figure 4.1 Route Map of the Senses

Note how full integration of all the senses is needed from in utero to ensure that a child is *able* to learn. This is identified by Davies et al. (2018: 25), who highlight the importance of controlling the peripheral skeleton, achieving motor-sensory integration by eight-years-old (which must be maintained and mastered), as well as crossing the mid-line and developing core strength. The implications of their work are clear for teachers and primary carers alike, who tend to place emphasis on "school-readiness" skills, like handwriting. They explain:

> Gross motor skills control needs to be in place in order for a child to properly develop fine motor skills control. Rushing straight to fine motor skills will restrict the proper development of gross motor skills control. Gross motor skills should be fully developed between the ages of six and eight-years-old.

It stands to reason, then, that handwriting skills must not be rushed – after all, developing handwriting skills is not a race (which, sadly, it has become in schools and homes, with teachers and parents "policing" children's dexterity and neatness). Yet, as Davies et al. (2018) bring to our attention, prioritizing the execution of fine motor skills ultimately inhibits healthy gross motor development. Figure 4.2 illustrates the striking difference between the seven-year-old child's more developed hand on the left compared to the four-year-old's hand on the right.

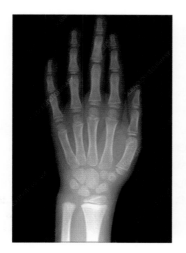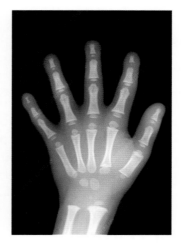

Figure 4.2 X-Ray of a Four-Year-Old's Hand Compared to a Seven-Year-Old's Hand

Source: Jones, J. (2013). Carpal Ossification. Case Study, Radiopaedia.org. (Accessed on 10th Mar 2022) https://doi.org/10.53347/rID-23244.

You will see that the hand in the image on the left contains a collection of small bones just above the wrist – eight small bones, in fact – and these are known as the carpal bones. These bones allow the wrist to move and rotate vertically. They are essential to handwriting, and when they are missing, a child will adapt their positioning in response. This typically looks like a child slumping or leaning on the table with their whole arm to prop up their shoulder – which increases the risk of injury.

Surely this is evidence enough to make every teacher and primary carer understand why *play before pencils* is a necessity! There are physical reasons children go through the phases of palmar supinate, digital pronate, static tripod and eventually to dynamic tripod while acquiring pencil grip mastery. Children also have to develop upper and core body strength and proprioceptor control in addition to fine motor control. The best way to achieve this is through play – particularly physical play, which involves climbing, pushing, crawling and creeping, which strengthens the shoulder and arm muscles. This in turn promotes the development of fine motor skills, including pencil grasp.

Rewind. Reflect. Write!

1a List the eight senses and their locations in the brain.

1b Outline the function of the eight senses.

1c Briefly explain the role of the eight senses in feeling regulated and "ready" to learn.

2 Discuss the importance of:

   a Interoception

   b Proprioception

   c The vestibular sense.

3 Supposing a parent approached you about her four-year-old child's "messy handwriting" and asked you to spend more time practicing handwriting skills in the setting. How would you support her to understand the importance of healthy gross motor development in acquiring handwriting skills?

Top Tips for Practice!

■ Do not expect – or demand that children sit still while listening

■ Bear in mind that the more uncomfortable a child is, the less they will be able to concentrate. With your team, re-assess your environment and resources

- Build in more time for physical play! Fun ideas include animal walking (bear walking, slithering like a snake or hopping like a frog!). You could also set up simple obstacle courses, hopscotch and ball games

- Writing should not be confined to tables – get creative and incorporate painting on foil, making marks using sand and sticks/brushes, easels, paper on walls and chalk on the floor/walls. These are just a few multi-sensory ways to build a love of writing.

Sensory Integration – The Sum Is Not Always Greater Than Its Parts

An examination of SI would not be complete without citing the ground-breaking work of occupational therapist and neuropsychologist Jean Ayres (1989, 1976). SI, or Ayres Sensory Integration, refers to how the brain registers, processes and discriminates information from the eight senses and consequently informs appropriate behaviours or responses to the stimuli from these senses. Ayres' (1972: 11) definition of SI, which is still widely used today, explains SI as:

> The neurological process that organizes sensation from one's own body and from the environment and makes it possible to use the body effectively with the environment and makes it possible to use the body effectively within the environment.

Although decades old, Ayres' work, which was initially informed by the available neurological knowledge of the 1960s and 1970s, is as relevant as ever. This is due to advances in neuroimaging technology, which have given Ayres' original theories (which stemmed from her neuroscientific knowledge and her observations of children's behaviour) new meaning. As Ayres (1972: 2) prophetically acknowledged:

> Just as the continued production of research results in constantly changing neurological concepts, so also will sensory integration theory need to undergo frequent revision.

In order for a child's senses to be correctly registered by the brain and to work optimally, their primitive reflexes need to be fully integrated. (This is further discussed in the following section.) Ayres (1979) proposed that the limbic system (which we looked at in Chapter 3) is partly responsible for SI. She also posited that this is atypical in some autistic children, which results in them not being able to register and process stimuli in the same way as "typically" developing children. While research continues to report contrasting findings, some reports continue to confirm this (Kilroy et al., 2019; Gibbard et al., 2018; Nair et al., 2015; Buxbaum et al., 2013; Harms et al., 2010; Courchesne et al., 2007).

Start at the Beginning – Primitive Reflexes and the Senses

Primitive reflexes are a set of automatic movement patterns that begin during pregnancy and are fully present when a baby is born. You will be familiar with most, if not all 10 of these reflexes, which include the startle, stepping, palmar and rooting reflexes. These reflexes lay the foundation for the child's nervous system, which is responsible for processing information through each of the senses. The reflexes should be fully integrated and disappear by roughly four-years-old, which will enable healthy holistic development, including gross-motor function (whole-body movements). Sometimes, however, integration does not automatically take place – and this commonly causes a host of challenges for children (which are addressed in this chapter). Possible causes of retained reflexes include:

■ Traumatic birth experience

■ Birth by caesarean section

■ Falls/traumas

■ Lack of tummy time

■ Delayed or skipped crawling

■ Chronic ear infections.

Retained reflexes can be easy to identify in a child's general behaviour. Some common signs/symptoms look like:

■ Sensitivity to sensory information (this could be hyper- or hypo-sensitivity, which are both examined in this chapter)

■ Poor impulse control

■ Posture issues

■ "Clumsiness"

■ Fidgeting and poor attention

■ Difficulties with visual tracking

■ Poor hand–eye coordination

■ Difficulties with fine motor skills

■ Walking on toes

■ Low muscle tone

■ Wriggling and fidgeting while sat down

■ W-sitting past age four. W-sitting is considered detrimental to physical development, as the position tightens muscles in the hips and legs. Tight muscles, in turn,
likely inhibit "typical" movement, affecting the child's developing coordination and
balance. An example of w-sitting is shown in Figure 4.3.

Figure 4.3 Child W-Sitting

Reflecting on these signs/symptoms, one can immediately appreciate how tough
daily life can be for children with retained reflexes – not least because many of the
resulting signs are too frequently mistaken for "laziness" or a general awkwardness or
"clumsiness."

A Word on Wiggles, Wobbles and Sitting Still

When you were little, you probably remember grown-ups telling you to "sit still." We
learn from an early age that wiggly legs and fidgety fingers are a problem. But that two-
word command to "sit still" invites a conversation about what "good" listening looks
like in the first place. Does a room full of silent, motionless toddlers really sound like
anyone's ideal learning environment? It is time we rethink those wiggles, what they
mean and how you should respond to them as a practitioner.

On some level, our response to children's fidgeting is an indication of how much we
trust them. In the command for children to "sit still," there is an unhelpful assumption
that we know children's own needs and impulses better than they do – and this is wrong
on various levels. Giving children more breaks and more freedom to move and engage in
the way that suits them best is a gesture of trust. It shows we trust children to lead their
own learning and to shape the conditions that make them most comfortable to learn.

If you fixate on whether children are sitting still, you can get too caught up in whether
they are complying and lose track of whether they are really engaged. When you
notice fidgeting, it is worth asking yourself whether it is causing trouble, distractions or
interruptions before you insist the child stops. After all, who is to say that learning looks
one way or another or that children must conform to a one-size-fits-all idea of attentive
listening? When we ask children to stamp out these self-regulatory behaviours, we are

setting them up to fail. So what can you do to help each child learn in the ways that work best for them? Removing "sit still" from your vocabulary would be a sound start.

Fidgeting, wiggling and struggling to sit still are children's way of showing you that they need a bit of help focusing. They might also be indicative of retained reflexes, particularly the spinal Galant reflex (this reflex causes babies to curve their hip outward if the lower back is stroked next to the spine). It supports the development of the muscles in the lower back, pelvic area and legs and is an integral part of preparation to help the child develop gross motor coordination.

When this reflex is retained, difficulty with leg control while walking and running is commonly experienced, along with challenges with focusing, concentration and general school performance. So asking children to stop wiggling is like asking them to quit breathing. It is how they self-regulate. We were children once, too. We must remember what it was like to sit with legs crossed, arms folded and getting reprimanded if you cannot. Sitting quietly is hard work for young children. They need to draw on their developing SR skills in order to regulate their impulses and to recognize and express their needs – and when that gets tough, it can help to wiggle their legs, zip the zipper on their jacket or fidget with the Velcro on their trainers.

When children are feeling a bit wobbly or wiggly inside, fidgeting can help them stay present, both cognitively and physically. So they fidget to focus, not because they are "messing around" or "pushing your buttons." You do not need to analyze fidgeting on an individual level. Instead, it is better to adjust your policies and practice to give children more healthy outlets for their wiggles. Digging too deep into these can drive us to over-analyze children and to lose track of the fact that fidgeting is a normal thing for some children to do in the first place. What you should do, however, is look for ways that your learning space can better support children's active impulses. You might ask yourself the following questions to help get an idea of what you might change:

- Are children sitting down for too long in one stretch? Try not to exceed a maximum of 15 minutes of sitting still for young children before it is time to change the pace

- Is a lot of your day based on sedentary activities? Could any of these be more active or allow children to stand or move how they like?

- Are there lots of desks and tables in your space, making it difficult for children to run and move about?

- Is your environment cramped, too bright or visually overstimulating for children?

- Does your daily schedule create some limits on when children can move?

If you answered "yes" to a lot of these questions, that is a sign that you might need some more brain breaks.

You'll find decades of research showing how getting up and active is a key ingredient in children's health, happiness and learning (Zeng et al., 2017; Becker et al., 2014) – and young children tend to be active in small, spontaneous bursts. This is why shorter, regular brain breaks can work better than a long, structured activity period. Even a break of a few minutes can make a big difference. The following are four ways to get up and active:

■ Try some yoga – run through a couple of simple yoga poses as a group

■ Move to music. Throw on a favourite song and have a little dance, or sing a song together!

■ Ditch the chairs. Try doing your next activity without your usual seating. Instead, give everyone the freedom to stand, squat, lie on their belly or lean against a wall as you play and learn

■ Get outside and play. Even if it is just for 10 minutes, a quick play in the garden does wonders to release those wiggles.

In the case of retained reflexes, as discussed previously, this needs to be diagnosed and assessed by an occupational therapist or physical therapist so that the reflexes can be fully integrated. Read on to find out how SI is commonly assessed.

Ayres' Sensory Integration and Praxis Test

Ayres' Sensory Integration and Praxis Test (SIPT), developed in 1989, is the most complete and flexible assessment of SI available. It remains the most commonly used assessment globally. The ultimate aim of this test is to enable the child to establish mastery of motor-sensory integration (MSI), which is the point where all senses and motor skills work coherently together in order to nurture calm, regulated behaviour and the consequent potential to learn efficiently. The test consists of 17 distinct tasks which are designed to assess certain aspects of sensory processing that are related to social behaviour, language development and academic achievement. At the end of the (approximately) two-hour test, children are scored on their ability to execute each of the tasks.

The following is a very brief outline of the four categories of tasks that are used during the test.

1   **Motor-free visual perception** – these assess the child's ability to visually perceive and discriminate form and space without involving motor coordination (fine or gross motor skills)

2   **Somatosensory** ("soma" meaning "body") – these tasks require the child to use their sense of touch more than their other senses. Any sensitivity to touch is noted

3   **Praxis** (refers to how effectively the child figures out how to use their hands and body in skilled tasks, such as playing with toys, holding a fork or a paintbrush and just about everything else). Praxis is assessed in six different ways in the test, each assessing a child's ability to listen to and execute instructions; draw; build with blocks and imitate movements and positions of the jaw, tongue and lips

4   **Sensorimotor** – four tasks are used, each of which is designed to assess a child's ability to integrate their senses by coordinating both sides of their body to execute specific actions.

Sensitivity to sensory information (as mentioned earlier) is not solely attributable to retained reflexes. Sensory overload (SO), SPD and SEND are also factors. Each will be discussed in the sections that follow.

Too Much! – The Effects of Sensory Overload

Anyone can get SO at any point of their lives. It occurs when our brain receives more sensory input from our eight senses than it can process. This might look like being sat on a packed bus, with people talking loudly, while others might be listening to music that is audible to those around them, being at a loud party or listening to multiple conversations go on simultaneously. It is important to note that SO is not the same as SPD, but it *is* most common with people who have PTSD, autism or sensory processing and other neurodevelopmental conditions. This will become clearer in the case studies further on in this chapter.

Just a few common signs of SO include:

■ Racing heartbeat

■ Uncontrollable crying

■ Covering ears

■ Aggression

■ Extreme sensitivity to sound and/or light

■ Refusing activities

■ Hiding or running away.

Again, many of the identified behaviours can easily be mistaken for "defiant" or "misbehaviour," which is often reprimanded, as opposed to understood and supported in schools (more on this in Chapter 5). Overcoming periods of SO is dependent on the individual child, their triggers, the measures put in place by the adult to help prevent exposure to triggers and how they co-regulate the child during times of dysregulation (as discussed in Chapter 2).

Sensory Processing Difficulties

Sensory processing difficulties (SPD) is a neurological condition that inhibits the proper processing of environmental stimuli, causing the individual to either be hyper-sensitive to common, everyday stimuli (like the sound from a washing machine or sunlight) or hypo-sensitive to stimuli (like not knowing when they are hungry or in pain) and hence needing to avoid or seek out additional sensory information to feel relief or content. SPD persists across the lifespan and, as previously stated, is more common among individuals who are autistic (Green et al., 2016), have PTSD, developmental delay, ADHD, self-regulatory difficulties or other neurodevelopmental conditions. It is these children who tend to be disproportionally referred for intervention, as well as those who generally struggle academically but with no clear reason – or diagnosis – as to why. Among those children diagnosed with autism, a large proportion also have SPD (Baum et al., 2015). Some studies (Ben-Sasson et al., 2019; Taylor et al., 2017) found that 90% showed symptoms of SPD.

Too Much or Not Enough – Hyper- and Hypo-sensitivities

SPD affects a child's fundamental experience of life – from eating, sleeping, getting dressed and playing to being at school and getting along with others. SPD means something different to each child, but the issues experienced and presented will generally fall into one – or both – of these categories and are caused by irregularities in the nervous system:

Hyper-sensitivity – "hyper" indicates excessive sensitivity, with children trying to avoid their senses being over-stimulated (for this reason, hyper-sensitivity is also referred to as sensory defensiveness). Children who tend to be overly sensitive often struggle with sleeping, eating, dressing or any form of sensory input. A well-intended comforting hug from a trusted adult or friend can feel extremely uncomfortable and cause dysregulation in a child who is hyper-sensitive.

Hypo-sensitivity – "Hypo" means that there is not enough sensation for any of the senses. Consequently, children who tend to be hypo-sensitive generally under-react to stimuli that should otherwise cause them some discomfort, such as pain or heat. This under-reaction causes them to seek sensory stimulation.

Examples of both hyper- and hypo-sensitivity are provided in Figure 4.4.

When we reflect on the signs of hyper- and hypo-sensitivity, we are better able to understand just how challenging the daily routine – and life itself – can be due to potential triggers being present in every aspect of the indoor and outdoor environment (think back to Shanker's five stressors). Let us hold in mind that all this dysregulation is further exacerbated by an education system that pays scant regard to the role of SI as a vital part of healthy holistic development. Instead, teachers are trained to either reward or punish behaviour – as opposed to equipping them to understand and support it.

The two case studies that follow have been provided by a mother of two boys, Ashley, aged 10-years-old, and Mark, aged five-years-old. Ashley has ADHD, is autistic and has SPD (and is hyper-sensitive), while Mark is autistic and also has SPD (and is hypo-sensitive). While reading, it will become apparent that the sensory triggers and overloads are mostly the opposite for her two children. The first case study concerns Ashley.

Easily distressed by noise

Avoids touch - slight touch can feel painful/uncomfortable

Highly sensitive to smell and bright lights

Wearing clothes and shoes can feel very uncomfortable

Bathing and brushing teeth/hair feel very uncomfortable

Tries to avoid extreme weather, like wind, rain and sun

Finds it difficult to balance (dizziness when using stairs)

Appears 'fussy' with foods, with many food aversions

Hearing – dysregulation in response to sudden, loud noises, even loud chewing noises at the dinner table

Aggression – difficulty concentrating, due to constant noise and distraction

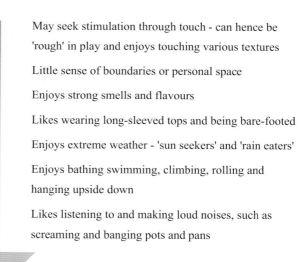

May seek stimulation through touch - can hence be 'rough' in play and enjoys touching various textures

Little sense of boundaries or personal space

Enjoys strong smells and flavours

Likes wearing long-sleeved tops and being bare-footed

Enjoys extreme weather - 'sun seekers' and 'rain eaters'

Enjoys bathing swimming, climbing, rolling and hanging upside down

Likes listening to and making loud noises, such as screaming and banging pots and pans

Figure 4.4 Signs of Hyper- and Hypo-Sensitivity

With regard to visual triggers, Ashley can hear colours. This hypersensitivity is called synaesthesia. Each colour has its own unique sound. He describes louder colours being the more intense shades, like red and purple. He explains this as a loud horn-like noise, whereas mellow colours sound more like a gentle tinkling sound. Visual sensory overload generally happens when there are lots of noisy colours in small spaces, such as bright multi-coloured lights and fireworks. When Ashley is overwhelmed, he tends to want to shut himself in a dark room and close his eyes, covering his ears. We handle this on a daily basis by simply reducing his exposure to such bright colours, and he has a neutrally decorated bedroom. At Christmas time, we buy warm lights, we do not use tinsel and we have minimal decorations.

Ashley struggles with bright lights, preferring cloud and rain to sunshine, because his eyes become sensitive to the level of brightness that the sun can produce. The greatest triggers for him are when the sun is particularly low in the sky, like in winter. He struggles with car journeys when the sun flickers in and out of the windows, and this can cause a meltdown.

Ashley has become good at identifying when this is a problem, and he takes a hooded top in the car with him and covers his head when he experiences this sensory overload.

With regard to auditory triggers, Ashley is extremely sensitive to sound. He can hear an aeroplane much sooner than myself or his brother can. The level of noise from things like bins being moved, me scraping his dinner plate, or even his brother chewing his food sends Ashley into sensory overload. He hears every sound at night time, which impacts his sleep, as he is easily woken. However, when it comes to making noise himself, he has a tendency to be very loud. That is, if he is watching a scene from his favourite film, he will turn the volume up to maximum on the television, or if he is taking part in a group activity, he will shout and try to drown out the sound of his peers. We handle these sensitivities by allowing him to have ear defenders wherever we go, or his favourite music on ear phones. We also use a fan for "white noise" in the evening. Ashley receives support through a teaching assistant at school to help him engage appropriately with his peers and when she identifies that he is becoming overwhelmed, she takes Ashley for a sensory break, where he is offered to roll on a gym ball in a quiet, empty space.

Ashley is highly sensitive to touch and hates to be touched. If I accidentally brush past him, he will say that it has physically hurt his skin. He hates brushing his teeth, his hair and washing, so personal care is a daily trigger for Ashley's sensory overload. Haircuts are also a "no-no," but we finally found someone he trusts, so he recently got his hair cut after well over a year! I purchased specific toothbrushes for Ashley which have softer bristles, we also have children's toothpaste, as the flavour isn't so strong, because he says that the mint burns his tongue. I do not force him to brush his hair because it's curly, so we are fortunate enough to condition it and leave it to dry curly. Instead of showering, he has baths and I let him choose the time of day the bathes and the scent of his bubble bath.

With regard to his proprioception, Ashley often needs to feel that he is using his muscles and joints when he is feeling cross. This type of feedback calms him, because it's a release of tension and he benefits from the physical feedback.

Punching bags, punching cushions and doing push kicks are an excellent way to get proprioceptive satisfaction. I enrolled him into a Muay Thai (martial art and combat sport) class and he is feeling the benefits from releasing this energy and feeling the after effects in his muscles. When we are at home, small triggers such as not being able to do what he wants, his brother annoying him, or change in circumstances can trigger his need for this feedback. When we are home, punching pillows, pushing against a wall, or my hands help to provide this feedback for him.

Now read the case study about Mark and then answer the questions that follow.

Triggers for Mark, particularly as a toddler and his gustatory sense, meant that he would only eat beige foods or toast. For every meal, he would want to eat plain boiled pasta with grated cheese on top. This stage lasted for a few months, until it transitioned to him only wanting to eat cucumber and strawberries. When offered a different meal he would wince, move the food around his plate and refuse to eat.

Now at five-years-old, he enjoys a healthy, balanced diet. He does, however, eat to excess, mainly because he enjoys the sensory experience of eating. He enjoys the taste and the crunch of certain foods, chewing the food and he likes the feeling of being full. Mark has, at times, over-eaten until he has made himself sick. We monitor his food intake and allow him a number of healthy snacks each day, limiting the amount of fatty, sugary or carbohydrate-heavy foods. I cook all his meals from scratch, so that I can ensure he is getting a healthy diet.

Mark loves to spin, climb, hang upside down, jump and run and has exceptional balance. Providing activities to satisfy his vestibular sense acts as a regulatory experience for him.

When Mark is becoming in need of vestibular feedback, we take him somewhere he can safely climb and swing. We let him jump, climb and hang on the sofa cushions. Jumping and holding hands also helps and allowing him to spin while holding his hands in the air. This satisfies his need for vestibular feedback and calms him down.

Mark loves touch and is very tactile. He will touch flowers, windows, any shop objects, sometimes licking objects to get that sensory feedback. He likes to chew on chew toys and he likes strong hugs. He nuzzles his forehead into ours and can be quite hard at times when he does this. As a younger child, Mark used to bite children. He liked the feedback of flesh on his teeth. His chew necklaces have helped to stop the biting. We allow him to have the freedom to touch things, but he has to be constantly supervised for his own safety.

Of course there will be many behaviours and traits within these too and given that the spectrum is so vast and complex (as I'm progressively learning), I am sure that a child can have a mixture of both hyper- and hypo-sensitivities. My eldest has more recently started to display behaviours from both categories.

As both case studies present, children with SPD generally respond to sensation more quickly and intensely than others, with some showing signs of both hyper- and hypo-sensitivities (as the children's mother highlighted). A child who is hypo-sensitive might also have:

■ Hypo-vision – experiencing trouble figuring out where objects are

■ Hypo-hearing – seeking sounds and enjoying the loudest places they can find in the home or setting

■ Hypo-taste/smell – chewing and/or smelling anything they can get hold of

■ Hypo-tactility – the inability to detect pain or temperature

■ Vestibular hyposensitivity – seeking out and enjoying all sorts of movement and spinning or swinging for a long time without feeling dizzy or nauseated

■ Proprioceptive hypo-sensitivity – difficulty knowing where their bodies are in space and often being unaware of their own body sensations (such as feeling hungry).

Now that you have read both case studies, respond to the following questions.

Rewind. Reflect. Write!

1a In your own words, explain what sensory integration is.

1b Why is it important to child development and learning? Discuss.

2 Conduct some desk-based research on primitive reflexes. Write at least two paragraphs on its role in achieving:

    a Healthy physical development

    b Self-regulation.

3a Reflecting on both case studies, note down the signs of hyper-sensitivity that you came across.

3b Now note the signs of hypo-sensitivity that you came across.

3c Were there any signs of SPD that you were not previously aware of? Discuss.

4a Outline the ways the boys' mother supported their respective sensitivities.

4b What behaviours of both children might be misinterpreted as "challenging"?

4c How could these children be supported at school?

5 How might policies embedded in self-regulation and co-regulation be helpful to children with SPD? Discuss.

6a Reflecting on the list of the signs of hyper- and hypo-sensitivity, do any more come to mind? Note these down.

6b Identify some in-the-moment strategies that could help children surmount these sensitivities.

7 Is sensory overload an issue for you? Discuss what triggers this in you.

Sensory Processing Difficulties and Learning Ability

As discussed in Chapter 1, SR and executive functioning skills are the bedrock of effective learning and life itself. Executive functioning skills in particular enable goal-directed behaviours, which are essential in all aspects of daily living. This includes school activities, playing and socializing. Yet recent studies (Brown et al., 2021; Pastor-Cerezuela et al., 2020; Romero-Ayuso et al., 2020; Hornix et al., 2019; Morgan et al., 2017; Case-Smith et al., 2015) found that sensory processing difficulties predicted executive and cognitive challenges in inhibitory control, auditory sustained attention and short-term verbal memory in autistic children and those who have ADHD within a school context. It is therefore perhaps expected that research findings continue to demonstrate a strong association between hyper- and hypo-sensitivity and poor academic performance and social functioning (Maciver et al., 2019; Miller et al., 2018; Blair and Raver, 2015).

As we know, SR and executive functioning skills depend on the development and maturation of the frontal areas of the brain, specifically the PFC, but the PFC of children with ADHD is under-active, whereas a larger PFC with excessive (but under-developed) neurons in this brain region are a key feature of autism, which might account for the ritualistic behaviours in the condition. Both skills are significantly impacted by the presence of ACEs, SEND and SPD. Thus, trying to navigate life and learning at school can be extremely challenging, as all those important higher-order, academic skills are more difficult to execute while the child tries to simultaneously process stimuli that they are bombarded with at school. Although legislation and policies have enabled more autistic children and children with SEND to engage in mainstream education, these children still have a constant battle, trying to manage (for example) SPD alongside cognitive, social and physical domains of wellbeing and learning.

Consider for a moment the many sensory triggers in school settings and their impact on a child: fluorescent lighting, loud and brightly decorated classrooms, smells of food and the hustle and bustle of a lunch hall – all this and much more can feel extremely uncomfortable for a child with SPD. If unsupported, SR and socialization skills become compromised – particularly making and maintaining friendships. In relation to these findings, Romero-Ayuso et al. (2020: 11) highlight the connection between SEND (including sensory processing difficulties) and socialization difficulties:

> Researchers continue to report that in children with neurodevelopmental conditions (for instance, autism and ADHD), deficiencies in executive functions, such as planning, organization, and working memory are associated with a greater degree of isolation in the schoolyard and with difficulties at managing friendships.

The presence of sensory impairments likely precede deficits in social functioning (Butera et al., 2020; van der Kruk et al., 2017; Cascio et al., 2016), with studies (Blair and Raver, 2015; Ausderau et al., 2014) concluding that, according to teachers, autistic children show more difficulty in social participation and that difficulties with social participation, alongside difficulties in proprioception, seem to be more characteristic of ADHD. Think back to Chapter 3 – the brain's "panic button," the amygdala, was discussed in relation to its primary role in triggering the fight or flight response: it is no different with SPD. When someone experiences sensitivity to sounds, it is thought that the amygdala pays more attention to sounds than it needs to, which results in the child entering a state of anxiety and dysregulation more readily, because they are very easily and quickly alerted by the sounds around them, which impedes their ability to focus and engage fully in the experience of school and all it offers. Imagine trying to listen to a teacher's instructions or engaging in a conversation with your friends, but because you perceive sounds with higher intensity, due to hyper-sensitivities, you find it too painful. Over time, avoidance will be drawn on as a coping mechanism, which will further compound the challenges in learning, socialization and holistic wellbeing.

The following case study was provided by a mother of an eight-year-old girl, whose SPD, she explains, pervades all areas of her life, as well as her family's. Her parents chose to home educate because they thought that the multi-sensory triggers of a typical school environment would be constantly overwhelming for their daughter. While reading, think about the all-encompassing nature of SPD that is presented and its impact on a child's quality of life.

My daughter has SPD. Her main triggers are around sound and smell. Sound is a big issue. She explains that it hurts her body and muffles her brain. She doesn't like loud noises or lots of different sounds at the same time. She finds the noise distracting, she is unable to concentrate and it can lead to heightened emotions. If we have to be in an environment with noise, we mainly get around this by using ear defenders. She often requests calm time when we get home, which is a time when no senses can be heightened.

Smell (I feel is the worse one for me) causes her to feel sick. She will sit by the toilet worrying that she will be sick — and sometimes she is. The smells of food cooking can lead to further distress and aversions, as she won't then look at or taste the meals due to their smell while cooking. Fish is a complete no-go for us, as the smell of fish is her biggest trigger and causes crying, gagging, screaming and a meltdown. She likes a very limited diet — beige foods that are the same each time. (What some call safe foods.) She is brand loyal as these foods are the same where ever we go. We also try to cook with the windows open to eliminate some of the smells. The occupational therapist has discharged her because although "she eats a limited diet, she is eating"!

Clothing doesn't seem as much of a problem for her as it once did. As a toddler she would strip as soon as my back was turned. Now it's mainly tightness, labels, itchiness and socks! We manage this by washing and drying her clothes quickly so that she can wear these again. Her dance uniform has various alternatives, which is helpful.

When we viewed schools, she couldn't cope with the walk around, the noises, smells and visuals, which were all too much for her. SPD controls her little life — it's more than just SPD, it is lack of confidence, self-doubt, worry, anxiety, lack of trust and general distress. Her SPD affects us as a whole family and can really limit what we do, where we eat and where we can go. At this age, she can express things much better now that she is getting older. Although she still has daily meltdowns, the more we build our knowledge, the more we are supporting and equipping her to overcome these more swiftly.

One key positive outcome which comes through this case study is the family building their knowledge of SPD and its signs and using this to support and equip their child to manage and overcome her triggers. As the child grows older, she too will be able to exert even more control and choice in navigating her way through life with SPD and, as a result, minimize the incidence of triggers and dysregulation.

As demonstrated, managing SPD can be particularly difficult to achieve at school – but it does not make the task insurmountable. Taking the time to get to know each unique child and their triggers is critical if they are to be supported to overcome these. No child needs to be excluded from any experience – it just requires due care and consideration – and a willingness to adapt what is offered. This simple truth was identified by founder of the highly regarded and innovative Children's Clinic in Vienna, Irwin Lazar, who firmly believed that the child's neurological condition was not the problem but that they were perpetually disadvantaged by a culture that had "written them off" and consequently failed to utilize teaching methods suited to these children's unique needs. When I ask teachers what they could do to meet the needs of a child with SPD, I am too frequently met with responses concerning the need for the child to adapt to the school environment, because a teacher cannot meet one child's needs in a class of 30. I beg to differ. It may at times be difficult, but I know that excellent, child-centred practice does exist.

Ongoing barriers such as a lack of sufficient training in SEND, SI, basic child development and neuroscience, alongside insufficient funding and resources, of course do not help, but we can nurture the growth, development and talents of each child when we make the effort to accept the child for who they are and "where they are at" and embrace all this involves. The following case study illustrates how one primary school teacher supports children with SPD in various ways, depending on the sensitivities they have.

In my current class, there is a high proportion of autistic children – all of whom have SPD. I support them in different ways, which varies from child to child and on a daily basis, but some things will always be triggering because we are in a classroom where everything is sensory heightened anyway (i.e. colours, lights, noise, people, children moving around and sitting in different places – all this happens constantly). So these are easy to identify and minimize. The more challenging triggers occur when a routine is altered, such as the lunch menu changing, or a packed lunch containing unexpected foods. Whatever the issue or how challenging a child finds it to express what their issue is, I believe it is always surmountable if we first know our children very well and seek to understand what their triggers are and how we can minimize these. I have created passports for children in close collaboration with their parents and previous teachers, so that I understand the child holistically. This way, I am aware of their triggers and am equipped to reduce them.

Sometimes it's information overload, let alone sensory overload! I therefore build in lots of brain breaks (like playing "Simon Says," "touch your toes" and doing simple exercises) and I always vary my lessons frequently – you will rarely see the whole group doing the same thing: some children will be sat down, while others walk around as they work. Seating presents an issue too – be it children disliking being sat at the front or back, or the feel of the chair, so these children can sit where they feel most comfortable and some choose to sit in the book corner while they work.

With the children's permission, I sometimes play music in the background – this is during creative lessons, like art, where we often listen to classical music. In other lessons, some children wear noise cancelling headphones. Other strategies I always use include visual timetables, using neutrally coloured backing paper, and the book area/quiet area, which is particularly popular among those children who are hyper-sensitive and need to take themselves away until they feel calmer.

As the child gets older, it tends to get easier to have conversations with them about their triggers and how I – and they – can help themselves too.

Both case studies underscore the importance of enabling the child to identify and express what their triggers are, how these make them feel and how they need to be supported.

Now have a go at answering these reflective questions.

Rewind. Reflect. Write!

1a Reflecting on the case study by the primary school teacher, what issues are familiar to you?

1b Which of her strategies do you find most effective? Discuss.

2 What is the difference between sensory overload and sensory processing difficulties?

3 Identify and explain at least three strategies to support a child with vestibular hyposensitivity.

4 Identify and explain at least three strategies to support a child with proprioceptive hypo-sensitivity.

Top Tips for Practice!

- Seek support from a Tomatis therapist (website address included in the Bibliography)

- Provide plenty of multi-sensory experiences which stimulate all eight senses and support overall sensory regulation

- Provide plenty of opportunities for movement, including balance, crawling, creeping, hopping, jumping, rolling, climbing, spinning and bear-walking

- Do rhythm work (such as dance, movement, music and drumming)

- Encourage the child to do finger and thumb exercises (including the use of Professional Putty to strengthen finger muscles and grip)

- Seek occupational therapy – be this at school or home

- Try tapping therapy (there are plenty of explainer videos on YouTube)

- Avoid trying to "change" the child – change your mindset instead!

- Build in frequent classroom breaks with movement experiences

- Adapt your provision to help minimize triggering children who have SPD (this requires close collaboration with primary carers)

- Build in lots of experiences/activities to build children's executive functioning skills (games which require turn-taking, sorting, categorizing and matching work well)

- Have noise-cancelling headphones available for the child/ren to use

- Give the child extra time between instructions and also more time before you repeat instructions, to avoid auditory overload

- Provide heavy work activities (those which push or pull on the body) with the child prior to going into noisy environments.

Self-Regulation in Children With SEND

The impact of the various stressors you looked at earlier is often more profound in children who have SEND.

What Do We Mean by SEND?

According to the SEND Code of Practice (Department for Education, 2015), a child or young person has SEND if they have a learning difficulty or disability that calls for special educational provision to be made for them. Children with SEND often have difficulty in at least one of the following four areas (in reality, many children experience difficulties that cut across these areas):

- Communication and interaction – Children with speech, language and communication difficulties may find it hard to express themselves or to understand others. This can make it challenging for a child to interact with others, make friends, communicate their thoughts effectively and understand what is being said to them. This might include children who experience speech and language delay. Autistic children are included in this area, due to potential difficulties with social interaction

- Cognition and learning – This area of SEND affects a child's ability to think, understand and learn. Some children have very complex and severe learning difficulties and will need support to access all areas of the curriculum. However, children with specific learning difficulties, such as dyslexia or dyspraxia, may only need support to learn specific skills

- Social, emotional and mental health – These difficulties can present themselves in a wide variety of ways. For example, a child may be extremely withdrawn, find it challenging to manage relationships with other people or demonstrate disruptive behaviours. Underlying mental health difficulties such as anxiety and depression may be the cause. Alternatively, a child may have been diagnosed with a condition such as ADHD, which means that they have difficulties with knowing what to focus on, maintaining attention and/or impulsive behaviour

- Sensory and/or physical needs – This area covers children who have a disability or medical condition that affects their learning and prevents them from making use of generally provided educational facilities. For example, children with sensory needs such as visual or hearing impairments may need additional support or equipment to access learning.

How Stressors Influence the Ability of a Child With SEND to Self-Regulate

Children with SEND are particularly sensitive to some of the stressors you looked at earlier. This will often be expressed through their behaviour. If you are presented with behaviour that you find difficult to understand, apply the five-domain model and think about whether their behaviour is a response to the stressors present at the time.

Let us look at some examples.

Joel is autistic and becomes overwhelmed by strong sensory stimulation. For example, he will put his hands over his ears if he hears a loud or sudden noise. If the noise persists, he becomes extremely distressed and staff find it hard to calm him. He cries and sometimes lies on the floor, kicking out at others.

In this example, a stressor in the **biological domain** (noise) stops Joel from being able to self-regulate his emotions and behaviour.

The need for order and routine is a common characteristic of autism and Joel is no different. In fact, he gets a great deal of comfort and security from his routine (for example, having his key worker meet him as he enters nursery each day and having certain toys available to play with). He becomes extremely anxious if this routine is changed. There have been occasions where his favourite toys have not been available and he has banged his head against the wall until suitable replacements could be found.

In these examples, we can see that the stressor is in the **cognitive domain**. Joel becomes cognitively dysregulated when his routine is changed. In other words, he finds it hard to rationalize (make sense of) the changes and problem-solve.

Joel finds it difficult to join in with the games that other children play, as he does not understand the social rules. He can become aggressive with others if he feels left out.

His difficulties in playing with his peers indicate that stressors in the **social domain** make it hard for him to regulate his mood and behaviour.

Rewind. Reflect. Write!

Have a look at the following scenarios and try to identify the stressors that are affecting each child and the domain to which they belong.

Katya

Katya has dyslexia and has been asked to write a short paragraph about what she did over the summer holidays. She finds it hard to get her thoughts down on paper, to think phonologically about words and to form certain letters. Her classmates get on with the task quickly, which makes Katya feel embarrassed and frustrated. One child laughs because she writes some of her letters backwards. She slams her pen down and rushes out of the classroom.

Ahmed

Ahmed has social anxiety and finds social situations quite traumatic, especially when he is asked to speak in front of others. As a very young child, he even went through a period of selective mutism. He now experiences panic attacks whenever he thinks a teacher might ask him a question in class or he has to speak to somebody that he does not know.

Molly

Molly has ADHD. Although she has difficulties with restlessness and impulsive behaviour, her main difficulties are with inattention. She finds it hard to focus and concentrate and has difficulty with retaining information and memory recall. This means she finds it hard to complete tasks and manage her time and she often loses things. Her teachers negatively label her a "daydreamer" and "lazy." This makes Molly feel angry and depressed, as she believes that she is trying her best, while trying to control the thoughts that stop her focusing on her work. Molly is often punished by missing out on playtime in order to complete tasks.

Many children with SEND struggle with SR, sensory processing and executive functioning. This means they have an increased risk of social isolation and behavioural difficulties such as disruptive and aggressive behaviour. Caregivers need to be patient and sensitive in their support. Taking the time to understand the child's individual stressors across each domain of SR is extremely important. We will now look at two common neurodevelopmental conditions, autism and ADHD, respectively.

Autism – Different. Not Deficient

Recent statistics from the Department for Education (2021) show there are 163,041 autistic children in schools – more than 70% of these children and young people attend mainstream schools. One recent study (Chance, 2021) demonstrated that 74% of parents were unhappy with the SEN support provided by their child's school. This may well be due to the complex nature of autism itself. Its history is one full of myths and conflicting information, which is compounded by the absence of any consistent teacher training and EY professional development programmes that could inform and equip practitioners – and children to better understand and meet the unique needs of autistic children (Chance, 2021; Department for Education, 2021; Hill et al., 2021; Bailey and Baker, 2020; Campbell et al., 2019; Ravet, 2015).

Neurobiological Understandings of Autism

The raft of evidence from neuroscience concerning the causes and multifaceted nature of autism is compelling (Grandin, 2020). Advances in technology and neuroimaging techniques are making things visible with incredible precision, to the extent that we can examine inside neurons to see how information travels. In line with these advances, contrary to long-held beliefs, neuroscience confirms that autism is a neurodevelopmental condition, with neural differences occurring on a large scale (Minshew and Williams, 2007). Muhle et al. (2017: 514) explain that:

> The advent of next-generation sequencing technology, advanced imaging techniques, and cutting-edge molecular techniques for modelling autism has allowed researchers to define autism risk-related biological pathways and circuits that may, for the first time, unify the effects of disparate risk factors into common neurobiological mechanisms.

Autism is multi-organ and multi-sensory in nature, with pervasive, lifelong impact on the nervous system, language, attention, communication and social interactions. Researchers Minshew and Williams (2007: 6) highlight the invaluable insights that continue to be provided by the use of functional magnetic resonance imaging (fMRI) studies, which are contributing to the advancement of understanding concerning the origins of autism. They explain:

> The structural imaging findings have led to the near general acceptance of autism as a condition originating in the brain rather than in behaviour, a subtle but significant distinction. (Social theories hold that lack of motivation to interact is the initiating event in autism and results in failure of brain circuitry to develop).

Note how the authors highlight a key myth here – that social theories attribute the condition to a lack of motivation to interact, which in turn causes the different functionality in the brain. This, of course, is not the case at all but, taken at face value, might lead to a dismissive attitude concerning the importance of nurturing the child's social skills and socialization – an attitude of "what's the point?"

The divergent brain development of autistic individuals is also attributable to the factors bullet-pointed in the following list. Please note that other factors were also considered but left out of this list, as the supporting evidence is inconclusive.

■ Over-growth of cortical brain regions (with increased head circumference). This brain overgrowth disrupts the development of normal brain structure and function in these regions

■ Mirror neuron system (MNS) differences, which reduce the ability to understand others' emotional states and intentions

- Reduced size in the corpus callosum (as discussed in Chapter 3 – the bundle of fibres that connects the left and right hemispheres of the brain, carrying information received in one hemisphere over to the other)

- Larger and over-aroused amygdala – which could result in hyper-sensitivity and difficulty in regulating emotions and behaviour (Tottenham et al., 2014)

- Specific changes in gene expression which contribute to symptoms of autism by altering the function of brain circuits (Velmeshev et al., 2019)

- Heritability – some studies demonstrate up to 80% heritability (Bai et al., 2019).

Emotional Dysregulation in Autism

As each of the previous factors highlights, autism manifests differently in each child, which is due to diverse factors, including but not confined to genetics, neurobiology, the presence of other conditions, the intensity of the condition and the support mechanisms the child has available to them. Inability to recognize facial expressions or tone, delays in recognition and processing of certain stimuli and heightened impact of and hyper-sensitivity to noises are common characteristics of autism – all of which can be misconstrued as "poor behaviour" to be dealt with, as opposed to emotional dysregulation (ED) that needs to be co-regulated and worked through. ED triggers a range of emotional and behavioural responses, from mild to severe, including anxiety and depression, dysregulation, aggressive and self-harming behaviours.

Some autistic children often experience ED because of various factors, including difficulty in:

- Recognizing emotions

- Understanding other perspectives

- Thinking flexibly

- Shifting attention

- Navigating the demands of a busy day

- Managing unexpected changes

- Regulating sensory experiences.

Awareness of the individual child's unique needs and triggers can be immensely powerful in minimizing incidents of ED, which, if left unaddressed, could increase the risk of a variety of psychiatric conditions across the life course. Reflecting on the five domains of SR and the stressors in each of these domains will enable you to effectively identify what the child needs in that moment to regain equilibrium.

Listed are some statements from parents who have shared their children's experiences of emotional and physical dysregulation in order to increase understanding of just a few of the behaviours that manifest in autism – behaviours that can easily be mistaken for "challenging" or "naughty." Read the statements and answer the questions that follow.

1 When L runs, shaking his head and grunting, I know that this is his way of telling me that his body does not feel OK. It might be due to frustration or anger. Some people may think he is having a "funny five minutes" or not listening, if he is asked to stop or sit down, but this is his way of self-regulating. I have a gym ball for him and an indoor trampoline. I also throw cushions on the floor from the sofa so that he can climb, jump and roll on the ball. I have put weights in a doll's push chair for him to push around the house so that he can achieve the sensory input he craves.

2 Many people view W's screaming meltdowns as negative behaviour or "tantruming." In fact, this is a classic meltdown. When he is in this zone, I keep him safe, his brother safe, stay close to him and reassure him until he is able to listen and respond. Can you imagine being a child exhibiting this deeply painful sensory experience and being punished on top of this?

3 N loves to lick my arm – he does this a lot to a range of objects. Some may incorrectly deem this behaviour as attention seeking. What I do to manage this is offer a range of diverse textures in foods and when he has an episode, I offer him ice lollies or chewy foods to occupy his mouth until he feels more regulated.

Rewind. Reflect. Write!

1a Which symptoms of autism do you think prove most challenging for teachers? Discuss.

1b How might these be overcome?

2 Ideally, how might schools generally better support autistic children's well-being and ability to learn?

3 Reflecting on W's dysregulation, how else might he be supported to reach calm?

4 How might we enable children to understand their feelings more, so that they can identify "big feelings" before their bodies spontaneously react?

5 Explain the benefits of encouraging shifting attention (such as focusing on a sensation in the body or thinking about an interest) during times of emotional dysregulation.

Let us now turn our attention to another common neurodevelopmental condition, ADHD.

ADHD – Busy Minds, Busy Bodies

This section explores ADHD, including its *aetiology* (its causes and the science explaining these causes) and symptoms. The advantages of having ADHD will also be included in this chapter.

ADHD is one of the most common problems in psychiatry, with up to five in every 100 children affected in the United Kingdom (Sayal et al., 2018), and left unchecked, childhood ADHD may lead to lower educational, occupational and social outcomes (Albrecht et al., 2015). Magnus et al. (2022: 1) explain that:

> Symptoms should be present before the age of 12, have lasted six months and interfere with daily life activities in order to be labelled as ADHD. This must be present in more than one setting (at home and at school, or at school and at afterschool activities).

These researchers emphasize the pervasive nature of ADHD, with all domains of a child's life being affected from early childhood. Albrecht et al. (2015: 3) further explain that its main symptoms persist across the life trajectory.

> The core symptoms of ADHD are present in approximately 5% of children and adolescents, irrespective of cultural background and with a strong overrepresentation of boys. In about one or two out of three of children with ADHD, the symptom may persist with clinical significance into adulthood, leading to a slightly lower prevalence of more than 3% in adults (larger in higher income countries), which makes ADHD a life-long problem for many patients.

We can all be a bit forgetful, restless or find ourselves drifting off at times. We might feel overwhelmed at the tasks ahead of us and find ourselves struggling to get organized and achieve goals. This does not necessarily indicate ADHD in children or adults. It is when these behaviours are developmentally inappropriate and persist over time that ADHD could be considered.

What Does ADHD Look Like?

The following are my "top 20" signs of ADHD. Some may be more familiar to you as a primary carer of someone who has ADHD or, indeed, as someone who has the condition themselves. While reading, more symptoms may come to your mind. Make a note to explore these and the reasons for their presence (such as any environmental influences that might be exacerbating these).

- Hyperactivity/restlessness

- Impulsivity

- Incessant talking/interrupting

- Hyper-focus

- Lack of attention

- Lack of concentration

- Disorganization/poor planning

- Difficulty completing tasks

- Forgetfulness

- Losing things

- Poor time management

- Problems focusing on a task

- Difficulty with multi-tasking

- Low frustration tolerance

- Frequent mood swings

- Low self-esteem

- Anxiety

- Depression

- Quick temper

- Trouble coping with stress.

Reflecting on that list, it can be easy to think of ADHD as a blight on one's life. It can be debilitating and consequently depressing, due to the simplest of tasks not being undertaken or being done too late. Homework can easily be forgotten, friends can be let down and thinking often comes after acting – much to the frustration of everyone concerned. Regulating one's emotions can also prove very challenging due to an overactive limbic system and dysfunctional frontal lobe (where those fundamentally important executive functions reside). When we consider that young children are already trying to acquire and master skills across a range of domains, having ADHD makes this all the more difficult – not least because they can barely regulate their attention long enough to learn anything. This is discussed further on in this chapter.

There are, however, advantages to having ADHD, and hence, some individuals with ADHD would not change their neurodivergence (myself included). Although I find it extremely difficult to concentrate for more than a few minutes, am forgetful, over-zealous in the projects I take on, hyper-sensitive and have excessive energy, I know that my industriousness is largely attributable to my having ADHD. I would not choose a life without it and over the years, I have learned to manage the more obstructive traits so that their interference is reduced.

Take a look at the more positive qualities in the following list and make a note of any more that come to mind.

- Authentic
- Rebellious
- Hyper-focus
- Sensitivity
- Risk-taking
- Creativity
- Attention to detail
- Lateral thinking
- High energy
- Abundant ideas
- Passionate
- Resilient
- Intuitive
- Inventive
- Imaginative
- Tenacious.

Looking at the qualities on this list, you may well think that some are self-limiting as opposed to being advantageous. Take, for example, high energy and rebelliousness – traits that can get a child or adult into trouble – but these traits allow us to eschew conformity, to dare to be and do different – and to channel our abundant energy into various projects simultaneously. We are undeniably complex – perhaps more so than the neurotypical individual – but the passion, along with the creative and industrious aspects to the condition somewhat compensate for the trickier ones that need to be navigated on a daily basis.

The Neurobiology of ADHD

ADHD is the most common neurodevelopmental condition (Wilens and Spencer, 2010). Approximately 9% of school aged children have ADHD, while 8% of adults have the condition, with traits such as restlessness and disorganization manifesting more than hyperactivity. It is largely genetic, with biological and environmental factors such as maternal smoking, prematurity, low birth weight and ACEs also being possible contributory factors.

ADHD impacts the way the brain regulates attention and impulse control. Research (Magnus et al., 2022; Leahy, 2018; Cortese et al., 2012; Swanson et al., 2007) indicates three main neurobiological causes of ADHD (but it is important to note that multiple brain pathways are implicated):

■ Dysfunctional reward centre

■ Reduced volume and activity in the frontal lobe

■ Reduced volume of the limbic system.

These causes will now be addressed.

Figure 4.5 highlights part of the reward network, in which the caudate nucleus and globus pallidus (both parts of the basal ganglia) reside. Both the caudate nucleus and globus pallidus contain a high density of dopamine receptors – but these are smaller in the ADHD brain. This difference can cause an individual to engage in immediately pleasurable activities to get that "dopamine kick" due to this consequent dopamine deficiency (Swanson et al., 2007).

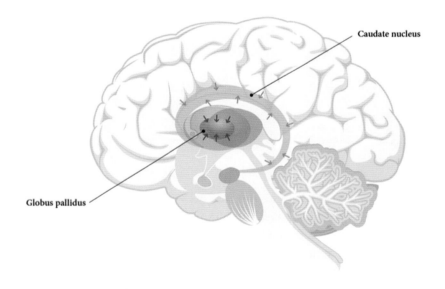

Reduced globus pallidus and caudate nucleus

Figure 4.5 The Reward Network

Source: Swanson, J. M., Kinsbourne, M., Nigg, J., Lanphear, B., Stefanatos, G., Volkow, N., Taylor, E., Casey, B., Castellanos, F. and Wadhwa, P. (2007). Biologic Sub-Types of ADHD: Brain Imaging, Molecular, Genetic and Environmental Factors and the Dopamine Hypothesis. *Neuropsychology Review*, 17(1), 31–59.

The nucleus accumbens (part of the basal ganglia), as shown in Figure 4.6, is the main component of the ventral striatum (part of the reward pathway and involved in reward processing). This is implicated as a cause of ADHD because it tends to be reduced in the ADHD brain. This is thought to be a contributory factor in hyperactivity and impulsivity (Tripp and Wickens, 2009).

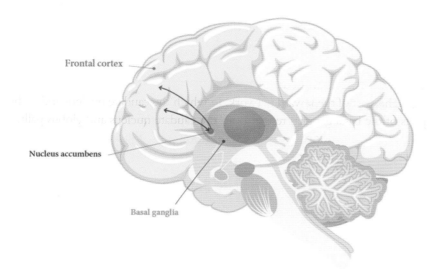

Frontal cortex

Nucleus accumbens

Basal ganglia

Reduced activation of prefrontal and striatal regions (nucleus accumbens and basal ganglia structures)

Figure 4.6 Reduced Activation of the Prefrontal Cortex

Source: Tripp, G. and Wickens, J. R. (2009). Neurobiology of ADHD. *Neuropharmacology*, 57(7–8): 579–589.

Low levels of two key neurotransmitters, dopamine and noradrenaline, are also indicated in ADHD. These neurotransmitters are also integral to maintaining thoughts; thus, a deficiency of noradrenaline within the frontal cortex, as highlighted in Figure 4.6, can cause inattention, diminished executive functioning and difficulties with organizing and evaluating actions – all critical skills for academic achievement and, indeed, in effectively managing daily life. SR of one's emotions and behaviour, including reaching calm and overcoming frustration will also prove difficult, due to deficient levels of dopamine in the limbic system and atypical function in the amygdala, the ventral striatum and the frontal cortex. Reduced volume and activity in the frontal lobe are also implicated in ADHD. This has a direct, pervasive impact on the individual's ability to concentrate and to filter out distractions – this is, of course, a recipe for disaster in all areas of life: in achieving effective communication and in getting along at school or at work. Shaw et al. (2014: 2) are unequivocal about the ubiquity of the adverse effects of emotional dysregulation, especially in children with ADHD:

> The combination of ADHD and emotion dysregulation represents a major source of impairment. In a study of 1,500 children, emotional problems had a greater impact than hyperactivity and inattention on wellbeing and self-esteem. Individuals with ADHD and emotion dysregulation were significantly more impaired in peer relationships, family life, occupational attainment and academic performance than those with ADHD alone.

Rewind. Reflect. Write!

1a Select three of the "top 20" signs of ADHD. What could be triggering these in a child?

1b Suggest three strategies to help minimize these in a child.

2 In your own words, explain the three neurobiological causes of ADHD.

3 Explain the implications of a lack of self-regulation in a child with ADHD.

4 Children with ADHD have trouble using their executive functioning skills. Suggest three ways in which you could help build these skills.

5 In your own words, describe the affected key brain regions in:

    a Autism

    b ADHD.

6a Outline some similarities between autism and ADHD.

6b Now outline the differences between the two.

Self-Regulation: Up or Down?

Reflecting on the possible causes of SI issues that have been presented throughout this chapter, the experiences/activities you choose to help the child self-regulate will differ, depending on the root cause and the sensory need at the time. It can also be very tricky trying to figure out what is suitable in-the-moment. Squeezing a stress ball, for example, will help to down-regulate a hyper-sensitive child, due to the rhythmic movement and distraction required to focus on squeezing, whereas for a hypo-sensitive child, it might be useful, as squeezing a stress ball requires energy and provides that necessary sensory feedback. The up- and down-regulatory activities will depend on the child and context, so sometimes an up-regulatory activity, such as crashing into a pillow, could help a hyper-sensitive child to re-focus their energy outlet and help them to calm down, while also helping a hypo-sensitive child to up-regulate, due to the energy required to crash into a pillow. Ultimately, the activities are not always either/or/clear cut, so your knowledge of the child and in-the-moment observations will guide you in terms of what they need. Some ideas are included in Table 4.2.

Table 4.2 Activities to Up-Regulate (Stimulate) or Down-Regulate (Calm) a Child

Ideas to Up-Regulate (Stimulate)	Ideas to Down-Regulate (Calm)
■ Hitting, kicking or bouncing a ball	■ Breathing exercises, such as blowing bubbles
■ Pushing, pulling or rocking	■ Having a cosy space to crawl into and relax
■ Singing/rapping	■ Big hugs and head and shoulder massages
■ Dancing	■ Tapping
■ Chewing crunchy foods	■ Picturing a happy place or favourite activity
■ Crashing into pillows or a crash pad	■ Naming five favourite things
■ Wheelbarrow walking	■ Breathing in a favourite or soothing scent
■ Squeezing a stress ball or making playdough	■ Practicing yoga/mindfulness
■ Shouting/screaming into a cushion	■ Identifying emotions with an adult
■ Ripping up or crumpling a piece of paper	■ Being in nature/outside
■ Chair push-ups	■ Listening to soothing music
■ Outdoor activities, like raking or sweeping	■ Repeating positive affirmations

Top Tips for Practice!

■ Seek free online training concerning SEND for you and your team

■ Create a (visual) routine and involve the child in its creation – this can help ease the anxiety of what is often a confusing and overwhelming world for autistic children and those who have ADHD

■ Use clocks and timers

■ Integrate the interests of the child into the learning experience – forming highly focused interests is a trait of both autism and ADHD. Use these as a gateway to their learning

- Use the activities to up-regulate or down-regulate children, as needed

- Permit fidget toys at home and in the setting. These can help to instil calm and focus

- Do not expect children to sit still for lengthy periods, listening to instructions – this will only heighten feelings of stress and anxiety while inhibiting attention

- Make learning fun! Invent games, incorporate fun songs and get children moving as much as possible!

- Keep your instructions brief, clear and bite-sized. Support the child to understand and redirect them if they go "wrong"

- For older children with ADHD, help them to make and use simple checklists, crossing items off as they accomplish them – a great way to build their organizational skills

- Provide children with responsibilities at home and in the setting, giving meaningful praise for their efforts. This can do wonders in boosting self-confidence

- Swap screen time for physical activity – a great emotion regulator while keeping children physically healthy

- Do not use threats of punishment or punish children when they do not conform to your expectations. More on this in Chapter 5.

Concluding Thoughts

As has been presented in this chapter, there exists a range of reasons some children experience SI issues. Having SI issues can hugely impact a child's ability to self-regulate, and if a child is placed in an environment that is not suited to their needs (while actually triggering them), they will feel unable to manage their feelings and become easily dysregulated. Equipping ourselves with up-to-date knowledge about the unique child and their neurodevelopmental condition(s) not only helps to minimize the stressors for these children but also maximizes their ability to learn. On this note, the take-away message from this chapter is that practitioners need to embrace ways of working with children that are child-led, because generally, this is how they learn most effectively. This means, for example, rethinking your indoor and outdoor environments, your expectations of children with SEND (ensuring that these are not low or misguided by any stereotypes) and your expectations of how children should listen when taking instructions. It is high time to eschew traditional ways of working and dare to do different – hopefully, this chapter has provided you with some simple strategies to take forward in your daily practice, which can make learning more accessible and enjoyable for every child.

Further Reading

- Abraham, D. (2017). *The Superkids Activity Guide to Conquering Every Day: Awesome Games and Crafts to Master Your Moods, Boost Focus, Hack Mealtimes and Help Grownups Understand Why You Do the Things You Do*. Boston: Page Street Publishing Co.

A practical guide for children and adults alike, which helps children who have sensory processing issues to better understand their bodies and their strengths (or superpowers). The book contains 75 activities to help children navigate the demands of the daily routine while giving children a sense of control through the activities and the self-regulatory skills that each one helps to develop.

- Ayres, J. (2005). *Sensory Integration and the Child*. Los Angeles: Western Psychological Services.

Ayres' seminal text on sensory integration is a must-read for anyone wanting to understand more about sensory integration. It is easy to navigate and read, packed full of information about the neuroscientific foundations of sensory integration by Ayres, alongside more contemporary commentaries by other researchers.

- Davies, C., Healy, M. and Smith, D. (2018). *The Maze of Learning. Developing Motor Skills*. Croydon: Fit-2-Learn CIC.

This book is vital reading for every school setting and home. The authors break down the subjects of primitive reflexes and sensory integration – fundamentally important subjects that are yet to be fully understood and embedded within the education system. It is written in a highly accessible style and is of immediate practical use, with a wide range of activities designed to promote development of gross motor skills, core strength, posture, mid-line crossing and proprioception – which all help to integrate all the primitive reflexes and enable the child to achieve sensory integration. Case studies and a suggested programme of activities are also included to support this process.

5 Time Out for Behaviour Management

Why We Must Move Towards Relational Approaches to Support Behaviour

Adults who choose to punish children physically or emotionally are making that flawed choice. It is *never* necessary – nor is it effective in re-directing behaviour. Perhaps if the pervasive impact of shaming, isolating and physically abusing children were better understood, adults would adopt more empathic and useful approaches to behaviour. As Siegel and Payne Bryson (2015: 32) elucidate:

> When the response is to isolate the child, an instinctual psychological need of the child goes unmet. Brain imaging shows that the experience of relational pain – like that caused by rejection – looks very similar to the experience of physical pain in terms of brain activity.

What to Expect in This Chapter

This chapter presents definitions of behaviour management and examines commonly utilized behaviour management approaches in homes, settings and schools. While it might be expected to present both the advantages and disadvantages of using any approach, this book makes it unequivocally clear that *behaviour management approaches are harmful to children's wellbeing and should be avoided in all homes, schools and settings* – and why. Alternative, relational approaches to nurturing children's behaviour will be presented, with a rationale as to why this must be the way forward for all primary carers and professionals. As part of this discussion, the role of stress in fuelling certain behaviours will be revisited, with emphasis on the short- and long-term neurobiological and physiological effects of toxic stress in particular – and the relevance of this to behaviour. The traditional antecedent, behaviour and consequence (ABC) of behaviour will also be examined, with alternative models provided for you to reflect on and use.

DOI: 10.4324/9781003327479-5

Zones of behaviour will be proposed as an alternative to (for example) the traffic light system, with a clear rationale. Alternatives to behaviour management are examined in detail, with real-life, proven ways to create more nurturing provision. Case studies and questions are included to help consolidate understanding and to help the reader to challenge particular arguments that are put forward. A Further Reading list ends the chapter.

By the End of This Chapter, You Will Be Able to:

- Define and explain what behaviour management is
- Discuss examples of behaviour management and explain how these can be psychologically damaging for children
- Understand why the use of punishments and rewards is ultimately ineffective
- Understand and discuss behaviour management as a safeguarding issue
- Understand behaviour as communication
- Explain the role of toxic stress in influencing behaviour
- Discuss the possible reasons underlying behaviours that are mislabelled as "challenging" (using the iceberg of behaviour)
- Distinguish between intrinsic and extrinsic motivators concerning behaviour
- Discuss alternative, more relational approaches to supporting behaviour
- Compare behaviourist and relational approaches to supporting behaviour
- Discuss the principles and benefits of trauma-informed care
- Outline and critique the key tenets of the zones of behaviour.

What Do We Mean by Behaviour Management?

Behaviour management. Read it back. What connotations does the term have for you? Are they positive or negative? Why? The EYFS (Department for Education, 2021: 34) is limited in its explanation of what behaviour management is, merely stating that:

> Providers are responsible for managing children's behaviour in an appropriate way.

What does this mean exactly? Apart from its clear stipulation that corporal punishment must not be used, it is not a positive definition. Instead, one could infer that it is solely about managing a child's behaviour – no nurturance, no support, no guidance – just objects to be controlled. In a recent article, the head of the regulating body Ofsted (the Office for Standards in Education, Children's Services and Skills), Spielman (2019), explains that:

> Effective behaviour management means that low-level disruption is not tolerated and pupils' behaviour does not disrupt lessons or the day-to-day life of the school.

If behaviour management were genuinely about supporting children to behave in ways that were prosocial and promoted personal growth, space would be provided to acknowledge the impact of poor mental health and the reasons for poor mental health; there would be understanding of ACEs and trauma and how these impact brain development, with due empathy and CR provided for children who are struggling to thrive. When we see words like "not tolerated," we know it means "zero tolerance." This is discussed further on.

Reports such as *Below the Radar* (Ofsted, 2014) and *Pupil Behaviour in Schools in England* (Department of Education, 2012) signified concerns about the impact of misbehaviour on attainment and wellbeing. Yet when we look to more recent guidance from the likes of the Department for Education (DfE), they still advocate *punishing poor behaviour, including detentions* (DfE, 2016: 7). It seems that there is still a long way to go in truly supporting children's ability to self-regulate in schools, with those regulating practice still promoting damaging, non-educational ways of responding to behaviour. There is no mention of the impact of ACEs or trauma on a child's mental health and consequent ability to behave in socially accepted ways or to learn effectively. You are invited to reflect on the message that this sends to children and their families.

A Brief History of Behaviour Management

This section provides an overview of the history of behaviour management in schools, with attention paid to some of the underpinning theories which continue to heavily influence policies and procedures in EY provision and schools.

Teachers have always had to "manage" behaviour in order to maintain a positive climate which is conducive to teaching and learning, and generally, this has meant enforcing behaviour management policies and procedures that attempt to control children's behaviour in order to achieve compliance. Such approaches are informed by key principles of behaviourist theories (Bandura, 1986; Skinner, 1976; Thorndike, 1932; Watson, 1913; Pavlov, 1897). While these will not be examined in any depth in this book, an overview is provided in Table 5.1 which can be used to help inform any further research.

Table 5.1 Behaviourist Theories

Theorist/Theory	Key Tenets of the Theory	What It Looks Like in Practice
Bandura/social learning theory	The idea that humans learn from observing and imitating the behaviour modelled by others. This was demonstrated through Bandura's Bobo doll experiments. (See Chapter 2 for further details on Bandura.)	Encouraging children to learn from each other – particularly in pairs or groups. Motivating children to learn and managing behaviour through the use of positive reinforcement and rewards. For example, a child who is reprimanded for an undesired behaviour is less likely to repeat that behaviour, as are their peers, who will also wish to avoid the negative consequence of replicating the action.
Skinner/operant conditioning	Modifying behaviour through the use of positive or negative reinforcement – operant conditioning occurs when an association is made between a particular behaviour and a consequence for that behaviour. Consequences need to be applied immediately following the behaviour to be effective.	Using rewards to acknowledge and reinforce "good" behaviour, to encourage repetition of the behaviour, and issuing punishments for "bad" behaviour, in the hope that this be extinguished or will occur less frequently.
Thorndike/three laws of learning	1 The law of effect – that pleasant consequences lead to repetition, while unpleasant outcomes extinguish behaviour. 2 The law of readiness – proposes that children will resist learning until they are ready. 3 The law of exercise – that idea that what is practiced strengthens, while what is not practiced becomes weaker.	1 Law of effect – engaging children in hands-on, relevant learning experiences, which provide intrinsic motivation. 2 The law of readiness – if a child is not developmentally ready to learn, rewards and punishments are not going to help: teachers should allow children to learn at their own pace without punishment or rewards. 3 Contrary to social learning theory, the law of exercise proposes that children learn by doing – observing others is not enough to learn a skill.

(Continued)

Table 5.1 (Continued)

Theorist/Theory	Key Tenets of the Theory	What It Looks Like in Practice
Watson/ Little Albert experiment	Watson developed classical behaviourism, having been influenced by Pavlov's earlier work. Watson believed that nurture plays a more significant role in a child's learning and development than nature and that all behaviour is a result of stimulation from the environment or a consequence of the individual's previous conditioning. In the Little Albert experiment, Watson and his colleagues induced a phobia of rats in nine-month-old Albert, who, prior to the experiments, was only scared of loud noises.	Behaviour modification through rewards and consequences. Ignoring or punishing undesired behaviours in order to decrease incidents.
Pavlov/"Pavlov's dogs" (1897)	Classical conditioning – demonstrated through his "Pavlov's dogs" experiment. Although initially accidental, Pavlov went on to show that dogs could be conditioned to salivate at the sound of a bell if that sound was repeatedly presented at the same time the dogs were given food.	Pavlovian conditioning techniques are still used to modify behaviour. Typically, this looks like teachers using positive reinforcement (such as rewards, good grades and verbal praise) to encourage more of the desired behaviour in children and using negative reinforcement (usually in the form of publicly shaming or isolating the child). It also includes removing "privileges," such as time to play.

What is immediately apparent is that much of behaviourist theories rest upon the manipulation of externally observable behaviour through the environment and stimuli within it – chiefly rewarding, ignoring or punishing the behaviour. There is scant regard for the child's mentalization (ability to understand the mental state of oneself or others) or their intrinsic motivation. This is evident in Skinner (1976), who argued that learning is a result of the reinforcement or punishment of behaviours within a context that is deliberately manipulated by the teacher. Thus, a teacher structures their teaching in order to receive the correct response (or behaviour) and uses punishments to ensure that the incorrect response (or behaviour) is avoided. On a superficial level, proponents of behaviour management approaches are correct – it seems to work. This is because the prospect of a reward or punishment is certainly effective in achieving compliance, but ultimately, they work on a superficial level and are only detrimental to children's psychological health and holistic wellbeing (Golding et al., 2021; Kohn, 2018; Dix, 2017). I am yet to meet a child or young adult who has been grateful for being reprimanded or physically abused in the name of behaviour management. I have, however, met countless people who remember teachers for showing understanding and kindness during their emotionally charged moments.

Fast-forward on from those foundational behaviourist theories over a century ago, and despite the plethora of more contemporary, evidence-based relational approaches to supporting behaviour, it remains the norm worldwide to bribe and threaten children and young adults into manipulating them to do what we demand – both in and out of school. This typically looks like promises of a sweet treat or extra screen time "rewarded" at home or "golden time" at school, where children have a limited selection of options to choose from in how they wish to spend some class time. "Winning" extra points or stars on a chart is also commonplace – both at home and at schools (which only serves to cause competitiveness and upset among children). We really must start asking why we persist with such archaic and cruel ways of treating children. As Kohn (2018: 4) says:

> The core of pop behaviourism is "Do this and you'll get that." The wisdom of this technique is very rarely held up for inspection.

Inside Out – Intrinsic Versus Extrinsic Motivation

Using operant conditioning in the classroom is considered an effective classroom management strategy (Dewsbury, 1997) and it is the staple of the majority of schools globally. However, relying on operant conditioning has its drawbacks. Operant conditioning in education relies on extrinsic motivation, or factors outside the students themselves used to motivate behaviours. The disadvantages of relying on extrinsic motivators (rewards) include the fact that they actually reduce intrinsic motivation (Kohn, 2018). We must also hold in mind that extrinsic motivation is less permanent than intrinsic motivation – motivation that comes from within the self and exists without the presence of external motivating factors. This is about children being motivated for reasons internally, such as for enjoyment, or because it makes them feel better about themselves, as opposed to extrinsic motivators, such as the prospect of being rewarded with stickers or privileges (Oxley, 2015). Essentially, if extrinsic motivators are relied on, when these are removed, the behaviours they shaped are more likely to decrease or disappear too – along with the children's interest in behaving in ways to get the reward.

Thus, the key tenets of all the summarized behaviourist theories tend to be interpreted very loosely – and traditionally, this has meant a reliance on the public humiliation and corporal punishment of children. This is captured succinctly by Kohn (2018: 42), who explains:

> Plenty of policies and programs limit our ability to do right by children. But perhaps the most restrictive virtual straitjacket that educators face is behaviourism – a

psychological theory that would have us focus exclusively on what can be seen and measured, that ignores or dismisses inner experience and reduces wholes to parts. It also suggests that everything people do can be explained as a quest for reinforcement – and, by implication, that we can control others by rewarding them selectively.

Essentially, behaviourist theories, with all their trinkets and humiliation, can actually reduce engagement over time. Providing students with unpleasant consequence for failure, such as missing out on "golden time" or time to play in the playground during breaks, is *negatively extrinsic*. If a child enjoys the feeling associated with not meeting the teacher's expectations – or enjoys the attention (particularly if it is negative), then it is negatively intrinsic. Punishment can also invoke other negative responses such as anger and resentment in the child, which, over time, is likely to prove detrimental to any positive relationship developing between them and the adult (be this their parent or teacher, for example). This brings to mind the cartoon character Bart Simpson (from the American animated sitcom *The Simpsons*). Despite the multiple, daily punishments Bart received such as detentions, having to write hundreds of lines or being physically abused, he never stopped "misbehaving" – in fact, he thrived on it!

Images of children wearing the "dunce" cap while sat at the front of the class as a reminder of what results if a child was "badly" behaved, as depicted in Figure 5.1, were standard practice well into the 1960s.

Figure 5.1 Child Wearing Dunce Cap

Figure 5.2 Child Being Hit With a Ruler

Being forced to stand facing a corner or writing lines; being hit on the head, hands or bare bottom by a teacher using a paddle, shoe, cane, ruler or ferule (a wide, flat metal ruler) as shown in Figure 5.2). All these were globally viewed as key features of the education system historically.

Indeed such punishments went on well into the 1970s and 1980s – and in some countries are still inflicted on children. One parent who went to school in the United Kingdom in the 1960s and 1970s recalls the various implements that teachers freely used to inflict pain on children. He explains:

> We often got hit with the slipper and cane at primary school back in the 60s and 70s. One teacher used to mark a chalk dot on the "offending" child's bottom then draw a chalk circle at the fulcrum of the blackboard compass and hit the child, trying to get the chalk circle over the chalk dot. At the time, we thought it was funny though a bit odd – and parents thought corporal punishment was correct.

Despite the Plowden Report recommending the abolition of corporal punishment in 1967, it was not until November 1986 that the 1986 Education Act abolished the use of corporal punishment in state schools, which became the law on 7th November 1986. On 15th August 1987, the use of corporal punishment in state schools became illegal, but it would take a further 11 years for corporal punishment to be outlawed in all private schools.

The education system has undeniably progressed in many ways since the 19th and 20th centuries, particularly with regard to its approach to behaviour. This is most evident in the abolishment of physical abuse of children in schools across Europe, which was commonplace until fairly recently. However, despite the unequivocal directive stipulated in Article 37 of the United Nations Convention on the Rights of the Child (United Nations Children's Fund, 1989), there is still much progress to be made, as some schools globally continue to physically abuse children in the name of behaviour management, with the physical and consequent mental abuse of children still being permitted in schools across South America, Australia, Africa, Southeast Asia and the Middle East (Gershoff, 2017). The article clearly specifies that any form of corporal or mental punishment must be not be tolerated by states:

> "No child shall be subjected to torture or other cruel, inhuman or degrading treatment or punishment." This is complemented and extended by Article 19, which requires States to "take all appropriate legislative, administrative, social and educational measures to protect the child from all forms of physical or mental violence, injury or abuse, neglect or negligent treatment, maltreatment or exploitation, including sexual abuse, while in the care of parent(s), legal guardian(s) or any other person who has the care of the child." There is no ambiguity: "all forms of physical or mental violence" does not leave room for any level of legalized violence against children. Corporal punishment and other cruel or degrading forms of punishment are forms of violence and States must take all appropriate legislative, administrative, social and educational measures to eliminate them.

While the physical abuse of children is no longer permitted in most countries, the hitting of children (predominantly spanking) in the home and in schools remains common worldwide (Cuartas et al., 2019; Ryan et al., 2016; Finkelhor et al., 2012). In one study conducted in the United States (Cuartas et al., 2021), approximately half of the parents reported spanking their children in the past year, and children globally are still routinely subjected to humiliation via "other cruel or degrading forms of punishment" as identified in the United Nations Children's Fund (1989), which also makes clear that these, too, are "forms of violence." These are discussed in the following section.

Moving forward, the 21st century is witnessing rapid advances in neuroscience, which are providing fascinating insights into the impact of corporal punishment (physical abuse) on the brain's development, structure and functioning and a child's consequent behaviour (Gershoff et al., 2018). Gershoff and Grogan-Kaylor (2016) conclude from their study that children who are spanked tend to exhibit higher levels of cognitive, behavioural and emotional problems than their never-spanked peers, with further findings including:

■ An increase in "delinquent" behaviours

■ Disruption to the parent/child relationship

■ Small increased risk of abuse towards their own spouse and/or children.

■ Poor child mental health

- Increased child-on-child physical abuse

- An increase in adult aggression

- Increased adult criminal behaviour.

Cuartas et al. (2021: 827) also reported similar findings in their more recent study:

> Our findings reveal that spanking was associated with greater activation to fearful versus neutral faces in multiple regions of the PFC.

Let us also hold in mind that children who are regularly threatened with being spanked/hit are in an almost constant state of fight or flight – and, as demonstrated throughout this book, stressed brains cannot learn, with stress derailing healthy brain development in the longer term (Nenia, 2022).

It is also critical to hold in mind that removing a child's underwear and placing them over your knee in order to spank their bare bottom is wholly unacceptable – and is rightly considered a form of sexual abuse. The common iliac artery and neurological pathways connect from the buttocks to the genital regions. Where childhood spanking causes involuntary sexual effects or stimulation in a child, this too, would be categorized as an ACE. The more frequently children are spanked by primary caregivers, the greater the probability that they will experience masochistic sexual arousal in adulthood. Linked to this – spanking (including with paddles – as used to inflict additional pain on a child) is a common fetishist activity, with adults paying for this service – have you ever paused to reflect why? It is never, ever acceptable to spank a child – or indeed, inflict *any* other type of punishment on them, in the name of discipline – or otherwise.

In conclusion, such evidence can and should be used to deter parents and professionals alike from inflicting harm on children. Just as public health campaigns exist for healthy eating and exercise, they are desperately needed to inform the public about the harm caused by inflicting physical and psychological harm on infants and children. Findings from the neurosciences are finally helping to pave new, child-centred approaches to supporting behaviour – as opposed to those derived from behaviourism and their negating of the inner psychological experience of learning and behaviour. Cuartas et al. (2021: 829) state:

> Growing evidence suggests that spanking is associated with deleterious cognitive and behavioural outcomes and changes in the neural processing of threatening emotional stimuli in children. The United States and other countries around the world should discourage the use of corporal punishment through public education and legal prohibition, following the Convention on the Rights of the Child, the United Nations Sustainable Development Goals and the robust scientific evidence on the harmful consequences of corporal punishment.

While we may not be able to exert influence on a wider, global scale, we can certainly positively influence the primary carers with whom we work and support them to make more child–centred and empathic choices when it comes to guiding their children's behaviour. In the long term, this can of course benefit families for generations to come, particularly if we are helping them to break free of archaic behaviour management–led approaches.

Rewind. Reflect. Write!

1   In your own words, provide a definition of behaviour management.

2a Discuss some of the common approaches used as part of behaviour management.

2b In your experience, how do children respond to the punishments?

3   Reflect on your setting's policies and procedures on children's behaviour. Would you say these follow a behaviourist or a relational model (or both)? Provide some examples and jot down what you think are the advantages and disadvantages of each of these approaches.

4   Why do you think it took a further 11 years for corporal punishment to be outlawed in all private schools? Conduct some online research to help inform your answer.

5   Given the evidence against behaviour management, why do you think adults insist on continuing to put children through various abusive practices in the name of behaviour management? Discuss.

6   Imagine a parent told you that she uses "time out" to "discipline" her four-year-old daughter, explaining that it works.

   a How would you respond?

   b What could you suggest as an alternative and why?

7   What more do you think should be done to prevent behaviour management in schools?

Top Tips for Practice!

■ Revisit your policies. How could these be improved? Make a plan of action with your team

■ Get families on board in banning behaviour management. Have non-judgmental conversations about their approaches to supporting their children's behaviour, with a view to guiding them on more nurturing and relational alternatives

■ Reflect on the systems in place to support the quality of relationships between staff and children. What needs to change and why?

■ Invest in resources that expand children's emotional vocabulary – this does not have to be costly (reflect on the ideas in this book and conduct an online search for resources that you could make with the children)

■ Speak with your team about how you could all reframe emotionally charged situations as opportunities to build children's ability to self-regulate

■ Re-direct behaviour by using more child-centred strategies, such as positive modelling, listening, empathizing and talking through alternative ways of responding to challenging situations.

Common Behaviour Management Approaches – What's the Harm?

This section explores some of the commonly used and widely accepted punishments and rewards that are utilized to control children's behaviour across settings – and, indeed, in some homes. As mentioned, the "success" of behaviour management approaches rests upon public shaming and humiliation, and there should be no room for this in any education system. Draconian and outmoded policies and procedures which advocate the use of ignoring, enforced "time out," isolation, exclusion or issuing red cards do nothing to change children's thinking or internal strategies, because there is no co-regulation of emotional responses and resulting behaviour. Instead, these forms of behaviour management put them in a state of further distress and derail self-confidence.

Rewards and Punishments

Let us start with the most ubiquitous form of managing behaviour – the use of manipulation and bribes to incentivize children with rewards or punishments. As parents, teachers and Early Years practitioners, we are all too familiar with these damaging strategies. Listed below are the "top 10" rewards and punishments utilized as part of behaviour management policies and procedures.

■ Sticker charts

■ Individual points and table points

■ "Star of the week"

■ Children's names being moved down on the class chart for "transgressions" which include not bringing their PE kit to school

■ "Time out"

■ Removal of "golden time"

- Detention

- Suspension

- Expulsion

- The traffic light system – makes clear what is acceptable and unacceptable behaviour. All children start on "green" and move to "amber," then "red" – some with a letter sent home. Some teachers also insist that children on "red" must start the following school day on "red"

- The weather chart – a system whereby well-behaved children get their photograph placed on the image of the sun and those who are deemed "naughty" or "disobedient" get their name and photograph placed on the thunder cloud.

Look at Figure 5.3. How does it make you feel? Enforced time out is a contentious issue, as many parents and educators that I continue to speak with advocate its use, stating that it does no harm and that it is a swift way to instil discipline. It is demoralization through (public) shaming and, in this regard, works. Is it relational or educational? No.

Figure 5.3 Time Out Chair

"Time out" chairs come in diverse designs, some engraved with a "loving" message for their child who is branded "naughty." Others are sexist, designed specifically for girls and boys. Some adults do not bother with a chair, instead sending (their) children to sit on the floor, facing the wall or on a "naughty step."

As for the removal of "golden time" – I do not know any child who enters school thinking "I wonder how I can lose my golden time today"! Nor have I ever encountered a child who was not distressed at having been isolated from their peers, as they sat alone in enforced "time out." I do, however, know of many children who, no matter how hard they try, cannot conform to the one-size-fits-all archaic behaviour management system of schools, for example, autistic children, those with ADHD and those who have been exposed to ACEs and trauma. These children tend to be the very children who are disproportionately told off and punished for "not doing as they are told." Kohn (2018: 2), who for decades has been an outspoken advocate against behaviour management, perfectly encapsulates the manipulative strategy of using reward and punishment as part of behaviour management, asserting that:

> Our basic strategy for raising children, teaching students, and managing workers can be summarized in six words: Do this and you'll get that.

This simply does not work in the longer term – if it did, the same children would not have to endure the shame of having their photographs on the thundercloud on a daily basis. Each child has their unique experience of being parented – some children are fortunate enough to have understanding and empathic parents, who take the time to model positive ways of behaving and responding to their own stressors and co-regulate their children's emotions and behaviours. Sadly, those who do not have this invaluable input find their own ways of managing in emotionally charged situations, and when these do not fit in with a school's rigid expectations, they are punished. Two deeply concerning strategies are discussed in the sections that follow.

Whole Class Punishments

A lazy approach which only serves to upset just about an entire class of children! It basically involves the teacher issuing a punishment to the whole class due to one child's "transgression" and tends to take the form of removing "golden time" for all the children, issuing a whole class detention or the whole class missing out on playtime (recess). All that children learn though this punishment is that school rules are unfair and that the teacher is unfair, while having nothing positive to take away at all in terms of how the world works and their place within it. What it does clearly demonstrate, however, is how to get what you want through adopting fear tactics to control everyone – while cleverly appropriating blame on that one child who has to now shoulder the blame for ruining everyone else's time at school too! If this were an effective way to "manage" behaviour, it would not be resorted to, along with other futile behaviour management approaches across schools, on a daily basis.

Zero Tolerance Approaches to Behaviour – Bin the Booths!

Zero tolerance approaches stem from policies that began in the United States, with the Gun-Free Schools Act of 1994 (Cerrone, 1999), which were designed to stamp out violence in schools.

Zero tolerance comes in the form of suspension, permanent exclusions (which iron-ically run counter to schools' rigid attendance policies and right to an education) and, just as worrying, isolation booths – which is the focus of this section.

In some schools and academy trusts, children are removed from class and taken to a referral or consequences room – or an isolation booth, where they are made to sit in silence for up to six hours a day as punishment for breaking school rules. They are phys-ically confined to a tiny cubicle where they are sat facing the front, with minimal room to move and no adult to co-regulate or help them. Further dysregulation is a common result of being forced into isolation.

When we reflect on the sheer rigidity of school rules, children are likely to end up in isolation for the most trivial of "transgressions." There is no educational worth in isolation – disaffected children need a trusted adult with whom they can talk through their issues. This requires engagement – not isolation. It also requires a space where that can happen. Containing a child in an isolation booth the size of a toilet cubicle makes that necessary dialogue impossible – and so the cycle of self-limiting behaviour and its damaging consequences continues. Figure 5.4 is just one type of isolation room, replete with its isolation booths.

Figure 5.4 Isolation Booths

Source: Independent News (2018). www.independent.co.uk/news/education/education-news/ isolation-booths-school-pupils-classroom-behaviour-special-educational-needs-bbc-a8630391.html.

One swift look at this isolation room and its claustrophobic booths and it is clear that they are designed to inflict further psychological damage to the child. Consider this with regard to the disproportionately high number of children with SEND, ACEs and trauma who end up in isolation and you can appreciate how utterly gruelling the experience is. It is little wonder that schools which enforce this type of zero toler-ance behaviour policies are known as a (unidirectional) "pipeline to prison." These schools are also notorious for their disproportionate numbers of children from disadvantaged and ethnic minority backgrounds being subjected to exclusions and iso-lation – children who have been set on a trajectory to prison (Owens and McLanahan, 2020; Gilliam et al., 2016; Skiba et al., 2011). As teacher and teacher trainer Paul Dix (2017: 114) brings to our attention:

> Look around inside any isolation room where children are separated for long periods of time from the rest of the school, and I would lay good money that more than 80% of the children in there have additional needs. . . . Others will be struggling with hidden needs that are all too obvious to those who work with them every day: trauma, anxiety, attachment, grief or plain old-fashioned neglect. The sins of the adult world are soaked up by a minority of children.

Siegel and Payne Bryson (2015: 32) are just as unequivocal about the harm caused by isolating children. They assert:

> When the response is to isolate the child, an instinctual psychological need of the child goes unmet. Brain imaging shows that the experience of relational pain – like that caused by rejection – looks very similar to the experience of physical pain in terms of brain activity.

While this statement might seem shocking to some, what is even more shocking is that regardless, some adults deem it appropriate to inflict such torture on children in the name of "managing behaviour." Take a look at the following case study. It was provided by a mother (and childminder) who had to battle for her son, who has SEND, to be better understood – and treated at school.

> My son started secondary school four weeks after turning 11. By this age he had been diagnosed with ADHD, ASD, dyspraxia and mild learning difficulties and was under CAMHS. He had been medicated for his ADHD since the age of seven.
>
> His secondary school was already his fourth school. He had been to two primary schools in Suffolk before being excluded from a Suffolk Middle school, at the age of nine. This occurred after they put him on a restricted timetable and insisted on teaching him in isolation, not in classes. After he was excluded from middle school, he then returned to the Essex Primary school system, for year six. When he started senior school, he had only had a statement of special educational needs for six months. My first parental application was rejected and my second attempt was successful.

I first started applying for a statement for him (now an education, health and care plan (EHC)), when he was six. When he arrived at secondary school he was not given the allocated 32 hours of support, a teaching assistant (TA) was simply in the classroom to help all the children with additional needs.

Two weeks in, he started to school refuse and had been sent to the Learning Resource Centre (LRC) (isolation) several times. This was a large secondary school with 1500 pupils and a good reputation.

In the third week, he ran away across the playing fields, climbed a tree and refused to come down. This was the start of his exclusions. They withdrew his full timetable, allowing him in the mornings only and he had to go straight to the LRC and they would "choose if he could go to lessons." After a few weeks of this, with most of his half day timetable in a room with no windows, only desks and chairs and expected to work alone he was at breaking point. He was screaming and refusing to go into school.

On the final occasion he attended school they had shut him in the LRC alone and he had a meltdown and he picked up a desk and threw it across the room. They then came in and tried to restrain him. By the time I got to school he had escaped to the school lobby and was trying to break the front door down to escape and smashing his head against the doors and windows. The headmaster was shouting at him that "they didn't want children like him" in their school.

I withdrew him from the school after that on the grounds they could not keep him safe. This was the start of 10 months with no school. The local education authority (LEA) provided an hour of education a week provided by a tutor, because he was too young to go to a pupil referral unit. I fought the LEA until the following July for a place at the local Special Educational Needs school. They finally agreed and he remained at this school until he was 16. He was finally happy and made friends. Unfortunately he suffered a nervous breakdown and very severe mental health problems for four years, which was the legacy of his educational experiences.

Thankfully he went on to do four years of NVQ qualifications at the local college. He is now 23 and works part time. He managed to get his English GCSE at college and remains friends with the people he met at SEND school. He is also in a long-term relationship. However, the damage that secondary school did to his self-esteem and wellbeing is immeasurable. I have three children, all now adults and all with ADHD! So many stories and so many battles over the last 25 years. That's why I started ADHD Kids UK on Facebook. There are thousands of parents with stories like mine.

Now answer the questions that follow.

Rewind. Reflect. Write!

I   What issues stand out for you in the mother's case study? Discuss.

2   Discuss your views on:

   a Zero tolerance policies and procedures

   b Isolation booths

   c How might it feel for a child who is frequently punished in the setting/ school?

   d How might this affect their holistic development?

3a What do you think are the wider implications of whole class punishments?

3b If whole class punishments were an effective way to "manage" behaviour, why do you think they (along with other futile behaviour management approaches) are resorted to across schools on a daily basis?

4   What might it take to create widespread and consistent change (towards more relational approaches) across schools?

Top Tips for Practice!

- Revisit your setting's behaviour policy and make a plan with your team (including the leadership team) to move away from all approaches that draw on punishments and rewards

- Create group rules with the children – this will also build individual and collective ownership

- Make every child know that they are valued and respected – talk through some strategies with your team

- Use meaningful, in-the-moment praise with children when children attempt to address behaviour

- Always separate the behaviour from the child. If a child is involved in an incident, address it supportively and then move on – make this a whole team approach so that no child is ever labelled

- Never shout at or threaten a child

- Include children in decisions that affect them – and give them a voice and choice.

Now that we have looked at some commonly used behaviour management approaches, let us critically think about behaviour management as a safeguarding issue.

Behaviour Management as a Safeguarding Issue

As has been made clear from the start of this chapter, behaviour management tends to draw upon methods of controlling children's behaviour by means which oppose child-centred approaches. Using manipulation, coercion, humiliation and threats of punishment, as well as physical punishment, to achieve compliance and control a child's behaviour *is* emotional and physical abuse, and this needs to be openly discussed as a key feature of behaviour management, as opposed to being mindlessly accepted. The NSPCC (2022) definition of emotional abuse makes it all the clearer:

> Emotional abuse is any type of abuse that involves the continual emotional mistreatment of a child. It's sometimes called psychological abuse. Emotional abuse can involve deliberately trying to scare, humiliate, isolate or ignore a child.

Definitions and descriptions of manipulation and coercion differ, depending on the literature. Hamberger et al. (2017) highlight how prevalent this inconsistency is. Terms such as "power," "control," "domination" and "controlling behaviour" are also interchangeably used to describe these terms. It can be useful to view coercive control as an intention, with the types of abuse a perpetrator uses as the strategies to create or maintain that control. Reflecting on the strategies commonly used under the guise of behaviour management, their use to establish and maintain control and power over children becomes all the clearer. The promises of a treat if a child stays silent or does whatever else the adult (teacher or parent) demands, or the threats of public shaming or punishment if a child fails to comply – be this in the setting or home, are sadly commonplace. Compliance is too readily accepted as a necessary part of most if not all education systems and classrooms – "children must do as they are told!" Must they? Obedient children obey whomever they might put above them – be this a teacher or a friend who is pressuring them into doing something they might not want to do or is dangerous. In older children who are compliant, this might look like participating in risky or illegal behaviour. As highlighted by Nenia (2022), *most cases of abuse begin with socially sanctioned discipline.* Allowances must never be made for abusing children – the "worse" the "transgression," the greater the need for time-in with a supportive adult who can show the child another, more positive way of responding – one which ultimately nurtures their personal growth.

What Lies Beneath – Understanding Behaviour as Communication

Reflect on all those behaviours that typically present as "frustrating" or "challenging." Do you reflect enough on their possible origins? Or do you dive right in with the behaviour management policy and threaten to reprimand the dysregulated child? Viewing the child through the lens of SR enables us to think that bit deeper and reframe what we see. Viewing behaviour as communication is becoming a common adage in some schools and therapeutic circles – and particularly as part of trauma-informed practices (which are discussed further on in this chapter). It is a perspective which ultimately serves us all well: by not immediately reacting to the child's behaviour, the adult not only creates the time and space for themselves to calm down before responding (as opposed to *reacting*), but they also afford the child the opportunity to express their feelings safely, with a view to problem-solving with the adult. This is also more beneficial to the child – and wider society in the longer term – because through co-regulating, the adult is equipping the child with those emotional tools to help them across the life trajectory.

As parents and educators, we must all bear in mind the fact that at a neurobiological and physiological level, children under stress cannot learn, and they *will* fail to thrive, with implications for their general mental wellbeing. Low self-confidence, depression, anxiety and self-harming are all affecting children from an alarmingly young age, and when we consider the current education system and all its excessive demands, we know that things must change.

Reflect on your learning from Chapter 3 concerning brain development. We know that everything is processed at a neural level, which then manifests at a physiological and behavioural level. Yet all too often, some parents and professionals alike dive in and react only to what they see, without due consideration of what lies beneath – picture an iceberg, if you will.

Beneath anger might be sadness; beneath aggression might be shame. Never take anything at face value. As we know, children's behaviour is communication – not misbehaviour. This finds support in Treismann (2017: 28), who explains:

> Rather than taking behaviours at face value, it is helpful to view behaviours as forms of multi-layered communication that tell a story and often provides us with a map of and clues about the child's inner worlds and unexpressed needs.

Linked to this, the role of stress as a key influencing factor in children's behaviour must be acknowledged. This is discussed in the section that follows.

What we see . . .

What we do not see . . .

Figure 5.5 The Iceberg of Behaviour

The Role of Stress and Toxic Stress in Influencing Behaviour: The Stress Response System

As discussed in previous chapters, our stress response (fight or flight) is our body's emergency reaction system. It is briefly summarized in the section that follows.

Our stress response system activates the body's SNS, setting off a series of physical and cognitive changes that prepare us to act by increasing our strength and stamina, speeding up our reaction time, enhancing our focus and preparing us to either fight or flee from the danger we are facing. They can also cause some people to freeze and even physically collapse (faint). This is why some commentators refer to the fight-flight-freeze response. Figure 5.6 depicts the stress response in action.

All of these changes happen so quickly that people are not usually aware of them. In fact, the wiring is so efficient that the amygdala and hypothalamus start this process even

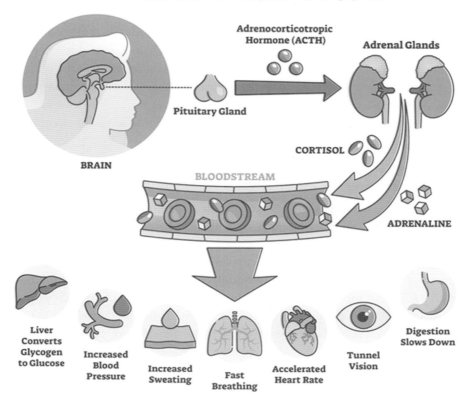

STRESS RESPONSE

Figure 5.6 The Stress Response

before the brain's visual centres have had a chance to fully process what is happening. It is this process that causes someone to "flip their lid" (as discussed earlier). It can also help to explain why a person may be able to jump out of the path of an oncoming car, for example, before they even think about what they are doing.

Scientists believe that the human stress response has evolved over thousands of years as humans learned to survive and adapt to the harsh realities of their environments. In prehistoric times, it would have helped our ancestors to escape from danger, such as being chased by a woolly mammoth! It gave us the alertness and energy to either fight our foe or take flight and remove ourselves from danger.

Though the woolly mammoths of our ancestors' time are long gone, the fight or flight response is still very much part of our instinctive behaviour. Sometimes, this is a good thing. In emergency situations, it can save our life. For example, it can give us extra strength to defend ourselves or spur us to slam on the car brakes to avoid an accident.

However, *being subjected to too much stress or prolonged periods of stress can mean that we become stuck in this fight or flight mode.* In other words, even though there may be no immediate danger, we remain in a hyper-aroused and hyper-vigilant state. This also applies to children. If they are exposed to excessive or prolonged levels of stress, their brains can become "primed" or "hard wired" for danger. This can make them anxious, fearful and suspicious of others. It can also make them react in ways that seem out of proportion to the reality of the situation. This is why it is necessary to eschew harmful behaviour management approaches in favour of trauma-informed care (TIC), which recognizes the child's past traumas while creating a climate of trust. We will now explore what TIC looks like in practice.

Trauma-Informed Care – Let Compassion Lead the Way

Now that we have looked at the impact of toxic stress on the developing brain, it is important to understand what a trauma-informed approach entails and its fundamental role in enabling healing and a child's capacity to thrive. We will start by defining trauma. While definitions of trauma particularly can vary according to personal interpretation and wider discourse, it is commonplace for the term to be used interchangeably with ACEs, but they are distinctly different. ACEs refer to the specific experience of adversity (some of these being the 10 types of ACEs originally identified by Felitti et al., 1998), whereas, generally, trauma refers to the stress response and the emotional, psychological, physical and behavioural responses to such deeply distressing or life-threatening experiences. Far greater understanding of the impact of ACEs, trauma and mental health conditions is needed by all school staff to better support every child to learn – and thrive. This is why we all need to embrace more relational, trauma-informed ways of nurturing children's wellbeing and ability to learn – ways that acknowledge trauma in the child instead of ways that only serve to re-traumatize and belittle children and young adults alike. With this in mind, it is essential to understand that a trauma-informed approach enables us to move away from the question *what's wrong with you?* to one that asks *what happened to you?* This can help us to be more curious about children's behaviour and the underlying causes for it – as opposed to reprimanding them for the behaviour we see. It's a bit like looking beyond the tip of an iceberg – think back to Figure 5.5.

When we consider the ways that trauma shows up in behaviour and how often these are misunderstood as misbehaviour, we know that the current education system must change. Figure 5.7 identifies the holistic impact of trauma on a child or young adult, all of which could be invisible or misunderstood to the uninformed eye.

Take a look at the signs/symptoms of trauma under the headings, brain development and cognition. You will note that cognitive processes and the stress response become impeded, along with changes in gene expression (which is addressed in Chapter 6). Difficulty in concentration and consequent struggles with learning also result. The integral role of SR is again highlighted under the headings emotions and behaviour – a traumatized child

Impact of Childhood Trauma

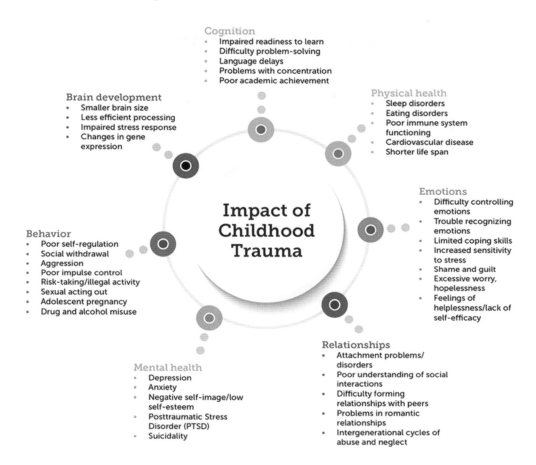

Cognition
- Impaired readiness to learn
- Difficulty problem-solving
- Language delays
- Problems with concentration
- Poor academic achievement

Brain development
- Smaller brain size
- Less efficient processing
- Impaired stress response
- Changes in gene expression

Physical health
- Sleep disorders
- Eating disorders
- Poor immune system functioning
- Cardiovascular disease
- Shorter life span

Behavior
- Poor self-regulation
- Social withdrawal
- Aggression
- Poor impulse control
- Risk-taking/illegal activity
- Sexual acting out
- Adolescent pregnancy
- Drug and alcohol misuse

Emotions
- Difficulty controlling emotions
- Trouble recognizing emotions
- Limited coping skills
- Increased sensitivity to stress
- Shame and guilt
- Excessive worry, hopelessness
- Feelings of helplessness/lack of self-efficacy

Impact of Childhood Trauma

Mental health
- Depression
- Anxiety
- Negative self-image/low self-esteem
- Posttraumatic Stress Disorder (PTSD)
- Suicidality

Relationships
- Attachment problems/disorders
- Poor understanding of social interactions
- Difficulty forming relationships with peers
- Problems in romantic relationships
- Intergenerational cycles of abuse and neglect

Figure 5.7 The Impact of Childhood Trauma

Source: Child Trends (2020).

or young adult may find it difficult to self-regulate and may "flip their lid" at seemingly innocuous events; they may often upset their peers and friends, partly due to not being adept at recognizing others' emotions, and they may prefer to spend much of their time alone.

The Four Rs of Trauma-Informed Care – The Key to Understanding the Impact of Trauma

TIC is an approach that is aware of and considers the pervasive nature of trauma and actively promotes environments of healing and recovery rather than practices and services that may inadvertently re-traumatize. This means that practice which is trauma-informed embodies the four Rs, as depicted in Figure 5.8.

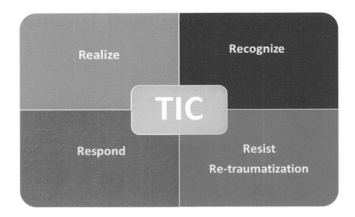

Figure 5.8 The Four Rs of Trauma-Informed Care

So a setting that is trauma-informed *realizes* the existence, impact and consequences of stress, adversity and trauma and understands potential strategies for recovery. It *recognizes* the signs and symptoms of trauma in staff, children, their family and all others connected to the setting, actively *resisting re-traumatization* by committing to reduce trauma as opposed to adopting policies and procedures that inadvertently induce traumatization. It *responds* by wholly and meaningfully embedding and infusing knowledge concerning trauma into its policies, procedures, language and culture.

But what else does being trauma-informed look like for primary carers and professionals alike?

The Five Principles of Trauma-Informed Care

1 Safety – ensuring everyone's emotional as well as physical safety

2 Trust – transparency in decision-making and building/maintaining everyone's trust

3 Choice – ensuring that everyone can make choices and exert control in planning

4 Collaboration – using "power with" as opposed to "power over" everyone

5 Empowerment – prioritizing skill-building and a sense of hope.

Embedding the five principles of TIC in all policies and provision will help to ensure that everyone in and associated with your setting understands what trauma, its signs and their role are in helping to heal trauma. Embracing parents as part of your approach to these principles will be vital if your efforts to heal are to be effective. After all, Bowlby acknowledged decades ago that "if we value our children, we must cherish their parents" (1951). This includes building their capacity to heal and be healed, as well as exploring ways to build resilience and the role of caring relationships within the family. What the five principles will look and feel like in practice will be unique to your setting and up to you and your team to create. Being trauma-informed cannot be achieved "overnight," nor is there a one-size-fits-all way to achieve it. To be meaningful, TIC must be infused in your organization's culture and ethos, providing that golden thread across all your policies and practices, with all stakeholders being aware of it and playing their part to achieve, maintain and continually build on it.

Why Adopt a Trauma-Informed Approach?

Adopting a trauma-informed approach will not only nurture the holistic and ever-evolving wellbeing of trauma survivors but will prove beneficial to everyone in the setting. When the wellbeing of all staff is prioritized as part of a mindful and compassionate trauma-informed approach, they too will feel much more emotionally contained and consequently be better equipped to reflect and respond – as opposed to react to potentially triggering situations. This also addresses the age-old response to TIC: "It's all very well taking about TIC for one child, but it's impossible when you have a class of 30 children!" Not so. When we are truly embedded in and guided by the principles of TIC, alongside those relational ways of supporting behaviour and setting expectations (as discussed in Chapter 2), teachers do not need to resort to punishments each time a child becomes dysregulated. This is because there will be a range of preventative measures in place, such as SR spaces and other resources and having a safe adult to problem-solve with – all in a climate of safety, instead of one guided by mass control.

A trauma-informed approach will also facilitate greater insight and understanding, which will allow for:

- Reframing behaviour
- Increased co-regulation, which is vital for the development of self-regulation
- Resilience
- Stability
- Sense of security
- Sense of belonging
- Emphasis on play and playfulness
- Creativity and imagination.

An understanding of trauma is yet to be integrated into the practice of education – and with mental health issues affecting children and teachers, who feel increasingly unable to meet children's needs due to a lack of trauma-informed training and support, there is an urgent need for a paradigm shift in education. Moving towards EY professional development programmes that are trauma-informed and embedded in the neuroscience of early brain development can equip lecturers, students and practitioners alike to identify the signs of trauma and help to minimize its impact while educating everyone in that community about trauma.

Remember to Take Five!

When we acknowledge those behaviours which are too frequently misunderstood and erroneously labelled misbehaviours, we are able to completely flip the narrative to one that is more empathic and reflective – one that actually provides children with alternatives to "flipping their lid" (or becoming dysregulated). On the contrary, behaviour management approaches do not afford the children such opportunities, while only serving to add to their distress. This is just one of the reasons you and your team should reflect on how you currently respond to the behaviours presented by children and how this could be improved. Shanker et al. (2017) outline these *five simple but vital steps when supporting children to overcome stress*. He advises to:

1   **Read** the signs of stress and reframe the behaviour (view it differently, as opposed to immediately making judgements about "misbehaviour")

2   **Recognize** the stressors

3   **Reduce** the stress

4   **Reflect** – enhance your (and the child's) stress awareness

5   **Respond** – help the child learn to respond to stressors and return to calm.

How to Calm a Child Who Is Stressed

The following are just a few strategies you could try with children to activate their PNS – that is, to decrease anxious feelings and help them return to a calm state.

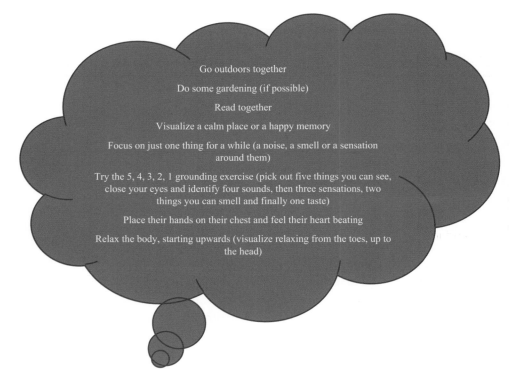

Go outdoors together

Do some gardening (if possible)

Read together

Visualize a calm place or a happy memory

Focus on just one thing for a while (a noise, a smell or a sensation around them)

Try the 5, 4, 3, 2, 1 grounding exercise (pick out five things you can see, close your eyes and identify four sounds, then three sensations, two things you can smell and finally one taste)

Place their hands on their chest and feel their heart beating

Relax the body, starting upwards (visualize relaxing from the toes, up to the head)

Stand up and shake their body for one minute

Lie on their back and stretch out their body

Listen to music

Drawing/doodling shapes

Deep breathing exercises

Cuddling someone they trust

Talk with someone about how they are feeling

Play a game or with a favourite toy (redirection of attention and emotions)

Push against a wall, imagining that they are pushing their negative energy away

Blow-painting with a straw (or blowing bubbles, blowing feathers across a table with a straw)

Rewind. Reflect. Write!

1 What are your thoughts on behaviour management as a safeguarding issue?

2a Reflecting on behaviour as communication, is this how you readily view children's behaviour in your setting? Discuss.

2b Outline any changes that you might need to make as a team to strengthen your approach.

3 Outline three more ways to activate the parasympathetic nervous system and instil calm.

4 Reflect upon a time when your child, or a child in your setting, experienced the fight or flight response. Explain what events triggered their stress response. How did they respond – what was their mood and behaviour, and what did they say? How did you (or others) try to calm them?

5a Revisit the four Rs of trauma-informed care. Outline how you will embed these in your provision and make a plan for implementation with your team.

5b Now revisit the five principles of trauma-informed care. Outline how you will embed these in your provision and make a plan for implementation with your team.

Top Tips for Practice!

■ Don't forget to revise your behaviour policies – think about how you will you inform families about this change

Once you have made this change:

■ Implement those four Rs of trauma-informed care!

■ Now set to planning and implementing the five principles of trauma-informed care

■ Reflecting on the five steps when supporting children to overcome stress, plan how you and your team will help children to identify their stressors

■ Revisit the list of strategies to instil calm. Make a plan to introduce these (as well as any others) to the children in ways that are meaningful.

Relational Approaches to Supporting Behaviour

As the term suggests, relational approaches emphasize the importance of adults gaining the child's trust by building an empathic and nurturing relationship with them. Once this is achieved, supportive and attuned adults can then investigate the factors that trigger a child's dysregulated emotions and subsequent behaviour and teach them (through CR) how to deal with these triggers in healthy ways. In contrast to the authoritarian behaviour management approaches, relational approaches draw inspiration from, among others, the work of Perry (2021), Porges (2018) and Siegel and Bryson (2018). There is now strong evidence to support the implementation of relational approaches in EY settings and schools (Golding et al., 2021; Sunderland, 2016; Rose et al., 2015).

Where to Start – Policy to Practice

With any new strategy you intend to introduce and embed, you must first ensure you discuss it with your team, involving parents where appropriate. Then, of course, you can make any necessary amendments or updates to the relevant policies. As I often remind practitioners:

Any decent behaviour policy will set clear expectations of the adult as co-regulator.

The following is an extract from the Promoting Children's Self-Regulation Through Co-Regulation Policy, provided by the head of Early Years at Thrive Childcare and Education, a large nursery chain of 46 nurseries across the United Kingdom. Critically, this was formerly their Promoting Positive Behaviour Policy, but since receiving training on SR, they eschewed it in favour of this current policy. While reading it, you will notice that this chain has fully embedded SR in all they do, from the very outset of the practitioner's career with them. This is achieved through their induction training and guidance on SR (which includes their approach to supporting behaviour through CR, as opposed to behaviour management).

Promoting Children's Self-Regulation Through Co-Regulation (Previously Promoting Positive Behaviour Policy)

At Thrive, we believe that all children are unique and the foundations for building self-regulation skills can only begin when a child feels safe, secure and motivated. Every child needs to be supported and nurtured through sensitive and trusting attachments in order to develop the skills to be aware of and in control of their emotions. We understand that all behaviours are communication and we need to be attuned to children's needs and emotions to support them.

Self-regulation

The period between birth and five-years-old is a sensitive period for children's developing brains; this period represents a window within which the effects of environmental stimulation on brain structure and function are maximized . . .

At Thrive, we will:

■ Gather as much information as possible about the child before they are inducted into nursery

■ Ensure all practitioners have access to the Thrive Self-Regulation Guidance through induction or training . . .

Co-regulation strategies we will use:

- "Name it to tame it" – acknowledge children's feelings. "I can see that makes you feel angry" rather than "Don't be silly, there's nothing to cry about"
- Age-appropriate rules and expectations that do not set children up to fail . . .

Environments to promote self-regulation

Children's natural desire to move and explore their own ideas and concepts is vital to learning, development and wellbeing; promoting this is highly effective in reducing children's frustrations . . .

Responding to dysregulated behaviours

Children who struggle to regulate their emotions often respond to a situation with anti-social behaviours . . .

In responding to dysregulated behaviour, we will:

- Never use physical punishment such as smacking or shaking
- Re-direct behaviour
- Have a named person who has overall responsibility for promoting self-regulation within the setting . . .

Any form of corporal punishment is not tolerated – anyone using such practice is committing an offence.

The named self-regulation advocate is . . .

They will . . .

Biting

Biting is a common behavioural stage that some young children experience . . .

Supporting children with additional needs

In addition to the above points, if a child with additional needs is demonstrating dysregulated behaviour, the key person must . . .

Related documents and reading:

- Thrive Self-Regulation Guidance
- Self-Regulation Support Plan
- ABCs Chart
- Why we shouldn't force children to say "sorry" article
- Thrive's Guide to Supporting Children with Additional Needs.

Integral to Thrive's recently embedded relational SR approach are two further documents – the ABCs Tracker and the Self-Regulation Support Plan (with the two generally used together). The Support Plan form is completed when it is decided (with parents) that additional support needs to be put in place to help children when they are struggling to self-regulate. This is in acknowledgement that all behaviours are a form of communication and that at times some children will require more support from adults as they develop SR. It is therefore vital that adults in the child's life work together in supporting children through this process instead of recording their behaviour on arbitrary forms as offences and reprimanding them.

Following is an extract from the ABCs tracker developed by Thrive.

ABCs Tracker

An ABCs tracker is an observational tool that allows us to record information about particular behaviours, to establish triggers and patterns that can help us understand the reasons for such behaviours and support the individual child appropriately. At Thrive, they have made space for additional information, which includes the additional Communication and Context column. This form tends to be used alongside their Self-Regulation Support Form.

Child's name

Child's age

Room

Date Time Location Activity	Staff Present	Antecedent (Before) What was going on right before the incident that may have triggered the behaviour?	Behaviour What actually happened? Actions, facial expressions, words. What were my peers doing at the time?	Consequence How did the child react afterwards? Actions, facial expressions, words?	Communication and Context What was the child trying to communicate? Any other contextual information?

The more relational and *curious* approach to children's behaviour is immediately clear from both policies. With an emphasis on SR, ascertaining the root cause of behaviour and working closely with parents to better support development of SR, these policies are more empowering for everyone involved.

Reflection Into Action

1   Discuss what you think the key enablers are to achieving the relational SR approach at Thrive.

2   Note any similarities and differences between your setting's behaviour policy.

3   At Thrive, children are not "forced" to say "sorry" when they have upset or hurt their peers. This runs contrary to adults' frequent demands of "getting" the child to apologise. What are your thoughts about this? Discuss.

4   Reflecting on your provision, do you think practitioners are sufficiently supported to reflect on their own responses toward challenging behaviours to ensure that their reactions are appropriate? What might need to change? Note these down to feed back to your team for action.

5   For children whose behaviour presents ongoing concern, the Self-Regulation Support Plan is put into place. This outlines the support needed for the child and its implementation, as opposed to recording any punishment for their behaviour. How might this benefit the child and their parent(s)?

6   Discuss the advantages of children having a self-regulation advocate in the setting.

7   What will you do to make your behaviour policy more informed by self-regulation and co-regulation?

Make a note to discuss your plans for action with your team.

Zones of Regulation

As a teacher, EY practitioner or parent, you are probably aware of the various zones of regulation which exist. Initially developed by occupational therapist Leah Kuypers (2011) – and not to be confused with a form of behaviour management – these zones are designed to help children identify how they are feeling and to take action to avoid (or get out of) the red/angry zone. One example is provided in Table 5.2.

Table 5.2 Zones of Regulation

Low Energy	Calm	High Energy That Feels Out of Control
Collapsed body	Cooperative	Yelling
Head hanging down	Content	Physical aggression
Head on desk	Prosocial language and behaviours	Opposition and defiance
Absence of eye contact	Able to learn	Stealing and lying
Limp limbs	May be high energy, but child is in control	Dysregulation (commonly referred to as a "tantrum")

Here is an overview of the three zones:

The green zone is where we would like to see the baby or child functioning from. Green zone behaviours including behaving prosocially – ways that encourage positive interactions and relationships with others – especially primary carers. Being in the green zone also enables a child to work from their "upstairs" brain – meaning that their PFC is engaged, enabling the child to tap into all those executive functions. It is these executive functions that enable a child to regulate their emotions, to think before they act and to receive rewards for "good" behaviour (bear this in mind).

The red zone is where children tend to operate from if they have been exposed to ACEs or unresponsive care-giving. Children who operate from the red zone have not had adults to model SR, nor have they had any CR in managing their emotional responses. Consequently, children in the red zone operate from their emotionally reactive "downstairs brain," with the limbic system being hyper-sensitive to threats (imagined or real). This ingrained fear leads children to behave in aggressive ways, as opposed to calm, prosocial ways. It is therefore critical that we do not further fuel this sense of danger in a child who is already rendered completely unable to return to and operate from a safe psychological place, having been in fight or flight mode. Siegel and Bryson (2015: 32) reminds us:

An overactive limbic system is a sign of a child who is a survivor! It was brilliant of their brain to organize in this way, and now they need our help in calming their limbic system so that their brain can grow connections to their prefrontal cortex.

The blue zone is where a child would operate if they had no ability to operate in fight or flight mode and all they could do was freeze. This mode of living results in body language being limp, with head hung low, with the child appearing listless and despondent. These behaviours must not be *(but often are)* confused with defiant, disinterest and "challenging" behaviour.

Although these three zones can help us to make sense of "where the child is at" in terms of their emotional state and subsequent behaviour, it is also important to note that they are not without criticism. One such critique comes from Walz (2021), who asserts:

> There is no "good zone" or "bad zone". . . . When we are dysregulated, we do not need to change zones, we need to regulate within, manage or take care of our zone. . . . When we deny the existence and need for this full emotional experience, we are teaching our learners that they need to "calm down" no matter the context or situation.

The key here is context. If a child, for example, has been accused of something they did not do, they have a right to feel angry at this injustice – but supporting them to gain perspective and a sense of equilibrium are also important. To do this and enable the child to move on, the adult needs to truly listen to and honour the child's feelings. Too often, we rush to cajole them out of it without giving the necessary time to explore and process these feelings (Diaz et al., 1990).

Rewind. Reflect. Write!

1   What impact might reward charts have on the fight/flight/freeze response in a child who is already dysregulated and fails to get a reward?

2   Are there areas of your existing provision that exacerbate dysregulated (red and blue zone) behaviours in babies/children? If so, note down how you will address these with your team.

3   Outline three strategies you aim to implement (with corresponding policy changes) to scaffold more regulated (or green zone) behaviours in babies and children.

4   With your team, discuss how you will all monitor the impact of the changes you make to decrease dysregulated (red and blue zone) behaviours and increase regulated (green zone) behaviours.

5   What are your thoughts about the zones of behaviour? Conduct some desk-based research to build your argument.

Top Tips for Practice!

- Ensure all staff know how to respond empathically and co-regulate
- Support children to identify their strengths: this helps to build their self-confidence

■ Build in time for mindfulness daily – this lowers cortisol activity and consequently reduces stress reactivity

■ Introduce the concept of the zones of behaviour to everyone, encouraging them to practice identifying the emotions that go with each zone and how each might feel

■ Try designing a zones of behaviour chart with the children for use in your setting, as a quick reminder for children and staff.

Concluding Thoughts

This chapter has examined the implications of adopting behaviour management policies and practices. The perspective taken is unapologetically anti-behaviour management, and it is hoped that the rationale informing this is clear.

Never has there been a period in the history of behaviourist theories marked by kindness (not bribes). Now, with the power of trauma-informed practices, alongside the scientific evidence base against behaviour management practices, we can all make that time now. Eschewing behaviour management is not an insurmountable task when we break it down and work together to embed SR in its truest sense (which far transcends its ELGs in the EYFS). Quite simply, SR-informed approaches to behaviour leave no room for behaviour management and this is what we must all strive for, to help safeguard our children's mental health and futures. When we *know* better, we can *do* better.

Further Reading

■ Dix, P. (2017). *When the Adults Change, Everything Changes: Seismic Shifts in School Behaviour*. Williston: Independent Thinking Press.

In this engaging book, behaviour training expert Dix draws on anecdotal case studies, scripted interventions and approaches which have been tried and tested in a range of contexts, from the most challenging urban comprehensives to the most privileged international schools, to illustrate that in order to change behaviour, ultimately the solution lies with the behaviour of the adults.

■ Kohn, A. (2018). *Punished by Rewards: The Trouble With Gold Stars, Incentive Plans, A's, Praise and Other Bribes*. New York: Houghton Mifflin.

A must-read for every parent and practitioner. This landmark anniversary edition makes an irrefutable case for eschewing rewards and punishments designed to control individuals in favour of more humane and effective alternatives to support behaviour.

■ Kuypers, L. (2011). *The Zones of Regulation*. Santa Clara, CA: Think Social Publishing.

Based on the zones of regulation curriculum, this book is full of activities designed to deepen children's understanding of how to self-regulate. Lessons focus on a range of skills, including how to read others' facial expressions and a broader range of emotions, as well as how to understand how others react to their behaviour. The book includes worksheets, handouts and visuals to display and share. These can be photocopied from the book or printed from the accompanying USB. This book is an excellent resource for all practitioners who work with children and young adults.

6 Concluding Thoughts – Building a Sustainable Future Through Self-Regulation

Creating a society that is truly informed by SR is not the business of "others" – it is up to you, me – all of us. As Shanker (2020: 281) explains:

> A just society is created by a united army of Just Societers. . . . Parents, relatives, siblings, friends, neighbours, doctors, educators, artists, musicians, philosophers, psychologists, complete strangers. Ultimately, a just society is created by those who don't just understand that there's no such thing as bad, lazy or stupid kid, but actually do something about it.

The aim of this book was to extend and challenge understanding of some key issues related to SR and how nurturing this set of life-essential skills in ourselves and others could save lives. The concept of SR was examined, with an attempt to capture its true essence while disentangling its emotional and cognitive domains. This included a discussion regarding why the cognitive domain (or executive functioning) is often erroneously prioritized at the expense of children's emotional wellbeing and ability to self-regulate, the role SR in EY curricula and the importance of making the language of neuroscience and SR as meaningful and accessible as possible. This was illustrated through the case studies in the book, some of which demonstrated how EY practitioners are successfully teaching children about their brains and getting parents involved in this important journey. After all, it is only deemed jargon for as long as we choose to stay away from, as opposed to grappling with, it. This is why I have always embedded knowledge from the neurosciences in all my work, particularly at the beginner levels – despite being discouraged from doing so "because it's better to just keep it basic at this level." Not on my watch! We each have a brain, mind and body, and we each need to know how these function and how we can help ourselves – and others – to function as optimally as possible. How to achieve SR-driven transformation in your home, EY setting or school has therefore been demonstrated throughout this book, while encouraging the reader to think deeply and critically about the issues presented.

DOI: 10.4324/9781003327479-6

What to Expect in This Chapter

An exploration of SR and its implications for living a fulfilled and optimal life would not be complete if those wider societal and global issues were not also considered as part of this.

Therefore, this final chapter focuses on the power of SR to support action on global challenges, primarily via the United Nations' (UN's) Sustainable Development Goals (SDGs) and as a key part of the Future Skills needed to live better. It is therefore important that we each spend some time thinking about SR in this broader context and what action is needed *now* to reframe what we deem important for children's wellbeing, learning and their future. The 17 SDGs, alongside Professor Pascal's 21st-century global challenges of participation, power, peace, planet, play and technology (five Ps and a T) (2021), hence frame much of the chapter through the lens of EY policy and practice.

Sustainability is a relatively new and all-encompassing subject yet to be consistently addressed and embedded in EY (just as SR remains). This chapter therefore contains many real-life examples of how EY practitioners organically weave through issues concerning sustainability and individual and collective responsibility concerning how the key messages from sustainable development and living sustainably can be actioned in EY settings and homes alike. It may be that you are already adopting some of these, but if you have yet to do so, the case studies and accompanying photographs are included to help you on your journey to achieving practice that not only best nurtures children's SR but is also holistically sustainable – and why this is necessary now more than ever.

By the End of This Chapter, You Will Be Able to:

- Give an overview of Pascal's five Ps and a T

- Discuss the relevance of the five Ps and a T to your provision

- Identify the 17 SDGs

- Plan for positive change around the 17 SDGs within your provision

- Discuss the relevance of the 17 SDGs to families' lives both in and out of the EY setting

- Use the Future Skills to frame practice in your setting.

The EY sector is a challenging place at present, but with challenges come opportunities for advancement – that is, if we are courageous and innovative enough to embrace change. It has long been widely accepted that the EY is viewed as *the* solution to addressing societal ills. This continues to be demonstrated in government initiatives such as the *Best Start for Life – A Vision for the 1001 Critical Days* (HM Government, 2021), Marmot (2020; 2010), the First 1001 Days Manifesto (2021) and Graham Allen's Review (2011), which followed the Field's Review on Poverty and Life Chances (2010). Yet despite all this cross-party acknowledgment of the invaluable role that the EY sector plays in building a more equitable experience for everyone, the sector remains under-valued, under-funded and under-resourced. Notwithstanding this chronic under-investment, the EY sector continues to provide an ideal platform from which societal and global issues can and should be tackled. The section that follows will begin to address how practitioners, along with children and their families, can achieve this on a daily basis.

The 17 Sustainable Development Goals – What's Early Years Got to Do With It?

Let us first ensure we understand what the term sustainability means. Living sustainably means living in ways and meeting our own needs without undermining the ability of future generations to meet their own needs. Living sustainably not only means looking after our environment, but it also requires us to think more carefully about how we treat each other and the opportunities available to help end inequality and disadvantage. Sustainability is therefore viewed as consisting of the following three elements:

- **Social justice** – concerns human rights, access to essential services and anti-discriminatory practices

- **Environmental protection** – this includes reducing our carbon footprints, packaging waste, water usage and other damage to the environment

- **Economic viability** – this centres around job creation and profitability, as well as the understanding that high rates of employment benefit both the economy and people's social wellbeing through the security that employment provides (Brewer et al., 2021).

The SDGs are a collection of 17 interlinked global goals designed to be a "blueprint" to help us all achieve a more sustainable future for everyone. They were set up in 2015 by the United Nations General Assembly and are intended to be achieved by 2030.

While the goals are not legally binding, they offer a clear framework of what must be achieved, how this can be done and by when. With only a few years left to achieve the goals, one cannot help but wonder whether signatories have done enough to meet these by 2030. It is my contention that there remain two key barriers to achieving these goals:

1   The lack of public awareness about what sustainability is (and a consequent lack of meaningful, sustained action)

2   The lack of public awareness of the existence of the 17 SDGs – which returns us to the consequent lack of public awareness and action.

Let us take a closer at these 17 goals. Figure 6.1 summarizes each of these goals.

Figure 6.1 How to Be Planet Positive – The 17 Sustainable Development Goals
Source: UNESCO (2022).

This global mission to meet the 17 goals might seem unrealistic or unattainable to some, but when we break these macro issues down into micro issues, we make them more manageable and achievable. After all, we are each accountable for helping to preserve the planet as best we can, and this can be done both in the work setting and at home. In line with the two key barriers identified previously, before even contemplating action on these 17 goals both in your provision and when encouraging families to take action, you must first consider how you will raise awareness and understanding of both sustainability and the SDGs before expecting people to change.

So what might these 17 SDGs look like for your provision? Following are just some suggestions. While reading, reflect on what you might already do or could do to be more sustainable in all areas of your policies and provision and general running of the setting, while also encouraging families to make choices that are more planet positive.

SDG 1: No Poverty

Poverty remains a major global issue. The Joseph Rowntree Foundation (2021) found that the following groups – who are already more likely than average to be in poverty – have been most impacted by the economic impacts of the pandemic:

■ Low-level and part-time workers

■ Lone parents

■ Minority ethnic groups

■ Private and social renters

■ People living in areas of the United Kingdom where there were already higher levels of unemployment, poverty and deprivation.

With the Resolution Foundation (Joseph Rowntree Foundation, 2021) projecting an increase in poverty by 1.2 million people over the next few years, childcare needs to be kept affordable. Where possible, some settings provide food parcels for the weekend, operate clothing schemes and signpost families to relevant organizations for support.

SDG 2: Zero Hunger

Is food wastage something that you ever reflect on? What are your views on eating foods that have exceeded their expiry date? Much of this food is perfectly edible but is thrown away. If you do not already, you could donate to local food banks – many supermarkets now have donation points were you can donate food items, or you could create one in your setting. What are your views on using food to make playdough, cornflour or using (for example) pasta and rice to make art with? While activities like these are common practice in some settings, what message is it giving children when trying to teach them about food wastage? EY settings and schools are ideal places to talk to children about how food is produced, how much is wasted and how we can all make choices that will help others and our planet. The following case study shows how one primary school teacher encourages children to think more deeply about their impact on the world and how they can live more sustainably.

In order to encourage the children to think more deeply about food, where it comes from and how much is wasted, I planned a range of hands-on activities which required them to not only engage intellectually and physically with the subject, but also emotionally. I wanted them to really understand how much food we all waste and the impact this has on our planet, so that they felt moved enough to do something about it – that is, to learn to self-regulate when it comes to what they eat, how much and how their choices impact the planet. Activities that have worked very well included an initial discussion about food waste, which we followed up by conducting an online search of what foods were most commonly wasted in the United Kingdom and in the world. Having found out that these were fruit, vegetables, milk, bread and potatoes, we talked about how much food poverty there is in the world and that actually a large part of the problem resides in the amount of viable food that continues to be wasted. The children then did a survey at home and we talked about how this waste could be reduced. This was followed by a visit from a lady who works at the local food bank, who came to the school to talk with the children about how many people within the locality use the food bank due to not having enough money to feed themselves or their families. This discussion led to the children drawing pictures about what they learned. You will see in the first image below, *You'll Never Know*, a row of children, some looking sad but with "full tummies," while the one child who looks happy is actually the one who is starving with an "empty" tummy. The second image shows perfectly edible food in a bin, while a child goes hungry. During other activities, the children searched for recipes to make foods by re-using old foods, such as fruit smoothies, fruit salads, bread and butter pudding, breadcrumbs, croutons and pizzas, which all the children thoroughly enjoyed making. We also spoke about how freezing some foods makes them last longer, which means that we do not have to throw them away. We will continue to revisit the subjects of hunger and food wastage while weaving in the children's particular interests, to make it all the more meaningful for them.

SDG 3: Good Health and Wellbeing

A discussion concerning holistic health and wellbeing would not be complete without drawing attention to the pandemic and the devasting impact that it continues to have on health and wellbeing globally. According to the UN (2021a), decades of progress in improving maternal and child health have been undermined by the impact of the pandemic, with 90% of countries still reporting at least one disruption to essential health services – which I am sure many of us can attest to. What about wellbeing? How do you nurture children's wellbeing as part of your daily provision? Like other diseases that spread rapidly across the globe, depression, too, affects millions of people on a global scale: 280 million people in the world suffer from depression, with approximately 700,000 dying due to suicide every year (Institute of Health Metrics and Evaluation.

World Health Organization, 2021). Depression is a leading cause of disability worldwide and is a major contributor to the overall global burden of disease. Yet, with greater SR, the onset/symptoms of depression can be minimized in individuals who are able to cope better with life's stressors. Emotion regulation is a protective factor against depressive symptoms and anxiety disorders while generally enriching individuals' lives. Research (O'Sullivan and Corlett, 2021; Hadland, 2020; Boyd et al., 2017; Chawla, 2006; Ewert et al., 2005) continues to show that the most important factor in raising children's appreciation of their environment while boosting wellbeing is being outdoors in nature (Jenkin et al., 2018). Do children have daily, free access to the outdoors in your setting? Do they have opportunities to do some gardening and grow their own food/herbs? Do you visit local allotments and green spaces? Getting primary carers involved in understanding and supporting their children's wellbeing is a key element of making your approach work in the long term. Reflect on how you currently achieve this and how this could be further built upon.

SDG 4: Quality Education

The EY setting is an excellent place to create equal access to lifelong learning opportunities, and this includes building everyone's understanding of sustainability. Think about the resources you use to as part of teaching and learning in your setting and whether these need to be revised to better extend stimulate and challenge children while capitalizing on their ever-changing preoccupations and interests. The pandemic severely disrupted the learning of children and young adults. By April 2020, roughly 1.6 billion children and youth were out of school and nearly 369 million children who rely on school meals needed to look to other sources for daily nutrition. Educators need to support families, ensuring that they work together in ameliorating the impact of time away from school on children's holistic wellbeing and development.

SDG 5: Gender Equality

While strides have taken place to drive gender equality, with fewer girls forced into early marriage, more women serving in positions of leadership and more girls going to school globally, much more needs to be done. The pandemic caused a sharp rise in violence against women and girls and with lockdown in place, they were trapped, with no support. In 18 countries, husbands can legally prevent their wives from working; in 39 countries, daughters and sons do not have equal inheritance rights; and 49 countries lack laws protecting women from domestic violence (United Nations Economic and Social Council, 2017). Educating children and families about such discrimination and battling gender stereotypes is integral in empowering them to break free of such oppression. The EY setting/school is an ideal place to do this. Here are some easy ways to build in gender equality and tackle discrimination:

- Give children the freedom to choose their own interests – if boys want to wear dresses in the dress-up corner and girls want to play football or with the cars – encourage this

- Introduce unexpected job roles. In a sector dominated by women, it is important to show children that women are fire fighters, astronauts, builders and mechanics – just as some men are ballet dancers and midwives. You could share real-life accounts through story books on the subject and inviting guests to speak with the children

- Mind your language! It is common to use endearments/pet names for children, especially in EY settings. "Honey," "sweetie," "fella" and "little man" are all gender-specific. Instead, use the child's name or use the same pet name for every child. "Friend" is a sound alternative

- Challenge any discriminatory views and behaviour immediately. If a group of girls tells a boy that he cannot play with them because he is a boy – speak with the children about why they think this is. Seek to understand what they think are boys' activities and what are girls' – and why. You can then tackle this in ways that are non-judgmental.

SDG 6: Clean Water and Sanitation

Teach children about water conservation in the setting by learning not to waste it. As with any strategy, this will be most effective if you get families on board. Consider the best ways to do this – it might be a letter home or a post on the setting's/school's communication platform (such as ClassDojo), outlining some easy ways they could do this. For example:

- Talking to the children about how to save water as a family and why this is important for the planet

- Encouraging everyone not to leave the tap water running while brushing their teeth or washing their hair

- Avoiding plastic bottled water

- Collecting rainwater in a bucket to water plants with

- Checking your taps and showerheads for leaks – one drip every second adds up to five gallons per day!

SDG 7: Affordable and Clean Electricity

Review your electricity consumption in the setting. Check the setting for old inefficient lighting. For example, old-style fluorescent light fitting burns roughly 120 watts, while LED replacements burn up to 60% less – commonly achieving 45% less energy use. Think about how you could encourage families to make the switch to more affordable energy sources too.

SDG 8: Decent Work and Economic Growth

The pandemic has led to a significant increase in unemployed young adults and those not in any education or training. Do you employ apprentices in your setting? What opportunities do staff (particularly younger and inexperienced staff) have for progression in your setting? Think about ways to provide staff with better benefits such as a good pension and decent training and development opportunities, regardless of the type of employment contract they have.

SDG 9: Industry, Innovation and Infrastructure

This might seem difficult to achieve, but to help achieve this goal, you might consider using trough sinks in the setting, rather than individual ones, as these waste a lot less water. You could also create an audit to measure your efforts to reduce your carbon footprint.

SDG 10: Reduced Inequalities

UN Secretary-General Antônio Guterres (2020) encapsulated this global issue most succinctly when he urged the world to: "Act now to strengthen the immunity of our societies against the virus of hate." Inclusion is often narrowly perceived to be about race, gender and disabilities, but it is much more than this and the EY sector must be aware of this in order to deliver real, meaningful inclusion. A report by Simpson (2017) found that some EY practitioners allowed their personal view of poverty to impact their responses to children, including whether to seek additional support for the child, as they believed the support would not be valued or continued at home.

SDG 11: Sustainable Cities and Communities

How can you contribute to making your neighbourhood greener and cleaner? Have you thought about joining a campaign to plant more trees? How about taking the children to use the local green space more? Some ideas for including children in helping to keep green spaces clean are provided further on in this chapter. Remember, people value these spaces when they see children enjoying and nurturing them.

SDG12: Responsible Consumption and Production

This encompasses the individual and collective attitudes and dispositions towards sustainability. Ideally this should begin with adults encouraging children to reflect on their responsibility in making planet-positive decisions around reducing waste (consumables, materials and resources), recycling and reusing "rubbish." Settings should therefore embed a culture of sustainability in all their policies as is relevant, so that all change has a clearly articulated rationale, procedure and expectations of everyone.

SDG 13: Climate Action

We can all help to achieve this goal by wearing an extra layer of clothing on colder days, walking instead of boarding transport where you can or even considering a bicycle scheme.

SDG 14: Life Below Water

An easy way to work towards achieving this goal is to ban single-use plastics, glitter and clingfilm and replace regular wet wipes with biodegradable wet wipes. All this would help to reduce plastic usage spreading to the oceans.

SDG 15: Life on Land

Encourage children to pay attention to the wildlife around them. Just a few ways to do this include inviting children to think creatively and critically about some solutions for how they can create positive change now – and an effective way to do this is to share books that address wildlife conservation. You could encourage children to spot any local wildlife during outings or, if they have one, in their garden (and in your setting's outdoor area). Where possible, you could encourage the children to create habitats for them. This might include making a small wildlife pond, making bird feeders or even starting a compost heap!

SDG 16: Peace, Justice and Strong Institutions

Recent global events have left children asking many questions about war and the possibility of war where they live. It is important to allay their fears and anxieties in these situations. You can do this by using age-appropriate language and avoiding sensation-alizing your descriptions of what is happening while watching their reactions and being sensitive to their level of anxiety. Conflict can often bring with it prejudice and discrimination – be this against people or a country. When talking to children, avoid labels like "bad" or "evil" people and instead use it as an opportunity to encourage compassion, such as for the families forced to flee their homes. Some children live in places where there is no peace and EY settings are often the only safe space in their community. Look at your inclusion policy and understand how you teach children to be respectful of each other within their communities. Take them out to visit local organizations and get involved in community activities.

SDG 17: Partnership for the Goals

Your planet needs *you*! This is the call to action for each and every one of us to play our role in protecting our planet. Remember – the small things we do (as outlined in this chapter) add up to make a big difference . . .

As Boyd et al. (2017: 21) bring to our attention, the sector still lags behind in mean-ingfully tackling issues around sustainability, yet as demonstrated in this chapter, EY providers are well positioned to do so. They explain:

> Activities supporting children's emerging awareness and understanding of eco-nomic sustainability are the least developed in early childhood education and care. Yet for most early childhood practitioners, parents and children, the day-to-day activities most significantly influencing sustainable development are at the level of consumption. Sustainable consumption is therefore a particularly important area upon which we should focus in the future.

We therefore need to re-evaluate our positions and agendas in and beyond the EY sector to better address sustainability issues in ways that are meaningful to everyone concerned. Consumption of services and goods (anything from transport to office supplies, nappies, clothing, food and drink) and services all need to be reconsidered and addressed. This directly relates to the 12th SDG, Responsible Consumption and Production. The chief executive officer (CEO) of London's largest and most successful charitable social enterprise, the London Early Years Foundation (LEYF), proposes some suggestions to addressing this SDG, which are woven through all aspects of provision across all their nurseries via the "Eight Rs":

1 **Reduce** – cut down consumption of food wastage, materials and resources

2 **Reuse** – use materials as many times as you can and for a range of purposes

3 **Repair** – fix things rather than discarding them or upcycle (repurpose) and fix things instead of throwing them away

4   **Recycle** – be aware of other ways of discarding rubbish and make sure you teach children and their families how to do this – and the difference they can make to the planet by doing so

5   **Rot** – let things return to the earth to enrich the next crop of plants, while providing a habitat for many insects

6   **Respect** – nurture an understanding and respect of nature and natural processes

7   **Reflect** – embed the habit of being thoughtful, asking questions and wondering about experiences

8   **Responsibility** – get in the habit of being socially and economically sustainable and making decisions that are sustainably responsible in all you do in the EY setting.

Reflecting on the 17 SDGs and some of the proposed ways that we should all be attempting to live more sustainably, the role of SR becomes all the more clearer. The power of SR to support action on the SDGs *and* as *the* foundation of Future Skills that are required to live better needs to be better understood by practitioners and parents alike if we are to meaningfully work towards the goals via SR. It is my contention that while it is so grossly misrepresented in the EYFS, we greatly risk this failing to happen. While there are various conceptual ideas about what these skills are, the Future Skills which consists of the four Cs, offers a sound place to start when reflecting on the skills that EY education and care should be cultivating. These are explored in the following section.

Future Skills for the 21st Century – The Four Cs

This section focuses on the Future Skills which are deemed to play an integral role in preparing children for a world that continues to rapidly evolve and rely upon technology – skills that will equip children to demonstrate resilience, innovation and the ability to get along with diverse groups of people in a range of contexts – not just in school, but across the life trajectory. The OECD Future of Education and Skills 2030 (2019b: 4) distinguishes between three different types of skills which are embodied in the four Cs. These are:

- Cognitive and meta-cognitive skills, which include critical thinking, creative thinking, learning-to-learn and SR

- Social and emotional skills, which include empathy, self-efficacy, responsibility and collaboration

- Practical and physical skills, which include using new information and communication technology devices.

Note how SR and its related emotional and social skills are considered a pivotal part of the 21st-century skill set. Not only underpinning cognitive skills but actually playing more of a significant role than these, in terms of building solid citizenship skills (which includes having personal and collective responsibility within society and collaborating locally, nationally and globally). This returns us to the need to adopt more relational, SR-informed approaches to behaviour from the start of children's academic careers, as opposed to adopting behaviour management, if we are serious about supporting the development of children to be resilient, global citizens. This is highlighted by the OECD (2019a: 1):

> Social and emotional skills can be equally – and in some cases even more – as important as cognitive skills in becoming a responsible citizen.

Now, let us turn our focus to the four Cs, which break down the Future Skills into finer detail. While reading, reflect on them in relation to the current education system and your provision.

- **Creative thinking** – where would we be without creativity? Sometimes referred to as "thinking outside the box," creativity supports self-expression in ways that cannot be deemed "wrong" while igniting curiosity and experimentation. It also fosters mental growth by providing opportunities for trying out new ideas, new ways of thinking and problem-solving. It is through creative experiences which children are able to express and process their feelings about things or people that may otherwise be too painful to convey. Yet, as Richard et al. (2021: 1/15) explain, although creativity is recognized as being a key component of success and individual actualization throughout life, contemporary childhood and lifestyles in general, the continued advances in technology have led to more sedentary lifestyles, which ultimately exert a detrimental impact on levels of physical activity in children and adults alike:

  > In a global and highly competitive world, the importance of creativity is increasing as it supports adaptability, health and actualization. . . . Yet while our world is in constant motion, forcing our mind to sprint to find new ideas, our bodies have never been in such a state of inertia.

  In the most watched TED Talk of all time, educationalist Sir Ken Robinson (2006) claimed that "schools kill creativity," arguing that "we don't grow into creativity, we grow out of it. Or rather we get educated out of it." A statement that, not only based on my experience as a mother of a child who receives no experiences in art or music at school, I wholly agree with. Creative skills and their experiences do not receive the same attention and investment in our current education system, which is myopically driven by academic outcomes and accountability, and yet, as Robinson asserted in this landmark talk, "creativity is as important as literacy and we should afford it the same status"

- **Critical thinking** – driven by active learning, critical thinking skills include being able to explain why things happen; predicting what will happen in the future and analysing a problem, why it exists and possible ways to solve it. It also involves remaining objective (that is, not allowing one's emotions or assumptions to influence thinking) when, for example, attempting to solve problems or overcoming conflict. Effective communication skills are an integral part of critical thinking, enabling the individual to handle difficult conversations, as well as to express their views and disagree in ways that are respectful.

■ **Communication skills** – effective communication skills in all areas of life are critical in enabling us to express our thoughts, feeling and ideas, as well as asking questions and sharing solutions to problems. Without it, we would find it nigh on impossible to get by in life. Just one of the positive aspects borne out of the pandemic and the numerous lockdowns was the opportunity afforded by technology to keep the majority of the world connected. This meant that children were able to keep connected with friends and relatives while resuming their learning remotely. With many children now owning a tablet or smartphone (some before they can even walk or talk), opportunities to communicate seem as endless as they are ubiquitous. It is therefore our responsibility to support effective communication skills through engaging in meaningful conversations with children, so that they build their vocabulary and confidence in communicating with diverse groups of people in a range of contexts. This finds support in Whitebread (2019: 7), who explains:

> Children's early development of self-regulation is highly dependent on the quality of their early social interactions, on their oral language development, and on the opportunities they have had to play with other children, their parents or other caregivers. As a consequence of variations in these factors, there are huge individual differences between the level and profiles of children's self-regulation abilities by the age of three.

■ **Collaboration** – skills such as taking turns, sharing, following rules, negotiating and compromising form a critical part of getting by in life and must be developed in early childhood. Experiences and activities which require children to work together on projects to reach a common goal such as playing games, collaborating on art projects, role play and music and dance are all great ways to build and extend children's competence and confidence in collaborating.

Just a few ways that these four Cs could be supported include the free movement of children in the setting/classroom, integrating age-appropriate technology with educational content and using media sources to explore children's interests and extending their learning in line with their interests. The four Cs can also be developed through encouraging children to exercise greater choice and facilitating greater child-led learning, where children are free to choose what they learn and how they learn it. Taking on leadership and mentoring roles is also integral to the 21st-century skill set. This might include children taking responsibility for certain areas of the setting, equipment or aspects of the routine, like being a "monitor" during tidy-up time, lunch time or visits to the local library – whatever applies to your provision. Creating situations and experiences for children to solve problems and work together and selecting materials and activities that reflect all cultures and families within the community are excellent ways to build citizenship and leadership skills while supporting children's communication, creativity and self-confidence in expressing their ideas and opinions. Part of your responsibility here will be to teach children how to see things from another's point of view and how to compromise in order to create a climate of respect and trust, where everyone is supported to voice their opinions without fear of being humiliated. Moreover, all these experiences will culminate in strengthening children's SR skills as they learn to better manage their own thoughts, feelings and behaviour – as well as co-regulating their peers' emotions and behaviour. This is why embedding a culture of SR in your setting is critical. We cannot strive to achieve a better society – world – without acknowledging the necessity of SR in this individual and collective endeavour. As Whitebread (2019: 4) highlights:

> Self-regulation skills have been shown to predict a range of academic and "soft" or "21st century" skills development through childhood into early adulthood more powerfully than any other aspect of early development.

Yet ironically, policymakers and the arbiters of the education system have for too long viewed SR as a "soft" skill – something unquantifiable and unimportant compared to the traditional three Rs of reading, writing and arithmetic, which are still prioritized at school – to the detriment of many children. The time has come for the four Cs to be put at the top of the agenda, to help ensure that every child develops the emotional, moral and intellectual maturity needed to help navigate their world.

Rewind. Reflect. Write!

I Is sustainability something that you consciously educate the children about? Discuss.

2a Note at least one thing you do with the children to achieve each of the 17 goals.

2b In which ways could this be improved? Make a plan to action.

2c Discuss some ways you could increase parental buy-in and involvement concerning sustainability.

3a Do you agree with the highlighted four Cs as being Future Skills? Discuss.

3b Are there other skills that would you add? Discuss.

3c How far in and in which ways do you think the current education system nurtures the four Cs in children?

3d Reflecting on the four Cs, how effectively do you and your team model each of these to children in your setting?

3e In which ways could this be improved? Note these down, with a view to action.

4 In which ways does SR provide the foundation of the four Cs?

5 Summarize how you provide experiences that are reflective of children's creative thinking and productivity.

6 Discuss the ways in which you and your team intentionally embed opportunities for children to collaborate and communicate with their peers.

7 Do you and your team empower children in your setting through opportunities for leadership? How could this be developed?

Five Ps and a T – The Key to Understanding Global Issues

Created by Pascal (2021), the 21st-century global challenges of participation, power, peace, planet, play and technology (five Ps and a T) (2021) provides a framework for us to critically reflect on pertinent global issues prismatically and through the lens of EY.

Power – this concerns children's agency, citizenship rights and voice in shaping their world and daily lives. After all, if they are not afforded the space and opportunities to express their voice and power (agency) to shape decisions about them, how can we honestly claim that they have rights and agency? Provision which does not actively facilitate children to exercise their power will ultimately diminish their experiences of autonomy and SR, which in turn will likely reduce their motivation to learn (Murray and Cousens, 2019).

Pedagogy – practitioners need to be confident in their approach to pedagogy and play, not least because play is at the heart of the pedagogic approach in EY. This is further explored as part of the following "P."

Play – is now widely understood to be critical to healthy child development and has been recognized by the United Nations' Convention of the Rights of the

Child (UNICEF, 1989) as a right of every child. Ideally (and in line with the concept of power), it should be up to children to decide how play is used and when. This can present both an opportunity and a worry for some practitioners and parents alike, who might feel that play is something to do once children have done something to "deserve" playing or once the "work" is done. Children learn best through their daily play and practitioners should be encouraging and facilitating this – as Vygotsky notes, children play at the edge of their capabilities when they are immersed in free-flow play and have the *agency* and *capacity* to do so. However, there is a discourse that runs contrary to this – a discourse, particularly post-pandemic, around "catching up," "lost learning" and a subsequent focus on language and vocabulary. While under-standable, the best vehicle to develop those skills is through high-quality, supported play. So, the onus is on practitioners to explain – or justify to regulatory bodies (such as Ofsted) – why play is prioritized as part of provision. We therefore need to take all staff through a process of confidence-building when instigating or engaging in pedagogical conversations. This can be done within team meetings, through role play, in discussion and in your general dialogue on a day-to-day basis in the setting. Such opportunities will enable practitioners to rehearse and practice in a safe place and have those reflective conversations about the children and why they have set up the environment in a particular way. Ultimately, if it works for children – why should it not be happening? There is no argument against ways of educating and caring for children that are child-centred and with practice, these pedagogical conversations with regulatory bodies, colleagues and primary carers ultimately help to build practitioners' confidence while further deepening the knowledge of all stakeholders in the process.

The two Ps that follow have come out of the wider global issues.

Planet – this is about how we reflect on issues of sustainability and how
we teach our children about these issues. It cannot be emphasized enough that we each have a responsibility to engage our children in thinking and talking about sus-tainability, as well as taking action on sustainability both at an individual and collective level. This includes EY providers being mindful and transparent about what they are actively doing to be sustainable, such as how they use plastics, which companies they source food from, which foods they include on the menu, choice of cleaning products, how energy efficient they are and how resources are maximized (as opposed to being wasted). Likewise, primary carers could reflect on and engage their children in conversations about how they too could live more sustainably. This predominantly revolves around the three Rs of:

- Reduce

- Reuse

- Recycle.

Typically, it includes getting the children involved in conversations and action around reducing waste during mealtimes; recycling; growing own produce where possible and considering a vegetarian/vegan diet, which can lower greenhouse gas emissions much more quickly; caring for local green spaces; and buying second-hand toys and clothes, as well as donating unwanted toys and clothes instead of throwing them away. With an estimated 8.5 million new, perfectly good toys thrown away every year in the United Kingdom (East Sussex County Council, 2019), it is vital that we all make more earth-conscious decisions about the way we live. We are the greatest role models for our children, so we must be more mindful of these issues, ensuring that we also engage them in finding solutions. The following case study was provided by an EY practitioner and mother of five children. The photograph in the case study depicts two of her children, Hiro, aged nine-years-old (left), and Mei, six-years-old (right), who have been raised to be planet-conscious and protective of their environment.

As a family, we are passionate about living in ways that are sustainable. Mei is on the Eco committee at school. Hiro isn't, as there is a restricted number of children on the committee, but he does support the project. They (and all our nurseries) follow this initiative, recycling and using only recycled resources where possible, having a compost, donating food to food banks and bringing unwanted clothes to clothing recycling stations. We also purchased litter pickers and a wagon to clear our local parks. My husband is Japanese and littering in Japan is frowned upon – respect for the natural and living/education environments is deeply embedded in their culture. Hiro is passionate about helping to keep the world clean and has even offered to clean the school on his lunch breaks! Living more mindfully about our planet helps to promote children's self-regulation skills too, as it builds prosocial behaviours and instils core values early on, therefore increasing a sense of responsibility, care, respect, love and connection to others and nature. It also builds skills in planning and implementing goals, delaying gratification (by making choices that put the planet first) and instilling moral values concerning the choices they make and the impact on the environment and the planet.

The next P to have come out of the wider global issues is:

Peace – this concerns how well we live together well – as was exemplified by the family in the preceding case study. The mother understands the importance of teaching her children to respect, love and connect to others and nurtures their ability to do so through every available opportunity. As this family demonstrates, efforts to live peacefully do not (and generally would not) have to start on a large scale but should instead focus on the immediate context and the people in it (which is further discussed in the following section, with regard to micro and macro issues). There exist many challenges at present, particularly around migration, diversity and inclusion. So how do we live peacefully and sustainably together while celebrating the richness and diversity of cultures, values and perspectives? The younger generation seems far more acutely aware of this than we readily acknowledge. When we reflect on the solutions in the longer term, the solutions reside in children, as they *are* the future, so the more we can build their awareness of these global issues and their responsibility as global citizens, the more beneficial for everyone. All these issues happen at a micro level but add up at a macro level – so it is about how we, with the children, whether a childminder or a large chain of nurseries, take the time to have these conversations (at an appropriate level) but also prepare them for the world which they inhabit – and will shape. This returns us to the need to consider the emotional climate that we create in the setting. We cannot expect children to make a positive impact and contribution across the life trajectory if we do not also support their developing ability to self-regulate. The Montessori School Peace Curriculum provides an appropriate example here, with its ultimate aim being to teach children how to grow up to contribute to world peace. According to the Curriculum, the three levels of experiencing peace are:

1   World peace

2   Community peace

3   Inner peace (achieving SR).

Granted, achieving world peace might seem like a vast, insurmountable undertaking, which is dominated by politics ingrained in inequality and difficult to address in the EY, but to reiterate, when we start on a micro level and work outwards, each of us *can* make a positive difference. Living peacefully concerns how children are encouraged to value and respect differences, to cooperate, negotiate, show empathy and overcome conflict. It is also about practitioners providing a positive role model when children are upset – and how effectively they listen, empathize and help them to feel connected.

Curricula frameworks like this are empowering for all children, through building their understanding of issues around peace, resilience and tolerance while encouraging unity. They also strengthen children's sense of identity concerning where they have come from but, more importantly, where they are going – at an individual and collective level. Issues surrounding peace become all the more easy to address when we include community (including classroom) peace. Similar to Bronfenbrenner's ecological systems theory (1989), this could include the adult addressing issues around peace, again, initially by tackling the micro issues before those more abstract concepts as part of the macro issues. This is illustrated in Figure 6.2.

Figure 6.2 Making the Macro Micro – Achieving Sustainability Through Self-Regulation

This simple diagram illustrates the first and most important step in co-constructing knowledge and action concerning sustainability issues: issues which present themselves in a child's daily life and affect them directly (that is, on a micro level). These are depicted in the centre of the diagram. Once these are addressed, practitioners and children can work together to tackle issues around sustainability on an environmental and global (macro) level. These are:

- Nurturing children's love and respect for themselves

- Nurturing children's love and respect for others and the community

- Nurturing children's love and respect for the planet.

Let us begin with nurturing children's love and respect for themselves. When we reflect on Bowlby's internal working model (1988), we know that this develops through those early interactions with significant others. A child who has an inconsistent or unresponsive attachment figure will likely develop a view of self as unacceptable and unworthy, resulting in a negative self-image, low self-esteem and low self-respect. Therefore, addressing this must be the first stage of teaching children about peace and their role in creating and maintaining peace in their lives. A robust key person system will be critical here, as well as embedding relational approaches to supporting behaviour (not managing behaviour!) Children who have not experienced CR from their primary carers may also have an impeded ability to self-regulate, and this plays a fundamentally important role in achieving emotional and physical calm – particularly in the face of triggers or conflict. In other words, it is all about how we support children to develop SR.

This initial step will prove all the more important to spend time on, because a child who does not love themselves will not find it easy to love and respect others – the next level of building knowledge and instilling values around peace. When children have love and respect for themselves, they will more readily demonstrate love and respect for their family, friends, environment and community – this encompasses respect for their school and neighbourhood and the people in it. Teaching children about conflict resolution and giving them simple ways to assert themselves without upsetting or physically hurting other children, as well as building their SR skills, are integral to nurturing love and respect for others and the community. When these principles and values are instilled, it is more likely that children will show love and respect for the planet. This includes taking greater responsibility about the choices they make while at the setting, at home and in the wider world – and the impact that their choices have on the planet. Thus, the adult's role is to constantly provoke and challenge their own, their team's and the children's thinking and behaviour. This could ultimately empower children to think about how they influence their future and the world that they go out into.

The following is a detailed case study of how the manager of a small rural nursery in the United Kingdom embeds knowledge and respect for the planet through organically weaving conversations and experiences around Pascal's five Ps, using SR-informed provision as the continual backdrop. Reflecting on Figure 6.2, you will also notice how everyone in this setting harnesses SR as *the* foundation to building understanding and achieving action concerning those micro sustainability issues first, before addressing the wider, macro issues.

For us, self-regulation and emotional intelligence provide the foundation of any nature-based practice. At our setting, we view global issues as a core part of all we do – so everything organically grows from this – "act local think global." Being connected with your local landscapes, even in your garden, attunes you to the wonders of nature and in doing so, you build that empathy and care of the natural world and community. I'm using the ACHUNAS framework (the Assessment framework for Children's Human Nature Situations), which is a framework that outlines a list-based set of criteria which is used to assess the how teachers are un/consciously fostering children's connection to the community and nature. In our setting, the children enjoy growing, preparing and eating the fruits and vegetables they grow – which is illustrated in the photograph below.

They also enjoy interactions with animals, making active time to just be in-the-moment, telling stories, utilizing books and generally feeling a part of their own space, with their friends in their garden, their community and their world. We also encourage honest conversations about positive and negative emotions towards others, to help nurture respect and empathy for others, as well as build their capacity to listen and negotiate in order to overcome disagreements. Ultimately, this teaches and fosters

gratitude and unconditional love as an active member of society, helping others, while protecting our local environment. It all provides a sense of purpose and liberation through small achievements.

As mentioned, we grow plentiful amounts of vegetables and fruits, bushes and trees – not just to harvest, but to support wildlife. We also have beehives, chickens and a fish pond that hosts frogs and toads. I think such experiences can be lacking for children in urban areas, which is a shame. We regularly visit the local woodlands and nature reserves to observe change, growth and decay, as well as exploring and investigating all the natural elements – wind, rain, fire and ice – and finding magic and joy in each of these. We also talk about forest fires, deforestation, saving the seas, the decline in biodiversity and climate activists. Importantly, although these were not introduced as topics (because I'm generally opposed to planning for learning in this way), we introduce these issues through play, during conversations and the questions we all ask as part of these interactions. It is embedded in our ethos and daily routines, rather than a topic to teach, which can be easily forgotten.

I believe that ecological identity cannot survive without a strong sense of self. Self-awareness and self-regulation need to be the foundation. Unconditional love of oneself will directly link to unconditional love of the community and the wider world. One way we do this which always proves effective is by using nature as a catalyst. For example, a rainy day and grey, dull clouds – which we link to emotions. We do this to encourage children to understand that we must regulate ourselves with love and acceptance of what we see as the "good" and "bad."

When we make time for mindfulness for ourselves and the wider world through supporting children's self-regulation skills, they can apply this resilience, strength and understanding, using skills like a self-regulation compass to navigate their way through the immediate environment and wider issues. It promotes empathy, compassion, forgiveness, creativity and critical thinking. . . . We use nature, such as forest bathing and meditation to self-regulate – which children and their parents now practice together at home, having observed the positive difference in their children's behaviour in the setting.

Children who struggle with their emotions blossom from connecting with all aspects of nature and are consequently able to feel that sense of acceptance, freedom and unity. Consequently, when their capacity to self-regulate increases, so does their resilience and compassion. Such qualities then motivate them to play their part in tackling global issues. Nature is all around us. So before language and full conversations, the natural world not only calms the brain and grounds the child, but enables personal growth, especially during times of dysregulation. The key is that the individual, unique self must be nurtured first, before the big issues. We achieve this through encouraging children to share their experiences with a teacher who can co-regulate and show them the magic in the world and listen to them, play beside them, no matter what they may say or how they feel. This is invaluable in nurturing self-regulation. I always encourage my team to imagine that they are seeing the world anew, just as these young children are, because we have to view nature from a child's perspective – with awe and wonder. Only then can we can teach care and compassion, for children to be there for each other in times of sadness and frustration and by planting such beautiful seeds, we can cultivate a much better chance of a more beautiful society – we have to nurture the self before we can help anyone else, just like Bronfenbrenner's ecological systems theory. As children grow, they will develop their critical thinking skills, which will not only affect the inner circle of that ecological system, but the wider systems too.

As I mentioned earlier, another key strategy we use is gratitude, along with dreams and wishes. Every day, we share gratitude, without fail – no matter how seemingly small, we encourage children to share their thoughts and express themselves artistically (or however they wish) to communicate their dreams, ideas and wishes. This has included their wishes for people to be kind to

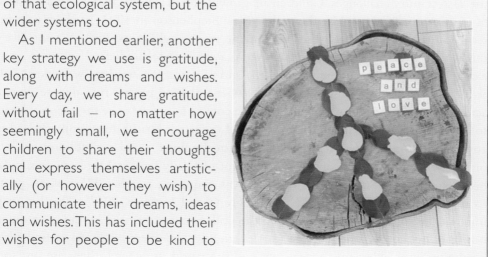

one and other, to help each other out, to be polite and to know it is okay to make mistakes. Through these experiences, they can contribute to their community and shape a safe space and an environment, filled with unconditional love and acceptance – as opposed to perfection – which is all too often frontloaded on social media. If we want to make change a reality, we must, because we feel something within us to create new habits and a more caring culture, which prioritizes peace and sustainabiltiy. Rigid behaviour policies will do nothing to achieve this. This beautiful piece of transient art was made by a group of children (mixed ages) on a sunny afternoon, following our conversations around peace.

Post-pandemic, we have reached a tipping point professionally and globally in how we move forward. We must therefore be mindful that any tipping point is not one isolated event but a cumulation of events that cause change. We should view it as a step at a time and a process which takes bravery, leadership and a clear vision to create the changes that we hope to see in our world and in our children. In conclusion, it is important that careful attention be paid to these global issues and that they are not just addressed in EY tokenistically, with a one-off, superficial topic planned, but are instead embedded and woven through curriculum planning and experiences in meaningful ways – ways that were beautifully demonstrated in the case study. Again, it is about viewing the curriculum prismatically – through pressing global issues which centre around sustainability and the future of the planet.

Technology – this focuses on the role of technology as part of the 21st-century challenges. Children are growing up in a digital world – or a metaverse (a term originally coined by the author Neal Stephenson in 1992. It describes a fully realized digital world that exists beyond the one in which we live). We too live in this world, which is seismically changing as a result of technological advances, prime examples being artificial intelligence (AI) and robotics. Referred to by Seldon (2018) as the fourth education revolution, AI has been making inroads into diverse domains across our lives for decades, and its uses have come a long way since the robots we came to know on shows such as *Tomorrow's World* (a former British television series about contemporary developments in science and technology – and a childhood favourite of mine). AI and robotics are core features of our daily lives and threaten to supplant between 400 and 800 million jobs by 2030, requiring roughly 375 million people to switch job categories entirely (McKinsey Global Institute, 2017). This has major implications for current education and the skills being prioritized by the government, not least because, as the OECD (2019a) rightly identifies, while AI is undeniably becoming invaluable across professions and the world in general, there are just some

skills that it cannot rival. This includes skills which (as mentioned earlier), paradoxically, are not viewed as important by the government – SR, imagination and creativity – highlighted earlier as part of the four Cs. For now, at least, the McKinsey Global Institute (2017: 7) reassures us that:

> AI appears less likely to replace jobs that require creativity. Workers in jobs that require originality – "the ability to come up with unusual or clever ideas about a given topic or situation, or to develop creative ways to solve a problem" – are substantially less likely to see themselves replaced by computer-controlled equipment, reflecting the current limitations of automation. Art directors, fashion designers and microbiologists are thus unlikely to be out of work anytime soon.

A recent report by Ofcom (2020) found that in the United Kingdom, 52% of three- to four-olds and 82% of five- to seven-year-olds are online. How do we give them the skills to navigate this virtual world, with an understanding of what is real and what is virtual? How do we use technology well? We need to bear all this mind while acknowledging that we are not digital natives – unlike our children, who are, and this brings its own challenges. One persistent challenge is that children seem to be more adept at navigating tech devices than adults, and in some EY settings and homes, these devices are used as a distraction as opposed to a teaching tool and consequently not used to their potential. This is due to a lack of staff training on the use of technology, which could equip them to be more confident about protecting children while maximizing the role of technology in their lives. Technology is (whether we like it or not) an integral part of almost all of our daily lives, changing as dynamically as it is rapidly. Yet there is also a discourse that we must keep children away from it, due to issues predominantly around safeguarding and screen time, but when effectively managed, the digital world can be a wonderful tool, giving instant access to knowledge about the world, people and experiences that we otherwise would not have access to. Children's mental health and wellbeing must be protected so that there is a balance between the real world and the digital world, knowing what is real and what is not – and, just as importantly, knowing when to withdraw and engage. While overstatements such as screentime rewiring children's brains are generally unlikely (Mills, 2014), the "Goldilocks effect" of screen time does seem to hold true (this is the "just right" amount of time for children/adolescents, when their sense of wellbeing is boosted by having "moderate" amounts of screen time). This currently stands at 1 hour and 40 minutes during the week. Difficulties set in when children have unlimited and unsupervised access – difficulties compounded by adults who do not have rules for themselves concerning when and how much they use their own tech devices. We need to understand that the impact of technology depends on the type of technology and what it is used for (for example, gaming or socializing) while setting very clear boundaries for ourselves and our children. This includes carving out time to enjoy these devices together while being clear about when we need to stop and why. We must also acknowledge that although technology was swiftly utilized to fill a gap for much of the two years during the pandemic and its numerous lockdowns, the challenges of online learning proved stressful for children and adults alike. There was minimal opportunity for conversation or bonding with peers or teachers and no remit for physical touch or comfort. Now that children have returned to school, reports evidence that while technology did fill a gap, the lack of real social contact with other children and trusted adults has affected children's ability to self-regulate and their behaviour in general, with heightened anxiety, irritability, anger, stress and disruption to sleep patterns and mood being commonplace (NHS Digital, 2021; United Nations Children's Fund [UNICEF], 2021b; Brooks et al., 2020; Francisco, 2020; WHO, 2020). Over time, this will exert detrimental effects on children's brain development and social skills (reflect on those stressors across the five domains of SR). We will, however, have to wait and see what future research findings tell us about the long-term impact of the pandemic on children's – as well as adults' – mental, emotional and social wellbeing. This is recognized by UNICEF (2021b: 16), which makes it clear that *it will be years before we can really assess the impact of COVID-19 on our mental health*. On a larger, global scale, we each have a responsibility to ensure that technology does not supplant our collective interest in and concern with sustainability issues: while it is undoubtedly propelling the human race forward, is it a world we want to embrace? when Freire (2016: xxiii) asserts that:

> While the volume of technological toys available increases, clean rivers for fishing and swimming, tree-shaded yards, clean air, clean drinking water, streets for playing or walking around, fruits eaten without fear of chemicals, free time, and spaces for informal socialization become more and more scarce.

Rewind. Reflect. Write!

1   In your own words, summarize the five Ps and a T.

2a Discuss the relevance of the five Ps and a T to your provision.

2b Which aspects of your provision do you think could be developed and how could you and your team do this?

3a Outline at least three ways you encourage your team to live peacefully and sustainably together while celebrating the richness and diversity of cultures, values and perspectives.

3b Now outline at least three ways you do this with children and their families.

4   Discuss the role of SR in the five Ps and a T. Your response can relate to children and adults alike.

5 Revisit the model *Making the Macro Micro – Achieving Sustainability Through Self-Regulation*. Now answer the following questions:

  a How do you nurture children's love and respect for themselves?

  b How do you nurture children's love and respect for others and the community?

  c How do you nurture children's love and respect for the planet?

  d In which ways and how far do you think SR underpins the model?

6 Do some online research into the Montessori School Peace Curriculum.

  a What aspects do you think are effective?

  b Are there any elements that could work in your provision? Discuss.

  c Are there any aspects that you think could be revised? Discuss.

Top Tips for Practice!

- With your team, carry out an audit of the resources you use, with a view to making planet-positive changes (for example, if you still use glitter, consider stopping this)

- What children's books do you have concerning sustainability? There are some fantastic choices available. Here are just a few ideas:

  - *Greta and the Giants*, by Zoë Tucker

  - *The Adventures of a Plastic Bottle*, by Alison Inches

  - *The Terrible Greedy Fossifoo*, by Charles Fuge

  - *Miss Fox's Class Goes Green*, by Eileen Spinelli

  - *10 Things I Can Do to Help My World*, by Melanie Walsh

- With your team, audit your indoor and outdoor environments – note down how these could be improved to support teaching around global issues

- With your team, audit your resources concerning peace and overcoming conflict – if these need to be updated and expanded, plan how you will do so

- Get parents/families on board! Start those non-judgemental, helpful conversations about how they could make small changes on a daily basis to live more sustainably

- Seek team training around effective use of technology to help ensure all staff are confident in maximizing its potential in the setting – as opposed to it being used as a distraction

- Support children to overcome conflict and help them to generate ideas of how they might solve the problem

- Focus on cultivating those Future Skills through planned and spontaneous learning experiences.

Concluding Thoughts

This book is dedicated to everyone who has made the decision to be more mindful of SR and is brave enough to do something about it. This might look like addressing their own mental health, building their own self-regulatory capacity and CR skills and eschewing behaviour management strategies professionally and personally. Every child deserves to be treated with respect and humility – cheap "quick wins" under the guise of behaviour management are not the way forward. We should no longer be guided by outmoded theories of child development that are hundreds of years old but instead make more consistent and meaningful attempts to include neuroscientific and evidence-based theories that are more suitable for a rapidly evolving life in the 21st century. The pandemic; sustainability; the omnipresent nature of the digital world with its unique risks and the reported rise in child and adolescent stress, anxiety and depression have culminated to make the world a very challenging place to inhabit. A related key theme throughout this book has been the critical role of SR in facilitating essential skills such as resilience, persistence and confidence as part of those Future Skills – which are indispensable in helping children and adolescents not only navigate these global challenges but take positive steps to surmount them.

It is up to each and every one of us to build a society that is guided by SR. It will not happen swiftly or easily – and we will encounter sceptics along the way – but we must never give up. The future of our children depends on it.

Further Reading

- Boyd, D., Hirst, N. and Siraj-Blatchford, J. (2017). *Understanding Sustainability in Early Childhood Education: Case Studies and Approaches From Across the UK*. Oxon. Routledge.

  This book provides a thorough examination of what education for sustainability looks like in practice across the four home nations of the United Kingdom. It discusses the different applications and positions of each region and considers the contribution of early childhood education to support the 17 SDGs. It is a useful resource for students, practitioners, leaders and researchers engaged in the study of education for sustainability in early childhood and the importance of the EYs for the development of life-long pro-environmental attitudes.

- Elliott, S., Ärlemalm-Hagsér, E. and Davis, J. (2020). *Researching Early Childhood Education for Sustainability: Challenging Assumptions and Orthodoxies*. Oxfordshire: Routledge.

This book presents diverse research and theory at a national and international level, providing a comprehensive guide to the role of sustainability in early childhood education, at a time when it is needed more than ever. The book serves as an effective resource which enables EY practitioners to practise sustainability with children, while also being useful to researchers, lecturers and students.

- O'Sullivan, J. and Corlett, N. (2021). 50 *Fantastic Ideas for Sustainability*. London: Featherstone.

This highly practical and easily accessible book is an excellent resource that supports teaching children how to reduce, reuse, recycle, repair and be respectful through the 50 fun activities which encourage environmental sustainability. The activities encourage children and practitioners to see the potential for creativity and fun using and reusing everyday, easy-to-source items, some of which might have otherwise gone to waste.

References

Abraham, D. (2017). *The Superkids Activity Guide to Conquering Every Day: Awesome Games and Crafts to Master Your Moods, Boost Focus, Hack Mealtimes and Help Grownups Understand Why You Do the Things You Do.* Boston: Page Street Publishing Co.

Ainsworth, M. D. S., Bell, S. M. and Stayton, D. J. (1971). Individual Differences in Strange-Situation Behaviour of One-Year-Olds. In H. R. Schaffer (Ed.), *The Origins of Human Social Relations* (pp. 17–58). London and New York: Academic Press.

Alberts, B., Johnson, A., Lewis, J., Morgan, D., Raff, M., Roberts, K. and Walter, P. (2014). *Molecular Biology of the Cell.* 4th ed. New York: Garland Science.

Albrecht, B., Uebel-von Sandersleben, H., Gevensleben, H. and Rothenberger, A. (2015). Pathophysiology of ADHD and Associated Problems-Starting Points for NF Interventions? *Front Hum Neurosci,* 9(359): 1–14.

Allen, G. (2011). *Early Intervention: The Next Steps.* London: Crown Copyright.

Allen, K. and van der Zwan, R. (2019). The Myth of Left- vs Right-Brain Learning. *Int J Innov Creativity Change,* 5(1): 189–200.

Almeida, R. G. and Lyons, D. A. (2017). On Myelinated Axon Plasticity and Neuronal Circuit Formation and Function. *J Neurosci,* 37: 10023–10034.

Anda, R. F., Porter, L. E. and Brown, D. W. (2020). Inside the Adverse Childhood Experience Score: Strengths, Limitations, and Misapplications. *Am J Prev Med,* 59(2): 93–295.

Arvay, C. G. (2018). *The Healing Code of Nature: Discovering the New Science of Eco-Psychosomatics.* Louisville, CO: Sounds True Inc.

Asmussen, K., Fischer, F., Drayton, E. and McBride, T. (2020). *Adverse Childhood Experiences. What We Know, What We Don't Know, and What Should Happen Next.* London: The Early Intervention Foundation (EIF).

Ausderau, K., Sideris, J., Furlong, M., Little, L. M., Bulluck, J. and Baranek, G. T. (2014). National Survey of Sensory Features in Children with ASD: Factor Structure of the Sensory Experience Questionnaire (3.0). *J Autism Dev Disord,* 44(4): 915–925.

Ayres, J. (2005). *Sensory Integration and the Child.* Los Angeles: Western Psychological Services.

Ayres, J. (1989). *Sensory Integration and Praxis Tests Manual.* Los Angeles, CA: Western Psychological Services.

Ayres, J. (1979). *Sensory Integration and the Child.* Torrance, CA: Western Psychological Services.

Ayres, J. (1976). *Sensory Integration Therapy. In Sensory Integration and the Child.* Los Angeles: Western Psychological Services.

Ayres, J. (1972). Improving Academic Scores Through Sensory Integration. *J Learn Disabil*, 5: 336–343.

Azevedo, F. A. C., Carvalho, L. R. B., Grinberg, L. T., Farfel, J. M., Ferretti, R. E. L., Leite, R. E. P., Filho, W. J., Lent, R. and Herculano-Houzel, S. (2009). Equal Number of Neuronal and Nonneuronal Cells Make the Human Brain an Isometrically Scaled-Up Primate Brain. *J Comp Neurol*, 513: 532–541. DOI: 10.1002/cne.21974.

Azevedo, R., Behnagh, R., Duffy, M., Harley, J. M. and Trevors, G. J. (2012). Metacognition and Self-Regulated Learning in Student-Centred Learning Environments. In D. Jonassen and S. Land (Eds.), *Theoretical Foundations of Student-Centred Learning Environments* (pp. 171–197). New York: Routledge.

Bai, D., Hon Kei Yip, B., Windham, G. C., Sourander, A., Francis, R., Yoffe, R., Glasson, E., Mahjani, B., Suominen, A., Leonard, H., Gissler, M., Buxbaum, J. D., Wong, K., Schendel, D., Kodesh, A., Breshnahan, M., Levine, S. Z., Parner, E. T., Hansen, S. N., Hultman, C., Reichenberg, A. and Sandin, S. (2019). Association of Genetic and Environmental Factors with Autism in a 5-Country Cohort. *JAMA Psychiatry*, 76(10): 1035–1043.

Bailey, J. and Baker, S. T. (2020). A Synthesis of the Quantitative Literature on Autistic Pupils' Experience of Barriers to Inclusion in Mainstream Schools. *J Res Special Edu Needs*, 20(4): 291–307.

Bambrough, R. (2011). *The Philosophy of Aristotle*. New York: Penguin Putnam Inc.

Bandura, A. (1992). Exercise of Personal Agency Through the Self-Efficacy Mechanism. In R. Schwarzer (Ed.), *Self-Efficacy: Thought Control of Action* (pp. 3–38). Washington, DC: Hemisphere.

Bandura, A. (1991). Social Cognitive Theory of Self-regulation. *Organ Behav Hum Decis Processes*, 50: 248–287.

Bandura, A. (1986). *Social Foundations of Thought and Action: A Social Cognitive Theory*. London: Prentice-Hall, Inc.

Bandura, A. (1977). *Social Learning Theory*. Englewood Cliffs, NJ: Prentice Hall.

Bandura, A. (1962). *Social Learning Through Imitation*. Lincoln, NE: University of Nebraska Press.

Bard, J. B. L. (2008). Waddington's Legacy to Developmental and Theoretical Biology. *Biol Theory*, 3: 188–197.

Barker, D. (1995). *Nutrition in the Womb*. London: The Random House Group Limited.

Barrett, L. F., Lindquist, K. A., Bliss-Moreau, E., Duncan, S., Gendron, M., Mize, J. and Brennan, L. (2007). Of Mice and Men: Natural Kinds of Emotions in the Mammalian Brain? A Response to Panksepp and Izard. *Perspect Psychol Sci*, 2(2007): 297–311.

Bassok, D., Latham, S. and Rorem, A. (2016). Is Kindergarten the New First Grade? *AERA Open*, 1: 1–13.

Bates, J. E., Schermerhorn, A. C. and Petersen, I. T. (2012). Temperament and Parenting in Developmental Perspective. In M. Zentner and R. L. Shiner (Eds.), *Handbook of Temperament* (pp. 425–441). New York: The Guilford Press.

Baum, S. H., Stevenson, R. A. and Wallace, M. T. (2015). Behavioural, Perceptual, and Neural Alterations in Sensory and Multisensory Function in Autism Spectrum Disorder. *Prog Neurobiol*, 134: 140–160.

Becker, D. R., McClelland, M. M., Loprinzi, P. and Trost, S. G. (2014). Physical Activity, Self-Regulation, and Early Academic Achievement in Preschool Children. *Early Educ Dev*, 25(1): 56–70.

Bell, C. D. and Wolfe, M. A. Brain (2007). The Integration of Cognition and Emotion During Infancy and Early Childhood: Regulatory Processes Associated with the Development of Working Memory. *Brain Cogn*, 65(1): 3–13.

Bellis, M. A., Hughes, K., Ford, K., Ramos, R. G., Sethi, D. and Passmore, J. (2019). Life Course Health Consequences and Associated Annual Costs of Adverse Childhood Experiences Across Europe and North America: A Systematic Review and Meta-Analysis. *Lancet Public Health*, 4: e517–528.

Ben-Sasson, A., Gal, E., Fluss, R., Katz-Zetler, N. and Cermak, S. A. (2019). Update of a Meta-Analysis of Sensory Symptoms in ASD: A New Decade of Research. *J Autism Dev Disord*, 49(12): 4974–4996.

Bengtsson, S. L., Nagy, Z., Skare, S., Forsman, L., Forssberg, H. and Ullén, F. (2005). Extensive Piano Practicing Has Regionally Specific Effects on White Matter Development. *Nat Neurosci*, 8: 1148–1150.

Blair, C. and Raver, C. (2015). School Readiness and Self-Regulation: A Developmental Psychobiological Approach. *Annu Rev Psychol*, 66: 711–731.

Bowlby, J. (1988). *A Secure Base: Clinical Applications of Attachment Theory*. Hove: Psychology Press.

Bowlby, J. (1953). *Child Care and the Growth of Love*. London: Penguin.

Bowlby, J. (1951). *Maternal Care and Mental Health*. Geneva: World Health Organization.

Boyd, D., Hirst, N. and Siraj-Blatchford, J. (2017). *Understanding Sustainability in Early Childhood Education: Case Studies and Approaches from Across the UK*. Oxon: Routledge.

Brewer, M., Corlett, A., Handscomb, K. and Tomlinson, D. (2021). *The Living Standards Outlook*. London: The Resolution Foundation.

Bronfenbrenner, U. (1989). Ecological Systems Theory. In R. Vasta (Ed.), *Annals of Child Development* (Vol. 6, pp. 187–249). Greenwich, CT: JAI Press.

Bronfenbrenner, U. (1979). *The Ecology of Human Development: Experiments by Nature and Design*. Cambridge, MA: Harvard University Press, The President and Fellows of Harvard College.

Bronson, M. B. (2000). *Self-Regulation in Early Childhood*. New York: The Guilford Press.

Brooks, S. K., Webster, R. K., Smith, L. E., Woodland, L., Wessely, S., Greenberg, N. and Rubin, J. (2020). The Psychological Impact of Quarantine and How to Reduce It: Rapid Review of the Evidence. *Lancet*, 395: 912–920.

Brown, H. M., Stahmer, A. C., Dwyer, P. and Rivera, S. (2021). Changing the Story: How Diagnosticians Can Support a Neurodiversity Perspective from the Start. *Autism*, 25: 1171–1174.

Bruner, J. S. (1977). *The Process of Education*. Cambridge, MA: Harvard University Press.

Bruner, J. S., Jolly, A. and Sylva, K. (1976). *Play: Its Role in Development and Evolution*. 1st ed. New York: Basic Books.

Burke Harris N. (2018). *The Deepest Well: Healing the Long-Term Effects of Childhood Adversity*. Boston: Houghton Mifflin Harcourt.

Burman, J. T., Green, C. D. and Shanker, S. (2015). On the Meanings of Self-Regulation: Digital Humanities in Service of Conceptual Clarity. *Child Dev*, 86(5): 1507–1521.

Bush, N. R., Jones-Mason, K., Coccia, M., Zoe Caron, Z., Alkon, A., Thomas, M., Coleman-Phox, K., Wadhwa, P. D., Laraia, B. A., Adler, N. E. and Epel, E. S. (2017). Effects of Pre- and Post-Natal Maternal Stress on Infant Temperament and Autonomic Nervous System Reactivity and Regulation in a Diverse, Low-Income Population. *Dev Psychopathol*, 29(5): 1–36.

Butera, C., Ring, P., Sideris, J., Jayashankar, A., Kilroy, E., Harrison, L., Cermak, S. and Aziz-Zadeh, L. (2020). Impact of Sensory Processing on School Performance Outcomes in High Functioning Individuals with Autism Spectrum Disorder. *Mind, Brain Educ*, 14(3): 243–254.

Buxbaum, J. D., Hof, P. R., Morgan, J. T., Nordahl, C. W. and Schumann, C. M. (2013). The Amygdala in Autism Spectrum Disorders. *Neurosci Autism Spectr Disord*, 297–312.

Cajal, S. R. (1899). *Comparative Study of the Sensory Areas of the Human Cortex*. Worcester, MA: Clark University.

Campbell, J., Lochner, O. and Railey, K. (2019). Educating Students About Autism Spectrum Disorder Using the Kit for Kids Curriculum: Effects on Knowledge and Attitudes. *Sch Psychol Rev,* 48(2): 145–156.

Carrasco, M. A., Delgado, B. and Holgado-Tello, F. P. (2020). Children's Temperament: A Bridge Between Mothers' Parenting and Aggression. *Int J Environ Res Public Health,* 17(6382): 1–17.

Cascio, C. J., Woynaroski, T., Baranek, G. T. and Wallace, M. T. (2016). Toward an Interdisciplinary Approach to Understanding Sensory Function in Autism Spectrum Disorder. *Autism Res,* 9(9): 920–925.

Case-Smith, J., Weaver, L. L. and Fristad, M. A. (2015). A Systematic Review of Sensory Processing Interventions for Children with Autism Spectrum Disorders. *Autism,* 19: 133–48.

Cazaly, E., Saad, J., Wang, W., Heckman, C., Ollikainen, M. and Tang, J. (2019). Making Sense of the Epigenome Using Data Integration Approaches. *Front Pharmacol,* 10(126): 1–15.

Central Advisory Council for Education (1967). *Children and Their Primary Schools.* The Plowden Report. London: HMSO.

Cerrone, K. M. (1999). The Gun-Free Schools Act of 1994: Zero Tolerance Takes Aim at Procedural Due Process. *Pace Law Rev,* 20(7): 1–58.

Chance, C. (2021). *National Autistic Society. School Report 2021.* London: National Autistic Society.

Chawla, L. (2006). Learning to Love the Natural World Enough to Protect It. *Norsk Senter for Barneforskning,* 2, 57–78.

Cleary, J. C. and Zimmerman, B. J. (2004). Self-regulation empowerment programme: A school-based programme to enhance self-regulation and self-motivation cycles of student learning. *Psychology in the Schools,* 41(5): 527–550.

Compas, B. E., Jaser, S. S., Bettis, A. H., Watson, K. H., Gruhn, M. A., Dunbar, J. P., Williams, E. and Thigpen, J. C. (2017). Coping, Emotion Regulation, and Psychopathology in Childhood and Adolescence: A Meta-Analysis and Narrative Review. *Psychol Bull,* 143(9): 939–991.

Conkbayir, M. (2021). *Early Childhood and Neuroscience: Theory, Research and Implications for Practice. Second Edition.* London: Bloomsbury.

Cook, S. J., Jarrell, T. J., Brittin, C. A., Wang, Y., Bloniarz, A. E., Yakovlev, M. A., Nguyen, K., Tang, L. T., Bayer, E. A., Duerr, J. S., Bülow, H. E., Hobert, O., Hall, D. H. and Emmons, S. W. (2019). Whole-Animal Connectomes of Both *Caenorhabditis Elegans* Sexes. *Nature,* 571(7763): 63–71.

Copple, C. and Bredekamp, S. (2009). *Developmentally Appropriate Practice.* Washington, DC: National Association for the Education of Young Children.

Corel, J. L. (1975). *The Postnatal Development of the Human Cerebral Cortex.* Cambridge, MA: Harvard University Press.

Cortese, S., Kelly, C., Chabernaud, C., Proal, E., Di Martino, A., Milham, M. and Castellanos, X. (2012). Toward Systems Neuroscience of ADHD: A Meta-Analysis of 55 fMRI Studies. *Am J Psychiatry,* 169: 1038–1055.

Courchesne, E., Pierce, K., Schumann, C. M., Redcay, E., Buckwalter, J. A., Kennedy, D. P. and Morgan, J. (2007). Mapping Early Brain Development in Autism. *Neuron,* 56: 399–413.

Cozolino, L. (2013). *The Social Neuroscience of Education: Optimizing Learning and Attachment in the Classroom.* London: Norton and Co.

Cuartas, J., McCoy, D. C., Rey-Guerra, C., Britto, P., Beatriz, E. and Salhi, C. (2019). Early Childhood Exposure to Non-Violent Discipline and Physical and Psychological Aggression in Low- and Middle-Income Countries: National, Regional, and Global Prevalence Estimates. *Child Abuse Neglect,* 92: 93–105.

Cuartas, J., Weissman, D. G., Sheridan, M. A., Lengua, L. and McLaughlin, K. A. (2021). Corporal Punishment and Elevated Neural Response to Threat in Children. *Child Dev*, 92(3): 821–832.

Davies, C., Healy, M. and Smith, D. (2018). *The Maze of Learning. Developing Motor Skills.* Croydon: Fit-2-Learn CIC.

Deak, J. (2010). *Your Fantastic Elastic Brain.* San Francisco: Little Pickle Press.

DeCasper, A. J. and Prescott, P. (2009). Lateralized Processes Constrain Auditory Reinforcement in Human Newborns. *Hear Res*, 255(1–2): 135–141.

DeCasper, A. J. and Spence, M. J. (1986). Prenatal Maternal Speech Influences Newborn's Perception of Speech Sounds. *Infant Behav Dev*, 9(2): 133–150.

Delahooke, M. (2019). *Beyond Behaviours: Using Brain Science and Compassion to Understand and Solve Children's Behavioural Challenges.* Eau Claire, WI: PESI Publishing.

Delgado, B., Carrasco, M. A., González-Peña, P. and Holgado-Tello, F. P. (2018). Temperament and Behavioural Problems in Young Children: The Protective Role of Extraversion and Effortful Control. *J Child Fam Stud*, 27: 3232–3240.

Department for Education (2021). *Statutory Framework for the Early Years Foundation Stage (EYFS).* London: Crown Copyright.

Department for Education (June 2021). Academic Year 2020/21. *Special Educational Needs in England.* London: Crown Copyright.

Department for Education (2016). *Behaviour and Discipline in Schools. Advice for Headteachers and School Staff.* London: Crown Copyright.

Department for Education (2015). *Special Educational Needs and Disability Code of Practice: 0 to 25 Years. Statutory Guidance for Organisations Which Work with and Support Children and Young People Who Have Special Educational Needs or Disabilities.* London: Crown Copyright.

Department of Education (2012). *Pupil Behaviour in Schools in England.* London: Crown Copyright.

Dewsbury, D. A. (1997). In Celebration of the Centennial of Ivan P. Pavlov's (1897/1902) the Work of the Digestive Glands. *Am Psychol*, 52(9): 933–935.

Dhana, K., Braun, K. V. E., Nano, J., Voortman, T., Demerath, E. W., Guan, W., Fornage, M., van Meurs, J., Uitterlinden, A., Hofman, A., Franco, O. and Dehghan, A. (2018). An Epigenome-Wide Association Study (EWAS) of Obesity-Related Traits. *Am J Epidemiol*, 187: 1662–1669.

Diaz, R. M., Neal, C. J. and Amaya-Williams, M. (1990). The Social Origins of Self-Regulation. In L. C. Moll (Ed.), *Vygotsky and Education: Instructional Implications and Applications of Sociohistorical Psychology* (pp. 127–154). New York: Cambridge University Press.

DiDonato, N. (2013). Effective Self- and Co-Regulation in Collaborative Learning Groups: An Analysis of How Students Regulate Problem Solving of Authentic Interdisciplinary Tasks. *Instr Sci*, 41: 25–47.

Dignath, C., Buettner, G. and Langfeldt, H-P. (2008). How Can Primary School Students Learn Self-Regulated Learning Strategies Most Effectively? A Meta-Analysis of Self-Regulation Training Programmes. *Educ Res Rev*, 3: 101–129.

Dix, P. (2017). *When the Adults Change, Everything Changes: Seismic Shifts in School Behaviour.* Williston: Independent Thinking Press.

Dollard, J. and Miller, N. E. (1950). *Personality and Psychotherapy.* New York: McGraw-Hill.

Dweck, C. (2017). *Mindset – Updated Edition: Changing the Way You Think to Fulfil Your Potential.* Edinburgh: Robinson.

Eagleman, D. (2015). *The Brain: The Story of You.* London: Canongate Books Ltd.

Early Years Coalition (2021). *Birth to Five Matters, Non-Statutory Guidance for the Early Years Foundation Stage.* St Albans: Early Education.

Elam, J., Glasser, M., Harms, M., Sotiropoulos, S., Andersson, J., Burgess, G., Curtiss, S., Oostenveld, R., Larson-Prior, L., Schoffelend, J. M., Hodge, M., Cler, E., Marcus, D., Barch, D., Yacoub, E., Smith, S., Ugurbil, K. and Van Essen, D. (2021). The Human Connectome Project: A Retrospective. *NeuroImage,* 244: 1–24.

Elliott, S., Ärlemalm-Hagsér, E. and Davis, J. (2020). *Researching Early Childhood Education for Sustainability: Challenging Assumptions and Orthodoxies.* Oxfordshire: Routledge.

Erber, R. and Erber, M. W. (2000). The Self-Regulation of Moods: Second Thoughts on the Importance of Happiness in Everyday Life. *Psychol Inq,* 11(3): 142–148.

Erikson, E. H. (1987). *A Way of Looking at Things: Selected Papers from 1930 to 1980.* New York: W.W. Norton and Company, Inc.

Erikson, E. H. (1959). Identity and the Life Cycle: Selected Papers. *Psychol Issues,* 1: 1–171.

Ewert, A., Sibthorp, J. and Place, G. (2005). Early-Life Outdoor Experiences and Individuals' Environmental Attitudes. *Leis Sci,* 27(3): 225–239.

Fani, N., King, T. Z., Jovanovic, T., Glover, E. M., Bradley, B., Choi, K. and Ressler, K. J. (2012). White Matter Integrity in Highly Traumatized Adults with and Without Post-Traumatic Stress Disorder. *Neuropsychopharmacology,* 37(12): 2740–2746.

Felitti, V. J., Anda, R. F., Nordenberg, D., Williamson, D. F., Spitz, A. M., Edwards, V., Koss, M. P. and Marks, J. S. (1998). Relationship of Childhood Abuse and Household Dysfunction to Many of the Leading Causes of Death in Adults. The Adverse Childhood Experiences (ACE) Study. *Am J Prev Med,* 14: 245–258.

Field, F. (2010). *The Foundation Years: Preventing Poor Children Becoming Poor Adults. The Report of the Independent Review on Poverty and Life Chances.* London: Crown Copyright.

Fields, R. D. (2008). White Matter in Learning, Cognition and Psychiatric Disorders. *Trends Neurosci,* 31(7): 361–370.

Finkelhor, D., Shattuck, A., Turner, H. A., and Hamby, S. L. (2012). Improving the Adverse Childhood Experiences Study Scale. *Arch Paediatr Adolesc Med,* 67(1): 70–75.

Fisher, S. E. (2013). Building Bridges Between Genes, Brains and Language. In J. J. Bolhuis and M. Everaert (Eds.), *Birdsong, Speech and Language: Exploring the Evolution of Mind and Brain* (pp. 425–454). Cambridge, MA: MIT Press.

Fonagy, P., Gergely, G., Jurist, E. L. and Target, M. (2004). *Affect Regulation, Mentalization and the Development of the Self.* Oxford: Routledge.

Fox, N. A. and Shonkoff, J. P. (2011). Violence and Development: How Persistent Fear and Anxiety Can Affect Young Children's Learning, Behaviour and Health. In Bernard van Leer Foundation (Ed.), *Early Childhood Matters, Hidden Violence: Protecting Young Children at Home* (Vol. 116, pp. 8–14). The Hague: Bernard van Leer Foundation

Francisco, R., Pedro, M., Delvecchio, E., Espada, P., Morales, A., Mazzeschi, C. and Orgilés, M. (2020). Psychological Symptoms and Behavioural Changes in Children and Adolescents During the Early Phase of COVID-19 Quarantine in Three European Countries. *Front Psychiatry,* 11(570164): 1–14.

Freire, P. (2016). *Pedagogy of the Heart.* London: Bloomsbury Academic.

Freud, S. (1989). The Mind and Its Workings. In James Strachey (Ed.), *An Outline of Psycho-Analysis* (pp. 13–48). London: W. W. Norton and Company.

Fuge, C. (2009). *The Terrible Greedy Fossifoo.* London: Simon and Schuster Children's UK.

Gazzaniga, M. S., Bogen, J. E. and Sperry, R. W. (1965). Observations of Visual Perception After Disconnection of the Cerebral Hemispheres in Man. *Brain,* 88: 221–230.

Genon, S., Reid, A., Langner, R., Amunts, K. and Eickhoff, S. B. (2018). How to Characterize the Function of a Brain Region. *Trends Cogn Sci,* 4: 350–364.

Gershoff, E. T. (2017). School Corporal Punishment in Global Perspective: Prevalence, Outcomes, and Efforts at Intervention. *Psychol Health Med,* 22(Sup1): 224–239.

Gershoff, E. T., Goodman, G. S., Miller-Perrin, C. L., Holden, G. W., Jackson, Y. and Kazdin, A. E. (2018). The Strength of the Causal Evidence Against Physical Punishment of Children and Its Implications for Parents, Psychologists, and Policymakers. *Am Psychol,* 73(5): 626–638.

Gershoff, E. T. and Grogan-Kaylor, A. (2016). Spanking and Child Outcomes: Old Controversies and New Meta-Analyses. *J Fam Psychol,* 30(4): 453–469.

Gibbard, C. R., Ren, J., Skuse, D. H., Clayden, J. D. and Clark, C. A. (2018). Structural Connectivity of the Amygdala in Young Adults with Autism Spectrum Disorder. *Hum Brain Mapp,* 39: 1270–1282.

Gilbert, L., Gus, L. and Rose, J. (2021). *Emotion Coaching with Children and Young People in Schools: Promoting Positive Behaviour, Wellbeing and Resilience.* London: Jessica Kingsley Publishers.

Gilbert, L., Gus, L. and Rose, J. (2015). Emotion Coaching, a Universal Strategy for Supporting and Promoting Sustainable Emotional and Behavioural Wellbeing. *Edu Child Psychol,* 32(1): 31–41.

Gilliam, W., Maupin, A., Reyes, C., Accavitti, M. and Shic, F. (2016). Do Early Educators' Implicit Biases Regarding Sex and Race Relate to Behaviour Expectations and Recommendations of Preschool Expulsions and Suspensions? *Yale University Child Study Centre,* 9(28): 1–18.

Golding, K. S., Phillips, S. and Bomber, L. M. (2021). *Working with Relational Trauma in Schools: An Educator's Guide to Using Dyadic Developmental Practice.* London: Jessica Kingsley Publishers.

Gordon, W. A. and Hibbard, M. R. (1992). Critical Issues in Cognitive Remediation. *Neuropsychology,* 6: 361–370.

Gottman, J. M. and DeClaire, J. (1997). *Raising an Emotionally Intelligent Child: The Heart of Parenting.* New York: Simon and Schuster.

Grandin, T. (2020). *The Way I See It: A Personal Look at Autism and Asperger's.* Arlington, TX: Future Horizons.

Gray, P. (2020a). *How Children Acquire "Academic" Skills Without Formal Instruction.* New York: The Alliance for Self-Directed Education.

Gray, P. (2020b). *The Harm of Coercive Schooling.* Cambridge, MA: The Alliance for Self-Directed Education.

Gray, P. (2011). The Decline of Play and the Rise of Psychopathology in Children and Adolescents. *Am J Play,* 3(4): 443–463.

Graziano, B. R., Town, J. P., Sitarska, E., Nagy, T. L., Fošnarič, M., Penič, S., Iglič, A., Kralj-Iglič, V., Gov, N. S., Diz-Muñoz, A. and Weiner, O. D. (2019). Cell confinement reveals a branched-actin independent circuit for neutrophil polarity. *PLoS Biology,* 17(10): e3000457.

Green, D., Chandler, S., Charman, T., Simonoff, E. and Baird, G. (2016). Brief Report: DSM-5 Sensory Behaviours in Children with and Without an Autism Spectrum Disorder. *J Autism Dev Disord,* 46(11): 3597–3606.

Hadland, C. (2020). *Creating an Eco-Friendly Early Years Setting: A Practical Guide.* Oxon: Routledge.

Hadwin, A. F., Järvelä, S. and Miller, M. (2017). Self-Regulation, Co-Regulation and Shared Regulation in Collaborative Learning Environments. In D. Schunk and J. Greene (Eds.), *Handbook of Self-Regulation of Learning and Performance. Second Edition.* New York: Routledge.

Hagmann, P. (2005). *From Diffusion MRI to Brain Connectomics* (Thesis). Lausanne: EPFL. http://doi.org/10.5075/epfl-thesis-3230 (Accessed 16th January 2014).

Hamberger, L., Larsen, S. and Lehrner, A. (2017). Coercive Control in Intimate Partner Violence. *Aggress Violent Behav,* 37: 1–11.

Harms, M. B., Martin, A. and Wallace, G. L. (2010). Facial Emotion Recognition in Autism Spectrum Disorders: A Review of Behavioural and Neuroimaging Studies. *Neuropsychol Rev,* 20: 290–322.

Hebb, D. O. (1949). *The Organization of Behaviour*. New York: Wiley and Sons.

Herculano-Houzel, S. (2009). The Human Brain in Numbers: A Linearly Scaled-Up Primate Brain. *Front Hum Neurosci,* 3(31): 1–11.

Hill, C., Keville, S. and Ludlow, K. A. (2021). Inclusivity for Children with Autism Spectrum Disorders: Parent's Reflections of the School Learning Environment Versus Home Learning During COVID-19. *Int J Dev Disabil,* 1–9. DOI: 10.1080/20473869.2021.1975253.

Hirsh-Pasek, K., Adamson, L. B., Bakeman, R., Tresch Owen, M., Michnick Golinkoff, R., Pace, A., Yust, P. K. S. and Suma, K. (2015). The Contribution of Early Communication Quality to Low-Income Children's Language Success. *Psychol Sci OnlineFirst,* 1–13.

HM Government (2021). *The Best Start for Life a Vision for the 1,001 Critical Days*. The Early Years Healthy Development Review Report. London: HM Government.

Hornix, B. E., Havekes, R. and Kas, M. J. H. (2019). Multisensory Cortical Processing and Dysfunction Across the Neuropsychiatric Spectrum. *Neurosci Biobehav Rev,* 97: 138–151.

Howard-Jones, P. (2009). Scepticism Is Not Enough. *Cortex,* 45: 550–551.

Hughes, D. A. and Baylin, J. (2012). *Brain-Based Parenting. The Neuroscience of Caregiving for Healthy Attachment*. London and New York: W. W. Norton and Company.

Immordino-Yang, M. H. and Damasio, A. (2007). We Feel, Therefore We Learn: The Relevance of Affective and Social Neuroscience to Education. *Mind Brain Educ,* 1: 3–10.

Inches, A. (2009). *The Adventures of a Plastic Bottle: A Story About Recycling*. New York: Little Simon.

Janssen, J., Erkens, G., Kirschner, P. and Kanselaar, G. (2012). Task-Related and Social Regulation During Online Collaborative Learning. *Metacogn Learn,* 7: 25–43.

Jenkin, R., Frampton, I., White, M. P. and Pahl, S. (2018). The Relationship Between Exposure to Natural and Urban Environments and Children's Self-Regulation. *Landsc Res,* 43(3): 315–328.

Joseph Rowntree Foundation (2021). *UK Poverty 2020/21. The Leading Independent Report*. York: The Joseph Rowntree Foundation.

Kaplan, R. (2001). The Nature of the View from Home: Psychological Benefits. *Environ Behav,* 33(4): 507–542.

Karpov, Y. V. and Haywood, H. C. (1998). Two Ways to Elaborate Vygotsky's Concept of Mediation. *Am Psychol,* 53(1): 27–36.

Kennis, M., van Rooij, S. J. H., Tromp, D. P. M., Fox, A. S., Rademaker, A. R., Kahn, R. S. and Geuze, E. (2015). Treatment Outcome-Related White Matter Differences in Veterans with Posttraumatic Stress Disorder. *Neuropsychopharmacology,* 40(10): 2434–2442.

Kilroy, E., Aziz-Zadeh, L. and Cermak, S. (2019). Ayres Theories of Autism and Sensory Integration Revisited: What Contemporary Neuroscience Has to Say. *Brain Sci,* 9(68): 1–20.

Kingsbury, M., Weeks, M., MacKinnon, N., Evans, J., Mahedy, L., Dykxhoorn, J. and Colman, I. (2016). Stressful Life Events During Pregnancy and Offspring Depression: Evidence from a Prospective Cohort Study. *J Am Acad Child Adolesc Psychiatry,* 55(8): 709–716.

Kitsantas, A., Zimmerman, B. J. and Cleary, T. (2000). The role of observation and emulation in the development of athletic self-regulation. *Journal of Educational Psychology,* 92(4): 811–817.

Kohn, A. (2018). *Punished by Rewards: Twenty-Fifth Anniversary Edition: The Trouble with Gold Stars, Incentive Plans, A's, Praise, and Other Bribes*. San Francisco: HarperOne.

Kuypers, L. (2011). *The Zones of Regulation*. Santa Clara, CA: Think Social Publishing.

La Marca-Ghaemmaghami, P., Dainese, S. M., Stalla, G., Haller, M., Zimmermann, R. and Ehlert, U. (2017). Second-Trimester Amniotic Fluid Corticotropin-Releasing Hormone and Urocortin in Relation to Maternal Stress and Foetal Growth in Human Pregnancy. *Stress,* 1. http://doi.org/10.1080/10253890.2017.1312336.

Larsen, R. (2000). Toward a Science of Mood Regulation. *Psychol Inq,* 11(3): 129–141.

Leahy, L. G. (2018). Diagnosis and Treatment of ADHD in Children vs Adults: What Nurses Should Know. *Arch Psychiatr Nurs*, 32(6): 890–895.

LeDoux, J. (2002). *Synaptic Self: How Our Brains Become Who We Are*. London: Penguin Books.

Lee Oh, D., Jerman, P., Purewal Boparai, S. K., Koita, K., Briner, S., Bucci, M. and Burke Harris, N. (2018). Review of Tools for Measuring Exposure to Adversity in Children and Adolescents. *Journal of Paediatric Health Care*, 32(6): 564–583.

Liberzon, I. and Abelson, J. L. (2016). Context Processing and the Neurobiology of Post-Traumatic Stress Disorder. *Neuron*, 92(1): 14–30.

Lieberman, M. D. (2015). *Social: Why Our Brains Are Wired to Connect*. Oxford: OUP Oxford.

Lifestyles Team, NHS Digital (2021). *Mental Health of Children and Young People in England 2021 – Wave 2 Follow Up to the 2017 Survey*. Leeds: Health and Social Care Information Centre.

Lifestyles Team, NHS Digital (2020). *Mental Health of Children and Young People in England, 2020: Wave 1 Follow Up to the 2017 survey*. London: NHS Digital, Part of the Government Statistical Service.

Lindell, A. K. and Kidd, E. (2011). Why Right-Brain Teaching Is Half-Witted: A Critique of the Misapplication of Neuroscience to Education. *Mind Brain Educ*, 5(3): 121–127.

Lockman, J. and Hazen, N. (1989). *Action in Social Context. Perspectives on Early Development*. New York: Plenum Press.

Maciver, D., Rutherford, M., Arakelyan, S., Kramer, J. M., Richmond, J., Todorova, L., Romero-Ayuso, D., Nakamura-Thomas, H., Ten Velden, M., Finlayson, I., O'Hare, A. and Forsyth, K. (2019). Participation of Children with Disabilities in School: A Realist Systematic Review of Psychosocial and Environmental Factors. *PLoS One*, 14(1): e0210511.

MacKinnon, N., Kingsbury, M., Mahedy, L., Evans, J. and Colman, I. (2018). The Association Between Prenatal Stress and Externalizing Symptoms in Childhood: Evidence from the Avon Longitudinal Study of Parents and Children. *Biol Psychiatry*, 83(2): 100–108.

Magnus, W., Nazir, S., Anilkumar, A. and Shaban, K. (2022). Attention Deficit Hyperactivity Disorder. *StatPearls*, Treasure Island, FL: StatPearls Publishing LLC. Available from: https://www.ncbi.nlm.nih.gov/books/NBK441838/.

Maltese, A., Gallai, B., Marotta, R., Lavano, F., Marianna Lavano, S., Tripi, G., Romano, P., D'Oro, L. and Salerno, M. (2017). The Synactive Theory of Development: The Keyword for Neurodevelopmental Disorders. *Acta Medica Mediterranea*, 33: 1257.

Marazziti, D. (2009). Neurobiology and Hormonal Aspects of Romantic Relationships. In M. deHaan and M. R. Gunnar (Eds.), *Hand-Book of Social Developmental Neuroscience* (pp. 265–280). New York: Guilford Press.

Marcus, G. and Freeman, J. (2015). *The Future of the Brain: Essays by the World's Leading Neuroscientists*. Princeton and Oxford: Princeton University Press.

Marmot, M. (2020). *Health Equity in England: The Marmot Review 10 Years On*. London: The Marmot Review.

Marmot, M. (2010). *Fair Society, Healthy Lives: The Marmot Review: Strategic Review of Health Inequalities in England Post-2010*. London: The Marmot Review.

Maté, G. (2019). *Scattered Minds the Origins and Healing of Attention Deficit Disorder*. Homebush West: Generic Publishing.

McCartney, D. L., Hillary, R. F., Stevenson, A. J., Ritchie, S. J., Walker, R. M., Zhang, Q., Morris, S. W., Bermingham, M. L., Campbell, A., Murray, A. D., Whalley, H. C., Gale, C. R., Porteous, D. J., Haley, C. S., McRae, A. F., Wray, N. R., Visscher, P. M., McIntosh, A. M., Evans, K. L., Deary, I. J. and Marioni, R. E. (2018). Epigenetic Prediction of Complex Traits and Death. *Genome Biol*, 19(1): 136.

McCaslin, M. and Burross, H. L. (2011). Research on Individual Differences within a Sociocultural Perspective: Co-regulation and Adaptive Learning. *Teachers College Record: The Voice of Scholarship in Education,* 113(2): 325–349.

McCaslin, M. and Good, T. L. (1996). The Informal Curriculum. In D. C. Berliner and R. C. Calfee (Eds.), *Handbook of Educational Psychology* (pp. 622–670). Macmillan Library Reference. New York: Prentice Hall International.

McCaslin, M. and Hickey, D. T. (2001). Self-Regulated Learning and Academic Achievement: A Vygotskian View. In B. J. Zimmerman and D. H. Schunk (Eds.), *Self-Regulated Learning and Academic Achievement: Theoretical Perspectives* (pp. 227–252). Mahwah, NJ: Lawrence Erlbaum Associates Publishers.

McClelland, M. M., Acock, A. C., Piccinin, A., Rhea, S. A. and Stallings, M. C. (2013). Relations Between Preschool Attention Span-Persistence and Age 25 Educational Outcomes. *Early Child Res Q,* 28(2): 314–324.

McClelland, M. M. and Wanless, S. B. (2012). Growing up with Assets and Risks: The Importance of Self-Regulation for Academic Achievement. *Res Hum Dev,* 9: 278–297.

McGilchrist, I. (2019). *The Master and His Emissary: The Divided Brain and the Making of the Western World.* London: Yale University Press.

McGowan, P. O., Sasaki, A., D'Alessio, A. C., Dymov, S., Labonte, B., Szyf, M., Turecki, G. and Meany, M. J. (2009). Epigenetic Regulation of the Glucocorticoid Receptor in Human Brain Associates with Childhood Abuse. *Nat Neurosc,* 12: 342–348. doi:10.1038/nn.2270.

McKinsey Global Institute. (2017). *Jobs Lost, Jobs Gained: Workforce Transitions in a Time of Automation.* London: McKinsey and Company.

McMurray, B. (2007). Defusing the Childhood Vocabulary Explosion. *Science,* 317: 631.

Meany, M. J. (2001). Maternal Care, Gene Expression and the Transmission of Individual Differences in Stress Reactivity Across Generations. *Annu Rev Neurosci,* 24: 1161–1192.

Mennin, D. S. (2006). Emotion Regulation Therapy: An Integrative Approach to Treatment-Resistant Anxiety Disorders. *J Contemp Psychother,* 36: 95–105.

Miller, A. L., Gearhardt, A. N., Fredericks, E. M., Katz, B., Shapiro, L. F., Holden, K., Kaciroti, N., Gonzalez R., Hunter, C. and Lumeng, J. C. (2018). Targeting Self-Regulation to Promote Health Behaviours in Children. *Behav Res Ther,* 101: 71–81.

Mills, K. (2014). Effects of Internet Use on the Adolescent Brain: Despite Popular Claims, Experimental Evidence Remains Scarce. *Trends Cogn Sci,* 18(8): 385–387.

Minshew, M. J. and Williams, D. L. (2007). The New Neurobiology of Autism: Cortex, Connectivity, and Neuronal Organization. *Arch Neurol,* 64(7): 945–950.

Morgan, P. L., Li, H., Farkas, G., Cook, M., Pun, W. H. and Hillemeier, M. M. (2017). Executive Functioning Deficits Increase Kindergarten Children's Risk for Reading and Mathematics Difficulties in First Grade. *Contemp Educ Psychol,* 50: 23–32.

Muhle, R. A., Reed, H. E., Chi Vo, L., Mehta, S., McGuire, K., Veenstra-VanderWeele, J. and Ernest Pedapati, E. (2017). Clinical Diagnostic Genetic Testing for Individuals with Developmental Disorders. *J Am Acad Child Adolesc Psychiatry,* 56(11): 910–913.

Murphy, L. K. (2021). *Co-Regulation Handbook: Creating Competent, Authentic Roles for Kids with Social Learning Differences, So We All Stay Positively Connected Through the Ups and Downs of Learning.* Seattle: Kindle.

Murray, D. W., Rosanbalm, K., Christopoulos, C. and Hamoudi, A. (2015). *Self-Regulation and Toxic Stress: Foundations for Understanding Self-Regulation from an Applied Developmental Perspective (Report #2015-21).* Washington, DC: Office of Planning, Research and Evaluation, Administration of Children and Families, US Department of Health and Human Services.

Murray, J. and Cousens, D. (2019). Primary School Children's Beliefs Associating Extra-Curricular Provision with Non-Cognitive Skills and Academic Achievement. *Educ, 3–13* 48(1): 37–53.

Music, G. (2019). *Nurturing Children: From Trauma to Growth Using Attachment Theory, Psychoanalysis and Neurobiology*. London: Routledge.

Nair, A., Carper, R. A., Abbott, A. E., Chen, C. P., Solders, S., Nakutin, S., Datko, M. C., Fishman, I. and Müller, R. A. (2015). Regional Specificity of Aberrant Thalamocortical Connectivity in Autism. *Hum Brain Mapp*, 36: 4497–4511.

National Scientific Council on the Developing Child (2011). *Children's Emotional Development Is Built into the Architecture of Their Brains. Working Paper 2*. Cambridge, MA: National Scientific Council on the Developing Child.

National Scientific Council on the Developing Child (2010). *Illustration by Betsy Hayes; Adapted with Permission from the Centre on the Developing Child*. New York: Centre on the Developing Child.

Nielson, J. A., Zielinski, B. A., Ferguson, M. A., Lainhart, J. E. and Anderson, J. S. (2013). An Evaluation of the Left-Brain vs. Right-Brain Hypothesis with Resting State Functional Connectivity Magnetic Resonance Imaging. *PLoS One*, 8(8): e71275.

OECD (2019a). *Trends Shaping Education*. Paris: OECD Publishing.

OECD (2019b). *OECD Future of Education and Skills 2030 (2019). Conceptual Learning Framework. Learning Compass 2030*. Paris: OECD Publishing.

O'Farrelly, C., Ailbhe Booth, A., Tatlow-Goldend, M. and Barkera, B. (2019). Reconstructing Readiness: Young Children's Priorities for Their Early School Adjustment. *Early Child Res Quart*, 1–30.

Ofcom (2020). *Children and Parents: Media Use and Attitudes Report 2019*. London: Ofcom.

Ofsted (2014). *Below the Radar: Low-level Disruption in the Country's Classrooms*. London: Crown Copyright.

O'Sullivan, J. and Corlett, N. (2021). *50 Fantastic Ideas for Sustainability*. London: Featherstone.

Owens, J. and McLanahan, S. (2020). Unpacking the Drivers of Racial Disparities in School Suspension and Expulsion. *Soc Forces*, 98(4): 1548–1577.

Oxley, L. (2015). New Voices: Do Schools Need Lessons on Motivation? *Psychol*, 28: 722–723.

Panksepp, J. (2012). *The Archaeology of Mind: Neuroevolutionary Origins of Human Emotion: Neuroevolutionary Origins of Human Emotions*. New York and London: W. W. Norton and Company.

Panksepp, J. (1998). *Affective Neuroscience: The Foundations of Human and Animal Emotions*. 1st ed. New York: Oxford University Press.

Panksepp, J., Lane, R., Solms, M. and Smith, R. (2017). Reconciling Cognitive and Affective Neuroscience Perspectives on the Brain Basis of Emotional Experience. *Neurosci Biobehav Rev*, 76(Part B): 187–215. http://doi.org/10.1016/j.neubiorev.2016.09.010.

Pascal, C. (2021). *Early Years EXPO Panel Session: Effective Delivery of the EYFS 2021 – Supported by Birth to 5 Matters* (22nd November, 2021). Online. https://www.youtube.com/watch?v=IG98O5PJn9g.

Pastor-Cerezuela, G., Fernández-Andrés, M. I., Sanz-Cervera, P. and Marín-Suelves, D. (2020). The Impact of Sensory Processing on Executive and Cognitive Functions in Children with Autism Spectrum Disorder in the School Context. *Res Dev Disabil*, 96(103540): 1–26.

Pavlov, I. (1897). *Digestive Glands*. Norfolk: Facsimile Publisher.

Pechtel, P. and Pizzagalli, D. A. (2011). Effects of Early Life Stress on Cognitive and Affective Function: An Integrated Review of Human Literature. *Psychopharmacology*, 214(1): 55–70.

Peddle, A. (2019). *TAM's Journey: The Beginning – Book 1*. Isle of Sheppey: TAM Publishing.

Perry, B. D. (2021). *What Happened to You? Conversations on Trauma, Resilience and Healing*. London: Bluebird.

Perry, B. D. (2014). The Neurosequential Model of Therapeutics in Young Children. In K. Brandt, B. D. Perry, S. Seligman and E. Tronick (Eds.), *Infant and Early Childhood Mental Health: Core Concepts and Clinical Practice* (pp. 21–54). Washington, DC: American Psychiatric Press.

Perry, B. D. (2009). Examining Child Maltreatment Through a Neurodevelopmental Lens: Clinical Applications of the Neurosequential Model of Therapeutics. *J Loss Trauma*, 14: 240–255.

Perry, B. D. (2006). Applying Principles of Neurodevelopment to Clinical Work with Maltreated and Traumatized Children: The Neurosequential Model of Therapeutics. In N. B. Webb (Ed.), *Social Work Practice with Children and Families. Working With Traumatized Youth in Child Welfare* (pp. 27–52). New York: The Guilford Press.

Pezzulo, G. and Castelfranchi, C. (2009). Thinking as the Control of Imagination: A Conceptual Framework for Goal-Directed Systems. *Psychol Res*, 73(4): 559–577.

Piaget, J. and Inhelder, B. (1972). *Psychology of the Child*. New York: Basic Books.

Pino-Pasternak, D., Basilio, M. and Whitebread, D. (2014). Intervention and Classroom Contexts That Promote Self-Regulated Learning: Two Intervention Studies in United Kingdom Primary Classrooms. *Psykhe*, 23(2): 1–13.

Porges, S. W. (2021). *Polyvagal Safety: Attachment, Communication, Self-Regulation*. New York: W. W Norton and Company.

Porges, S. W. (2018). *Clinical Applications of the Polyvagal Theory – The Emergence of Polyvagal-Informed Therapies*. London: W. W. Norton and Company

Porges, S. W. (2017). *The Pocket Guide to the Polyvagal Theory: The Transformative Power of Feeling Safe*. New York: W. W. Norton and Company.

Porges, S. W. (2003). Social Engagement and Attachment: A Phylo-Genetic Perspective. *Ann N Y Acad Sci*, 1008: 31–47.

Powell, E. M., Campbell, D. B., Stanwood, G. D., Davis, C., Noebels, J. L. and Levitt, P. (2003). Genetic Disruption of Cortical Interneuron Development Causes Region- and GABA Cell Type-Specific Deficits, Epilepsy, and Behavioural Dysfunction. *J Neurosci*, 23: 622–631.

Raney, M. A., Hendry, C. F. and Yee, S. A. (2019). Physical Activity and Social Behaviours of Urban Children in Green Playgrounds. *Am J Prev Med*, 56(4): 522–529.

Raver, C. C. (2004). Placing Emotional Self-Regulation in Sociocultural and Socioeconomic Contexts. *Child Dev*, 75: 346–353.

Ravet, J. (2015). Inclusive/Exclusive? Contradictory Perspectives on Autism and Inclusion: The Case for an Integrative Position. *Autism Educ*, 15(6): 667–682.

Reed, J. and Parish, N. (2021). *Working for Babies. Lockdown Lessons from Local Systems*. London: Parent Infant Foundation.

Richard, V., Holder, D. and Cairney, J. (2021). Creativity in Motion: Examining the Creative Potential System and Enriched Movement Activities as a Way to Ignite It. *Front Psychol*, 12(690710): 1–18.

Robson, D., Allen, S. and Howard, S. (2020). Self-Regulation in Childhood as a Predictor of Future Outcomes: A Meta-Analytic Review. *Faculty of Social Sciences – Papers* 4656. https://ro.uow.edu.au/sspapers/4656.

Rodriguez, E. T. and Tamis-LeMonda, C. S. (2011). Trajectories of the Home Learning Environment Across the First 5 Years: Associations with Children's Vocabulary and Literacy Skills at Prekindergarten. *Child Dev*, 82(4): 1058–1075.

Rollins, E. M. and Crandall, A. (2021). Self-Regulation and Shame as Mediators Between Childhood Experiences and Young Adult Health. *Front Psychiatry*, 12(649911): 1–9.

Romeo, R. R., Segaran, J., Leonard, J. A., Robinson, S. T., West, M. R., Mackey, A. P., Yendiki, A., Rowe, M. L. and Gabrieli, J. D. E. (2018). Language Exposure Relates to Structural Neural Connectivity in Childhood. *J Neurosci*, 38(36): 7870–7877.

Romero-Ayuso, D., Toledano-González, A., Segura-Fragoso, A., Triviño-Juárez, J. M. and Rodríguez-Martínez, M. C. (2020). Assessment of Sensory Processing and Executive Functions at the School: Development, Reliability, and Validity of EPYFEI-Escolar. *Front. Pediatr*, 8(275): 1–16.

Rose, J., Gilbert, L. and Richards, V. (2015). *Health and Wellbeing in Early Childhood*. London: Sage Publishing.

Rose, R. and Abi-Rached, J. M. (2013). *Neuro: The New Brain Sciences and the Management of the Mind*. Princeton, NJ: Princeton University Press.

Rowe, M. L. (2012). A Longitudinal Investigation of the Role of Quantity and Quality of Child-Directed Speech in Vocabulary Development. *Child Dev*, 83(5): 1762–1774.

Ruisch, I. H., Buitelaar, J. K., Glennon, J. C., Hoekstra, P. J. and Dietrich, A. (2018). Pregnancy Risk Factors in Relation to Oppositional-Defiant and Conduct Disorder Symptoms in the Avon Longitudinal Study of Parents and Children. *J Psychiatr Res*, 101: 63–71.

Ryan, R., Kalil, A., Ziol-Guest, K. and Padilla, C. (2016). Socioeconomic Gaps in Parents' Discipline Strategies from 1998 to 2011. *Paediatrics*, 138(6): 1–10. https://doi.org/10. 1542/peds.2016-0720.

Sandman, C. A. and Glynn, L. M. (2009). Corticotropin-Releasing Hormone (CRH) Programs the Foetal and Maternal Brain. *Future Neurol*, 4(3): 257–261.

Sayal, K., Prasad, V., Daley, D., Ford, T. and Coghill, D. (2018). ADHD in Children and Young People: Prevalence, Care Pathways, and Service Provision. *Lancet Psychiatry*, 5(2): 175–186.

Schaffer, H. R. (1996). *Social Development: An Introduction*. Hoboken, NJ: Wiley-Blackwell.

Scheffer, L. K., Xu, C. S., Januszewski, M., Lu, Z., Takemura, S. Y., Hayworth, K. J., Huang, G. B., Shinomiya, K., Maitlin-Shepard, J., Berg, S., Clements, J., Hubbard, P. M., Katz, W. T., Umayam, L., Zhao, T., Ackerman, D., Blakely, T., Bogovic, J., Dolafi, T., Kainmueller, D., Kawase, T., Khairy, K. A., Leavitt, L., Li, P. H., Lindsey, L., Neubarth, N., Olbris, D. J., Otsuna, H., Trautman, E. T., Ito, M., Bates, A. S., Goldammer, J., Wolff, T., Svirskas, R., Schlegel, P., Neace, E., Knecht, C. J., Alvarado, C. X., Bailey, D. A., Ballinger, S., Borycz, J. A., Canino, B. S., Cheatham, N., Cook, M., Dreher, M., Duclos, O., Eubanks, B., Fairbanks, K., Finley, S., Forknal L, N., Francis, A., Hopkins, G. P., Joyce, E. M., SungJin Kim, S., Kirk, N. A., Kovalyak, J., Lauchie, S. A., Alanna Lohff, A., Maldonado, C., Manley, E. A., McLin, S., Mooney, C., Ndama, M., Ogundeyi, O., Nneoma Okeoma, N., Ordish, C., Nicholas Padilla, N., Patrick, C. M., Paterson, T., Phillips, E. E., Emily M Phillips, E. M., Rampally, N., Ribeiro, C., Robertson, M. K., Rymer, J. T., Ryan, S. M., Sammons, M., Scott, A. K., Scott, A. L., Shinomiya, A., Smith, C., Smith, K., Smith, N. L., Sobeski, M. A., Suleiman, A., Swift, J., Takemura, S., Talebi, I., Tarnogorska, D., Tenshaw, E., Temour Tokhi, T., Walsh, J. J., Yang, T., Horne, J., Li, F., Ruchi Parekh, R., Rivlin, P. K., Jayaraman, V., Marta Costa, M., Jefferis, G., Ito, K., Saalfeld, S., George, R., Meinertzhagen, I. A., Rubin, G. M., Hess, H. F., Jain, V. and Plaza, S. M. (2020). A Connectome and Analysis of the Adult *Drosophila* Central Brain. *eLife*, 9: e57443, 1–83.

Schermerhorn, A. C., Bates, J. E., Goodnight, J. A., Lansford, J. E., Dodge, K. A. and Pettit, G. S. (2013). Temperament Moderates Associations Between Exposure to Stress and Children's Externalizing Problems. *Child Dev*, 84: 1579–1593.

Schmitz, D., Muenzing, S. E. A., Schober, M., Schubert, N., Minnerop, M., Lippert, T., Amunts, K. and Axer, M. (2018). Derivation of Fibre Orientations from Oblique Views Through Human Brain Sections in 3D-Polarized Light Imaging. *Front Neuroanat*, 12(75): 1–15.

Schore, A. N. (2021). The Interpersonal Neurobiology of Intersubjectivity. *Front Psychol*, 12(648616): 1–19.

Schore, A. N. (2003). *Affect Regulation and the Repair of the Self*. New York: W. W. Norton and Company.

Schunk, D. H. and Zimmerman, B. J. (1997). Social Origins of Self-Regulatory Competence. *Educ Psychol*, 32: 195–208.

Schunk, D. H. and Zimmerman, B. J. (1994). *Self-Regulation of Learning and Performance: Issues and Educational Applications*. Hillsdale, NJ: Lawrence Erlbaum Associates.

Seldon, A. (2018). *The Fourth Education Revolution*. London: University of Buckingham Press.

Sen-Bhattacharya, B., Serrano-Gotarredona, T., Balassa, L., Bhattacharya, A., Stokes, A. B., Rowley, A., Sugiarto, I. and Furber, S. (2017). A Spiking Neural Network Model of the Lateral Geniculate Nucleus on the SpiNNaker Machine. *Front Neurosci*, 11(454): 1–18.

Seung, S. (2013). *Connectome: How the Brain's Wiring Makes Us Who We Are*. Boston and New York: Houghton Mifflin Harcourt.

Shanker, S. (2020). *Reframed*. Toronto, Buffalo and London: University of Toronto Press.

Shanker, S. and Barker, S. (2018a). *Self-Reg. How to Help Your Child (and You) Break the Stress Cycle and Fully Engage with Life*. Ontario, CA: The MEHRIT Centre.

Shanker, S. and Barker, T. (2018b). *Help Your Child Deal with Stress – and Thrive: The Transformative Power of Self-Reg*. London: Yellow Kite.

Shanker, S. and Hopkins, S. (2019). *Self-Reg Schools: A Handbook for Educators*. Melbourne: Pearson Education.

Shanker, S., Hopkins, S. and Davidson, S. (2015). *Self-Regulation: A Discussion Paper for Goodstart Early Learning in Australia*. Peterborough, ON: The MEHRIT Centre, Ltd.

Shanker, S., Hopkins, S. and Showalter, A. (2017). Ontario: Self-Regulation Institute. *Refram J Self-Reg*, 1(1): 1–116.

Shaw, P., Stringaris, A., Nigg, J. and Leibenluft, E. (2014). Emotion Dysregulation in Attention Deficit Hyperactivity Disorder. *Am J Psychiatry*, 171(3): 276–293.

Sidpra, J., Abomeli, D., Hameed, B., Baker, J. and Mankad, K. (2021). Rise in the Incidence of Abusive Head Trauma During the COVID-19 Pandemic. *Arch Dis Child*, 106: e14. http://dx.doi.org/10.1136/archdischild-2020-319872.

Siegel, D. J. (2012). *The Developing Mind: How Relationships and the Brain Interact to Shape Who We Are*. New York: Guildford Press.

Siegel, D. J. (1999). *The Developing Mind*. New York: Guilford.

Siegel, D. J. and Bryson, T. (2018). *Yes Brain: How to Cultivate Resilience, Encourage Curiosity, and Inspire*. New York: Bantam Books.

Siegel, D. J. and Bryson, T. (2012). *The Whole-Brain Child: 12 Proven Strategies to Nurture Your Child's Developing Mind*. London: Robinson.

Siegel, D. J. and Bryson, T. (2011). *No-Drama Discipline: The Whole-Brain Way to Calm the Chaos and Nurture Your Child's Developing Mind*. London: Scribe.

Siegel, D. J., Score, A. N. and Cozolino, L. (2021). *Interpersonal Neurobiology and Clinical Practice*. London: W. W. Norton and Co.

Siehl, S., King, J. A., Burgess, N., Flor, H. and Nees, F. (2018). Structural White Matter Changes in Adults and Children with Post-Traumatic Stress Disorder: A Systematic Review and Meta-analysis. *NeuroImage: Clinical*, 19: 581–598.

Simpson, D. (2017). A UK–US Investigation of Early Education Practitioners' Opinions About Child Poverty and Its Prioritizing Within Their Practice. *Soc Educ Stud*.

Skiba, R. J., Horner, R. H., Chung, C. G., Rausch, M., May, S. L. and Tobin, T. (2011). Race Is Not Neutral: A National Investigation of African American and Latino Disproportionality in School Discipline. *Sch Psychol Rev*, 40: 85–107.

Skinner, B. F. (1976). *About Behaviourism*. Manhattan: Random House USA Inc.

Sperry, R. W. (1982). Some Effects of Disconnecting the Cerebral Hemispheres. *Science*, 217: 1223–1227.

Sperry, R. W. (1965). Corpus Callosum and Intermodal Visuo-Tactile Integration in the Monkey. *Anat Rec*, 151(3): 476 (Abstr.).

Spinelli, E. (2011). *Miss Fox's Class Goes Green*. Morton Grove, IL: Albert Whitman and Company.

Sporns, O., Tononi, G. and Kötter, R. (2005). The Human Connectome: A Structural Description of the Human Brain. *PLOS Comput Biol*, 1(4): e42.

Sroufe, L. A. (1995). *Emotional Development: The Organization of Emotional Life in the Early Years.* Cambridge: Cambridge University Press.

Stephenson, N. (1992). *Snow Crash.* New York: Penguin.

Sunderland, M. (2016). *What Every Parent Needs to Know: Love, Nurture and Play with Your Child.* London: Dorling Kindersley Publishing.

Swanson, J. M., Kinsbourne, M., Nigg, J., Lanphear, B., Stefanatos, G., Volkow, N., Taylor, E., Casey, B., Castellanos, F. and Wadhwa, P. (2007). Biologic Sub-Types of ADHD: Brain Imaging, Molecular, Genetic and Environmental Factors and the Dopamine Hypothesis. *Neuropsychol Rev,* 17(1): 31–59.

Szyf, M., McGowan, P. and Meaney, M. L. (2008). The Social Environment and the Epigenome. *Environ Mol Mutagen,* 49(1): 46–60.

Taylor, M. J., Gustafsson, P., Larsson, H., Gillberg, C., Lundström, S. and Lichstenstein, P. (2017). Examining the Association Between Autistic Traits and Atypical Sensory Reactivity: A Twin Study. *JAACAP,* 57(2): 96–102.

Teicher, M. H. and Samson, J. A. (2016). Annual Research Review: Enduring Neurobiological Effects of Childhood Abuse and Neglect. *J Child Psychol Psychiatry Allied Disc,* 57(3): 241–266.

Thomson, M. (2013). The Physiological Roles of Placental Corticotropin Releasing Hormone in Pregnancy and Childbirth. *J Physiol Biochem,* 69(3): 559–573.

Thorndike, E. (1932). *The Fundamentals of Learning.* New York: AMS Press Inc.

Tice, D. M. and Bratslavsky, E. (2000). Giving in to Feel Good: The Place of Emotion Regulation in the Context of General Self-Control. *Psychol Inq,* 11(3): 149–159.

Tierney, A. L. and Nelson, C. A. (2009). Brain Development and the Role of Experience in the Early Years. *Zero Three,* 30(2): 9–13.

Tottenham, N., Hertzig, M. E., Gillespie-Lynch, K., Gilhooly, T., Millner, A. J. and Casey, B. J. (2014). Elevated Amygdala Response to Faces and Gaze Aversion in Autism Spectrum Disorder. *Soc Cogn Affect Neurosci,* 9(1): 106–117.

Tozzi, L., Staveland, B., Holt-Gosselin, B., Chesnut, M., Chang, S. E., Choi, D., Shiner, M., Wu, H., Lerma-Usabiaga, G., Sporns, O., Barch, D. M., Gotlib, I. H., Hastie, T. J., Kerr, A. B., Poldrack, R. A., Wandell, B. A., Wintermark, M. and Williams, L. M. (2020). The Human Connectome Project for Disordered Emotional States: Protocol and Rationale for a Research Domain Criteria Study of Brain Connectivity in Young Adult Anxiety and Depression. *Neuroimage,* 214(116715): 1–38.

Tranter, M. (2021). *A Million Things to Ask a Neuroscientist: The Brain Made Easy.* London: Mike Tranter.

Treismann, K. (2017). *A Therapeutic Treasure Box for Working with Children and Adolescents with Developmental Trauma: Creative Techniques and Activities (Therapeutic Treasures Collection).* London: Jessica Kingsley Publishers.

Trevarthen, C. (2011b). What Is It Like to Be a Person Who Knows Nothing? Defining the Active Intersubjective Mind of a New-Born Human Being. *Infant Child Dev,* 20(1): 119–135.

Trevarthen, C. and Aitken, K. J. (2001). Infant Intersubjectivity: Research, Theory, and Clinical Applications. *J Child Psychol Psychiatry,* 42(1): 3–48.

Trevarthen, C., Aitken, K. J., Vandekerckhove, M., Delafield-Butt, J. and Nagy, E. (2006). Collaborative Regulations of Vitality in Early Childhood: Stress in Intimate Relationships and Postnatal Psychopathology. In D. Cicchetti and D. J. Cohen (Eds.) *Developmental Psychopathology,* Volume 2 Developmental Neuroscience, Second Edition, Chapter 2 (pp.65–126). New York: Wileys.

Trevarthen, C. and Delafield-Butt, J. (2016). Intersubjectivity in the Imagination and Feelings of the Infant: Implications for Education in the Early Years. In *Under-Three-Year-Olds in Policy and Practice* (pp. 17–39). New York: Springer Publishing.

Trevarthen, C. and Delafield-Butt, J. (2013). Biology of Shared Experience and Language Development: Regulations for the Intersubjective Life of Narratives. In M. Legerstee, D. W.

Haley and M. H. Bornstein (Eds.), *The Infant Mind: Origins of the Social Brain* (pp. 167–199). New York: The Guilford Press.

Tripp, G. and Wickens, J. R. (2009). Neurobiology of ADHD. *Neuropharmacology,* 57(7–8): 579–589.

Tronick, E. and Gold, C. M. (2020). *The Power of Discord: Why the Ups and Downs of Relationships Are the Secret to Building Intimacy, Resilience, and Trust.* New York: Little, Brown and Company.

Tucker, Z. (2019). *Greta and the Giants.* London: Frances Lincoln Children's Books.

United Nations Children's Fund (UNICEF) (2021a). *School Readiness and Transitions.* New York: UNICEF.

United Nations Children's Fund (UNICEF) (2021b). *The State of the World's Children: On My Mind – Promoting, Protecting and Caring for Children's Mental Health.* New York: UNICEF.

United Nations Children's Fund (UNICEF) (1989). *The United Nations Convention on the Rights of the Child.* London: UNICEF UK.

United Nations Economic and Social Council (2017). *Progress Towards the Sustainable Development Goals: Report of the Secretary-General.* E66, 1–19. https://unstats.un.org/sdgs/files/report/2017/secretary-general-sdg-report-2017--EN.pdf.

van Albada, S., Rowley, A. G., Senk, J., Hopkins, M., Schmidt, M., Stokes, A. B., Lester, D. R., Diesmann, M. and Furber, S. (2018). Performance Comparison of the Digital Neuromorphic Hardware SpiNNaker and the Neural Network Simulation Software NEST for a Full-Scale Cortical Microcircuit Model. *Front Neurosci,* 12(291): 1–20.

van der Kruk, Y., Wilson, Y. J., Palghat, K., Downing, C., Harper-Hill, K. and Ashburner, J. (2017). Improved Signal-to-Noise Ratio and Classroom Performance in Children with Autism Spectrum Disorder: A Systematic Review. *Review Journal of Autism and Developmental Disorders,* 4(3).

VanTieghem, M., Korom, M., Flannery, J., Choy, T., Caldera, C., Humphreys, K. L., Gabard-Durnam, L., Goff, B., Gee, D. G., Telzer, E. H., Shapiro, M., Louie, J. Y., Fareri, D. S., Bolger, N. and Tottenham, N. (2021). Longitudinal Changes in Amygdala, Hippocampus and Cortisol Development Following Early Caregiving Adversity. *Dev Cognit Neurosci,* 48(100916): 1–11.

Velmeshev, D., Schirmer, L., Jung, D., Haeussler, M., Perez, Y., Mayer, S., Bhaduri, A., Goyal, N., Rowitch, D. H. and Kriegstein, A. R. (2019). Single-Cell Genomics Identifies Cell Type–Specific Molecular Changes in Autism. *Science,* 364(6441): 685–689.

Vygotsky, L. S. (1987). Thinking and Speech. In L. S. Vygotsky, R. W. Rieber (Series Eds.) and A. S. Carton (Vol. Ed.), *The Collected Works of L. S. Vygotsky. Vol. 1: Problems in General Psychology* (N. Minick, Trans.). New York: Plenum.

Vygotsky, L. S. (1978). *Mind in Society.* Cambridge, MA: Harvard University Press.

Walder, D. J., Laplante, D. P., Sousa-Pires, A., Very, F., Brunet, A. and King, S. (2014). Prenatal Maternal Stress Predicts Autism Traits in 6 ½ Year-Old Children: Project Ice Storm. *Psychiatry Res,* 219(2): 353–360.

Walker, S. P., Chang, S. M., Vera-Hernández, M. and Grantham-McGregor, S. (2011). Early Childhood Stimulation Benefits Adult Competence and Reduces Violent Behaviour. *Paediatrics,* 127(5): 849–857.

Walsh, M. (2009). *Ten Things I Can Do to Help My World.* London: Walker Books.

Watson, J. B. (1913). Psychology as the Behaviourist Views It. *Psychol Rev,* 20: 158–177.

Wave Trust (2014). *Healthy Child Programme and Age of Opportunity Compared.* London: Department of Health.

Weaver, I. C. G., Cervoni, N., Champagne, F. A., D'Alessio, A. C., Sharma, S., Seckl, J. R., Dymov, S., Szyf, M. and Meaney, M. J. (2004). Epigenetic Programming by Maternal Behaviour. *Nat Neurosci,* 7: 847–854. https://doi.org/10.1038/nn1276.

Weeland, J., Moensa, M. A., Beute, F., Assink, M., Staaks, J. and Overbeek, G. (2019). A Dose of Nature: Two Three-Level Meta-Analyses of the Beneficial Effects of Exposure to Nature on Children's Self-Regulation. *J Environ Psychol,* 65(101326): 1–25.

Weisleder, A. and Fernald, A. (2013). Talking to Children Matters: Early Language Experience Strengthens Processing and Builds Vocabulary. *Psychol Sci*, 24(11): 2143–2152.

White, M. P., Alcock, I., Grellier, J., Wheeler, B. W., Hartig, T., Warber, S. L., Bone, A., Depledge, M. H. and Fleming, L. E. (2019). Spending at least 120 minutes a week in nature is associated with good health and wellbeing. *Scientific Reports*, 9(7730): 1–11.

White, R. (1963). *Ego and Reality in Psychoanalytic Theory: A Proposal Regarding the Independent Ego Energies*. Madison, CT: International Universities Press.

Whitebread, D. (2019). *Developing Essential Skills Supporting Self-Regulation in 3–4 Year Olds Early Years Teachers Handbook*. London: The Headley Trust.

Whitebread, D. (2016). Editorial: Self-Regulation in Early Childhood Education. *Early Educ J*, 80. https://early-education.org.uk/wp-content/uploads/2021/12/EE_Journal_-Autumn-lo-res-version.pdf.

Whitebread, D., Bingham, S., Grau, V., Pino Pasternak, D. and Sangster, C. (2007). Development of Metacognition and Self-Regulated Learning in Young Children: The Role of Collaborative and Peer-Assisted Learning. *J Cognit Edu Psychol*, 6: 433–455.

Whitebread, D. and Coltman, P. (2011). Young Children as Self-Regulating Learners. In J. Moyles, J. Georgeson and J. Payler (Eds.), *Beginning Teaching: Beginning Learning: In Early Years and Primary Education* (pp. 122–138). Maidenhead: Open University Press.

Wilens, T. E. and Spencer, T. J. (2010). Understanding Attention-Deficit/Hyperactivity Disorder from Childhood to Adulthood. *Postgrad Med*, 122(5): 97–109.

Williams, F. (2018). *The Nature Fix: Why Nature Makes Us Happier, Healthier, and More Creative*. New York: W. W. Norton and Company.

Williamson, J. M. and Lyons, D. A. (2018). Myelin Dynamics Throughout Life: An Ever-Changing Landscape? *Front Cell Neurosci*, 12(424): 1–8.

Wilson, D., Gottfredson, D. and Najaka, S. (2001). School-Based Prevention of Problem Behaviours: A Meta-Analysis. *J Quant Criminol*, 17(3): 274–272.

Winston, R. and Chicot, R. (2016). The Importance of Early Bonding on the Long-Term Mental Health and Resilience of Children. *Lond J Prim Care*, 8(1): 12–14.

Yendiki, A., Aggarwal, M., A., Howard, A., van Cappellen van Walsum, A.-M. and Haber, S. (2021). Post-Mortem Mapping of Connectional Anatomy for the Validation of Diffusion MRI. *BioRxiv*, 1–53.

Yowell, C. M. and Smylie, M. A. (1999). Self-Regulation in Democratic Countries. *Elem Sch J*, 99(5): 469–490.

Zeegers, M. A. J., de Vente, W., Nikolić, M., Majdandžić, M., Bögels, S. M. and Colonnesi, C. (2018). Mothers' and Fathers' Mind-Mindedness Influences Physiological Emotion Regulation of Infants Across the First Year of Life. *Dev Sci*, 21(6): 1–18.

Zeng, N., Ayyub, M., Sun, H., Wen, X., Xiang, P. and Zan Gao, Z. (2017). Effects of Physical Activity on Motor Skills and Cognitive Development in Early Childhood: A Systematic Review. *BioMed Res Int*, 1–13.

Zimmerman, B. and Schunk, D. (2011). *Handbook of Self-Regulation of Learning and Performance*. New York: Routledge.

Websites

Arm Research (2022). https://community.arm.com/arm-research/b/articles/posts/spinnaker-next-level-thinking (Accessed 5th January 2022).

Begley, S. (2020). A 'Landmark' Achievement: Scientists Trace Full Wiring Diagram of the Fly Brain's Core. *In the Lab*. www.statnews.com/2020/01/22/landmark-achievement-fruit-fly-wiring-diagram-connectome-mapped/ (Accessed 2nd January 2022).

The Centre for Social Justice (2021). *Early Years Healthy Development Review Launch.* https://www.centreforsocialjustice.org.uk/events/early-years-healthy-development-review-launch-with-rt-hon-andrea-leadsom-mp (Accessed 2nd January 2022).

Child Trends (2020). www.childtrends.org/publications/how-to-implement-trauma-informed-care-to-build-resilience-to-childhood-trauma (Accessed 2nd January 2022).

Cross Party Manifesto (2013, revised 2015 and 2019). *The 1001 Critical Days – The Importance of the Conception to Age Two Period.* www.wavetrust.org/1001-critical-days-the-importance-of-the-conception-to-age-two-period (Accessed 3rd January 2022).

Daniel Siegel – 'Flipping Your Lid:' A Scientific Explanation. www.youtube.com/watch?v=G0T_2NNoC68 (Accessed 29th November 2021).

Daniel Siegel's Hand Model of the Brain. www.youtube.com/watch?v=f-m2YcdMdFw (Accessed 29th November 2021).

Daniel Siegel Hand Model of the Brain. www.youtube.com/watch?v=qFTljLo1bK8 (Accessed 29th November 2021).

East Sussex County Council (2019). https://new.eastsussex.gov.uk/rubbish-recycling/how-we-manage-our-waste/recycling-facts#:~:text=8.5%20million%20new%2C%20perfectly%20good,every%20year%20in%20the%20UK (Accessed 5th January 2022).

The Free Printable Brain Hemisphere Hat (2021). https://homeschoolgiveaways.com/2017/08/free-printable-brain-hemisphere-hat/ (Accessed 3rd January 2022).

Guterres, A. (2020). www.un.org/en/coronavirus/covid-19-un-counters-pandemic-related-hate-and-xenophobia (Accessed 10th March 2022).

Harvard Centre on the Developing Child (2021). https://developingchild.harvard.edu/science/key-concepts/brain-architecture/ (Accessed 10th April 2021).

https://self-reg.ca/learn/online-courses-with-dr-shanker/early-childhood-development/ (Accessed 15th March 2022).

https://self-reg.ca/learn/self-reg-parenting-course/ (Accessed 15th March 2022).

https://unstats.un.org/sdgs/report/2021 (Accessed 5th January 2022).

Independent News (2018). www.independent.co.uk/news/education/education-news/isolation-booths-school-pupils-classroom-behaviour-special-educational-needs-bbc-a8630391.html (Accessed 2nd January 2022).

Jones, J. (2013). *Carpal Ossification. Case Study.* Radiopaedia.org. https://doi.org/10.53347/rID-23244 (Accessed 10th March 2022).

Keep Your Cool Toolbox. https://keepyourcooltoolbox.com/ (Accessed 29th November 2021). (This resource is also available as a free app on Google Play.)

Lincoln, D. (2020). www.thegreatcoursesdaily.com/solving-the-mystery-of-the-left-brain-and-right-brain-myth/ (Accessed 29th November 2021).

Living Montessori Now (2018). https://livingmontessorinow.com/brain-hemisphere-hat-and-montessori-activities-to-learn-about-parts-of-the-brain/ (Accessed 2nd January 2022).

McCalla, A. (2020). https://www.rainbowrehab.com/executive-functioning/ (Accessed 2nd January 2022).

Nenia, K. (2022). *Alternatives to Spanking.* Northern Illinois University Child Development and Family Centre. www.chhs.niu.edu/child-center/resources/articles/alternatives-to-spanking.shtml (Accessed 15th March 2022).

Neuroscience for Kids (2022). https://faculty.washington.edu/chudler/outside.html (Accessed 2nd January 2022).

Nitty Gritty Science (2021). *Cauliflower Brain – Make a Brain Model Using Entire Head of Cauliflower and Label Functions.* www.youtube.com/watch?v=MIhfstdnxLY (Accessed 5th January 2022).

NSPCC. (2022). www.nspcc.org.uk/what-is-child-abuse/types-of-abuse/emotional-abuse/ (Accessed 15th March 2022).

Robinson, K. (2006) *Do Schools Kill Creativity?* www.youtube.com/watch?v=iG9CE55wbtY (Accessed 10th April 2021).

Siegel, S. (2020). *"Interpersonal Neurobiology: Daniel Siegel" on YouTube.* www.youtube.com/watch?v=sr78UgNqs-c (Accessed 29th November 2021).

Spielman, A. (2019). https://www.gov.uk/government/speeches/research-commentary-managing-behaviour. (Accessed 29th November 2021).

UNESCO (2022). https://en.unesco.org/sustainabledevelopmentgoals (Accessed 3rd January 2022).

Walz, E. (2021). *Do We Really Need to "Get Back to the Green Zone"? We Think Not.* www.zonesofregulation.com/uploads/3/4/1/7/34178767/do_we_really_need_to_get_back_to_the_green_zone_article.pdf (Accessed 5th January 2022).

World Health Organization (WHO) (2020). *Mental Health and Psychosocial Considerations During COVID-19 Outbreak.* www.who.int/docs/default-source/coronaviruse/mental-health-considerations.pdf (Accessed 5th January 2022).

www.bmj.com/company/newsroom/surge-in-domestic-child-abuse-during-pandemic-reports-specialist-uk-childrens-hospital/ (Accessed 25th March 2021).

www.nhs.uk/start4life/pregnancy/week-by-week (Accessed 29th November 2021).

Index

Note: Page numbers in *italic* indicate a figure and page numbers in **bold** indicate a table on the corresponding page.

right-brain dominance 113
Robinson, Sir Ken 231
robotics 242

sadness, represented by blue resources 86
sanitation and water conservation, as
    SDG 226
say "sorry" 213, 214
scaffolding, and co-regulation 47
school readiness 11, 13–15
Self-Reg Global xv, xvi
self-regulation (SR) 1–38; adult ability to
    self-regulate 68; brain development 18–22;
    children's play 31–33; defined xvi, 2–6;
    develops how 28–31; develops when
    24–27; dysregulation 5, 17, 24, 36; five
    domains of 6, **7,** 8; *see also* domains of
    self-regulation (SR); interconnectedness
    of emotional and cognitive capacities 4,
    17–24; as predictor of 21st Century skills
    233; Stream of Self-Regulation 68–70, *69*;
    up- and down-regulation 178–180, **179**;
    what SR is not 34–36
SEND (special educational needs or
    disabilities) 3; connection between SPD
    and socialization 162; difficulty with
    cognitive self-regulation 11; effects of
    behaviour management 197–198; self-
    regulation in children with SEND 166–
    169; teaching self-regulation skills to 66
SEND Code of Practice 166
senses of human body 144–149, **145,** *146*
sensorimotor, as category in SIPT 154
sensory defensiveness 155
sensory integration (SI) 143–181; assessment
    with SIPT 153–154; defined 149; eight
    senses 144–149, **145,** *146*; fidgeting and
    wiggles 151–153; reflexes, primitive and
    retained 150–153; self-regulation, up or
    down 178–180, **179**; sensory overload
    154–161; sensory processing difficulties
    (SPD) 154–155, 161–166; *see also* ADHD;
    autism; SEND (special educational needs
    or disabilities)
Sensory Integration and Praxis Test (SIPT)
    153–154
sensory overload 154–161; hyper- and
    hypo-sensitivities 155–160, *157*

sensory processing difficulties (SPD): and
    learning ability 161–166; as sensory
    overload 154–155
seventeen Sustainable Development Goals
    221–229
Shanker, Stuart x, xvi–xix, 1, 5, 6, 64, 219
SI *see* sensory integration (SI)
Siegel, Daniel 23, 119, 120
sight *see* vision, sense of
Simpsons, The (TV show) 188
SIPT (Sensory Integration and Praxis Test)
    153–154
"sit still" 151–152
Skinner, B. F. **185,** 186
smell, sense of *see* olfactory sense
social anxiety 169
social cognitive perspectives of co-regulation
    46–47
social domain of SR **7,** 15, 168
socialization and friendships: as difficulty for
    children with SEND 167, 169; and sensory
    processing difficulties (SPD) 162–163
social justice, as element of sustainability 221
social learning theory 46, **185**
social skills for future 230, 231
somatosensory, as category in SIPT 153
somatosensory cortex **145**
sound *see* auditory sense
spanking children 190–191
SPD *see* sensory processing difficulties (SPD)
special educational needs or disabilities
    see SEND
Spiking Neural Network Architecture
    (SpiNNaker) computer 129–130
spinal cord 95, *95*
spinal Galant reflex 152
SR *see* self-regulation (SR)
Stephenson, Neal 242
stimulation (up-regulation) 178–180, **179**
Stream of Self-Regulation 68–70, *69*
stress: brain development and learning
    18–19, 20; calming a child under stress
    208–210; in children xvi–xvii; five steps
    in supporting children 208; four Fs for
    dealing with 9; as inhibitor to learning 8,
    11, 18, 41, 191, 201, *205*; maternal, effect
    on children 25, 127–128
stress hormones 9–10, *26,* 95, 119–120